Table of Contents

Introduction
Definition of Terms
Trusting Our Children to Our Enemies: The Beginning of
"Detrimental Reliance" – The Fairy Tale

- *Battle for the Black Mind*
- *Introduction*
- *The Legend of John Henry*
- *The Ugly Duckling*

  - ✓ *Differences Are Deficits*
  - ✓ *The Story and its Theme*
  - ✓ *Conclusion*

- *The Story of Little Black Sambo*

  - ✓ *Black Sambo as Tip of the Iceberg*
  - ✓ *Black Mingo*
  - ✓ *Little Black Quasha*
  - ✓ *Little Black Quibba*
  - ✓ *Color- and Race-Coded Storytelling*
  - ✓ *Popularity of Little Black Sambo*
  - ✓ *The Minds of Black Folk*
  - ✓ *Closing Remarks*
  - ✓ *About the Author*

- *Ten Little Niggers*

  - ✓ *Introduction*
  - ✓ *Critique and Commentary*
  - ✓ *Impact on Black Children: Detrimental Reliance as Learned Behavior*

- *Sinter Klaus and "Black Pete"*

- ✓ *Introduction to Black Pete*
- ✓ *St. Nicholas, Sinter Klaus, Santa Clause*
- ✓ *Conclusion*

Food Diversion, the Marketplace and the Black Community

Detrimental Reliance: Omaha's Black Community, "Race Commissions" and "Human Relations"

- The Name of the Organization
- "Cultural Tenderizing:" Inclusion, Diversity, Engagement, etc.

  - Multiculturalism
  - Cultural Competency
  - Diversity

    - o .1. The Ideological Response Approach
    - o .2. The Federal Compliance Reaction
    - o .3. The Oasis Syndrome
    - o .4. The Qualified Intentions Approach
  - Inclusion
  - Empowerment
  - Community Engagement

1. Make it easy to participate
2. Be a leader
3. Interact with community
4. Welcome newbies
5. Identify and nurture power users
6. Showcase and cross-promote UGC
7. Reward contributors
8. Be timely about posting UGC
9. Allow profile creation
10. Engage with popular existing communities

Detrimental Reliance: The Farmland Crisis and Blacks
Detrimental Reliance: Re-Drawing of Political Districts

- *District 2: Political Evolution and North Omaha*
- *Redistricting and the Decline: A Response to a World-Herald Article*
- *The Yale Apartment Evacuation of October 2018*

Relocation Realized: An Afterword
Conclusion
References

INTRODUCTION

Let me begin by saying from the outset that "detrimental reliance" is the fault of those doing the relying, not necessarily the ones who created and fostered the reliance with a history of lies and trickery. As the saying goes, "Fool me once, it's on you; fool me twice, it's on me."

Black people in Omaha, as in many parts of the country, have grown (read: been programmed) to believe in the white race and that it is "changing" and that race relations "are improving." These idiots come to these conclusions because of a mass media campaign that allows them to see black and white kids playing together at school, black men kissing on white bitches, and black people walking around in expensive suits and driving expensive cars. All this, despite the fact that racial and residential segregation remain as pervasive as ever and the racial gap between blacks and whites is actually widening.

This then, serves as the ideological basis for what I view as "detrimental reliance" on the part of black people, a "syndrome" that only serves to muddy the waters that prevent clear and coherent racial analyses and discussions from taking place. In sum the white people have a view that is imposed on those who they appoint and hire to serve as "black leadership." As a result, the black masses think that they have a perspective being presented when in reality, what is being offered up by these coons posing as black people is nothing more than scripted statements and actions laid out by their white masters.

Because of this "relationship." Detrimental reliance" is the key. Before moving on, functional and operational definitions of what constitutes 'detrimental alliance' is provided once the variable of "race" is interjected. And as I hope to show, it all begins during the formative years with those "fairy tales" that boost white self-concept and promote the consequent debasement of the black child's self-esteem. I will show how this is done and continues on through life.

First, let us learn a little bit more about "detrimental reliance."

DEFINITION OF TERMS

Legal websites, put together by actual law firms, provide the following legal definition of what constitutes "detrimental reliance":

> Detrimental reliance is a term **commonly used to force another to perform their obligations under a contract**, using the theory of promissory estoppel. Promissory estoppel may apply when the following elements are proven:
>
> - A promise was made
> - Relying on the promise was reasonable or foreseeable
> - There was actual and reasonable reliance on the promise
> - The reliance was detrimental
> - Injustice can only be prevented by enforcing the promise

I believe that a case of "detrimental reliance" can be made because the four factors just listed are in effect. First, a promise was made in the Constitution of the United States, and even though black people weren't considered human, later documents and laws attempted to include black people as "citizens" and are therefore entitled to certain "inalienable rights."

The second is a reliance on the promise and that the promise was reasonable or foreseeable. Black people have evolved and white folks got scared and passed laws that paid lip service – a form of a promise – that black people would not be singled out and harassed. As a result, point three came into fruition: black people responded by relying on the promise that was made. Our expectations were not met and still black people foolishly petition, picket and pray in public begging that the promise be kept. This reality in itself shows that the promise, on some level, does exist. Abraham Lincoln once said, "A promise, once made, must be kept."

The fourth factor is where the reliance on the promise was somehow detrimental. Look at where black people, as a grouping, are today and then look back to 1954. Do you see any real "integration"? For that matter, segregation remains alive and well. Relying on the civil rights act of 1964 was a mistake, and relying on these various presidents who lie and talk about black rights is an exercise in futility. In light of this and much more, any reliance that black people continue to have on white people and their promises of "change" in terms of more equitable race relations, is bullshit and therefore detrimental to black people./

Fifth and finally, and read this one well: "Injustice can only be prevented by enforcing the promise." I have always said that I understand white people being envious and hateful of people of color, but what I don 't like is their ongoing lies and promises that they harbor no ill will. All around us we can see it and yet they want to either blame the victims or deny that any racism or discrimination is taking place. As a result, the only way that "injustice" can be prevented is by enforcing the promise. And like Malcolm X, I am with those who believe that the promise that was made will be enforced *"by any means necessary."*

Moving on, "Detrimental means that some type of harm is suffered." And hasn't harm been suffered in Omaha by a reliance on these outside forces that have an obligation to provide equal care and concern for all residents? And hasn't the city shown an on-going disdain and disregard for the residents of North Omaha (the black community), much to their (the residents') detriment?

In The Complete Real Estate Encyclopedia, the authors define "detrimental reliance" as, "Taking an action or failing to take an action because of a representation made by another person that turned out to be untrue." (Evans & Evans, 2007). Is this not the history of race relations in this country? Black people continue to go around claiming to be "Americans" and about their "rights" being violated when in reality, it is clear that neither is really valid. We rely on pieces of paper that talk about "man" this and "man" that when black people were not even considered human beings. To this day we fall prey to a belief in a system that does not believe in us. This is the most clear-cut example of "detrimental reliance." We care more about a race of people that oppresses us and sees us as nothing more than crippling liabilities.

With both operational and functional definitions out of the way, we can now interject the variables of "racism" and "segregation" and gain a more profound understanding of the nature and scope of detrimental reliance as it relates to the city of Omaha's majority population and a section of the city that is located on an 8-square mile section of the city known as "North Omaha."

TRUST OUR CHILDREN TO OUR ENEMIES: THE BEGINNINGS OF "DETRIMENTAL RELIANCE" – THE FAIRY TALE

Detrimental reliance begins with programming the oppressed to believe they are "beholden" to the majority group. At one time this process began in kindergarten, but in these more current "microwave type" educational terms, that process now starts with what is called pre-school.

It was Debasish Mridha who once wrote, "Most of us are brainwashed by our society so we become the reflection of that society." This quote speaks directly to the gist and thrust of this book and the brainwashing that is taking place has been and continues to be directly aimed at our future: the children.

THE BATTLE FOR THE BLACK MIND

"He know he took it. As sho' as Jesus' eyes is blue, he know it."
--Esther Rolle
"Rosewood"

Jesus – blue eyed? If you've seen the movie "Rosewood," you know it was about how a white woman's lie about being raped by a black man (when in reality a white boy did it) led to the destruction of an entire black town and the lynchings of numerous black men. And despite all this, the matriarch of the town, played by Esther Rolle, still had a belief that the Supreme Being was a white man, hence the opening quote. How sick and confused can a race be?

Africentric scholar Molefi Asante correctly argued that, "myth, conventionally defined as a traditional story or tale that has functional value for society, usually serves as a way of dealing with mystery." And that's what this bitch Bannerman was all about: she was probably fucking around with some man of color, got turned out and then rejected, and decided to take it out on the race.

The "mystery" that is at the foundation and root of the racist patterns I have documented in this work is one that is rooted in the naiveté of the European, his fear of what he discovered about skin color, and his envy of it. From there, as Welsing made clear, he evolved an entire system that glorified what he perceived and defined himself to be: white. The myths then came in abundance to not only rationalizes or justify this "whiteness," but to systematically devalue any human of "color." Both European and American history are replete with examples.

What this book and all of my works have been about is evidence, providing proof positive that race relations, despite the convenient veneer, the convincing façade and the money spent on programs that don't work (such as busing), is as strong today as it was during the days of institutional slavery. And racism is kept alive through simple observance of day-to-day actions of white people. In another book I've written, I show how their love for their pets is superior to any affection they show toward black human beings. That was evidence. Like that book, this book is an analysis of a long-valued "tale" about black kids who literally do not know their asses from a hole in the ground, black parents who are negligent, and jungle animals that can talk. White people are not about to change their actions, because the IMAGES that they paint of that which is not "white" continue to be negative – as in the case of Little Black Sambo, Little Black Mingo, Little Black Quasha and the others.

Some might say that their aversion to the goes back to their original fear of and concern about the night:

> Another theory suggests that both the general white-black
> evaluative tendency and the individual differences in the
> strength of the tendency may be an elaboration of an averse
> response to darkness of night. Fear of the dark is common
> in young children, fear of the light has yet to be
> documented... (Williams & Stabler, 1973: 52)

Euroamerican mythology is packed with incidents where Caucasian ADULTS are afraid of the dark. As part of the promotion and success of their movies and popular culture media, the "night" is still a place for suspense, action, murder, sex and more recently, 'urban adventure.' They are afraid of it and their attempts to show mastery of it appear in all forms. It is also a time when they take advantage of the defenseless and a time when their action-heroes, mostly white males, can appear to be more courageous than they are in real life.

The "mythology" of the 21st Century is as rooted in the "color line" as it was during the 20th Century, as DuBois so aptly predicted. The "functional value' of the myths that buttress the "white is good and black is bad" ethos is that it enables white people to retain their belief that they are in control and represent standards by which all other people should be judged. This function is very important in this, a world economy, where more and more persons of color from developing nations are seizing their freedom. Here in America, the myth of white superiority continues and manifests itself in the programming and literature now as much as it ever has.

James Baldwin once wrote in *The Fire Next Time* that, "The glorification of one race and the consequent debasement of another has been and always will be, a recipe for murder." For every "Little Black Mingo," "Little Black Quasha," "Little Black Quibba" and "Little Black Sambo" that the Anglo mind has concocted, there is also a flip side glorifying their pale skin: "Cinderella," "Little Red Riding Hood," "Snow White," "Seven With One Blow," and so on.

It has been going on for a long time, from nursery school, preschool and elementary school through middle school. When my youngest son brought home the story of "Sinter Klaus and Black Pete," my audacity and challenging of first, the Milwaukee Public Schools and then a year later, the Omaha Public Schools, got that crap stricken from the "take home assignments" given to the elementary school children in both districts – districts more than 500 miles apart. Hence, the pervasiveness of white supremacy and the brainwashing of children which, in turn, perpetuates white supremacy.

Following are my contributions to this system's own understanding of itself, and a literary sword for black people to defend their children with.

<u>INTRODUCTION</u>

I am a member of perhaps the most feared and envied group that exists on this planet: African-American males. We are the most copied, the coolest, the most creative and the sexually mystified people of the human species and as a result, those who have power over us have spent an inordinate amount of time and huge sums of money attempting to dehumanize, control, "thingify" and otherwise minimize our human potential.

From the belief that we are lazy and shiftless to the myth of the super masculine menial to a group with a high pain threshold or as President Jefferson said, "No emotional attachment to the [black] female," we have been the subjects of studies, reports, analyses, books, movies, documentaries and stolen ideas.

One of the ways that white folks and their Negro lackeys have been able to slice into Black self-esteem (the way we think and feel about ourselves) is through literature. From pre-kindergarten through graduate school, the myths persist. Let me share a short story with you before proceeding.

In 1991 and once again in 1993, I had children who were attending public school. In fact, the same child came home to me in 1989 and handed me a booklet that had the theme of showing these kids how Christmas was celebrated around the world. I perused it, as I did all of his materials (as a teacher myself) and I came to Norway's version. In it, there was a white man on a white horse wearing a Pope's hat. His name was Sinter Klaus. If the children were good, he gave the presents and candy and the like. But for the kids who behaved badly, Klaus called upon his side kick, none other than BLACK PETE, to chastise the children, including beating them with a birch rod!

As the editor of the major Black newspaper, *The Milwaukee Courier*, I used my considerable "juice" to chastise the Milwaukee Public Schools and go them to extract that imagery from the handout. Less than two years later I had to do it again, as the Omaha Public Schools was distributing the same image! I wrote in using my status as a professor in the Department of Black Studies at the University of Nebraska at Omaha, and Mel Clancy (a Black man), then the Director of Elementary Education, pledged it would be removed and thanked me for my diligence.

What, you may ask, does this have to do with John Henry?

You've got a school system that is using every trick in the book to make it appear as if the kids are the problem. And the parents, most of whom never attend parent-teacher meetings by the way, are falling for it. School has become nothing more than eight hours of free day care for many parents. And while you're at home kicking it with your buddies or even at work, the kid is being subjected to a curriculum that at one time, included the likes of "Black Pete."

But merely look at their social studies book and even third grade readers: as long as stories like "The Ugly Duckling," "Tar Baby," "the Bre'r Rabbit Tales" are still around, the school system has a way to make a young Black or minority person hate him or herself. They're systematically taking over the minds of our children. I have included eight (8) books for children in this analysis, courtesy of Atlanta Blackstar.com, that provides the titles of even more atrocious and racist contributions to the literature. And it is part of a long-time strategy and design.

One of my favorite *Black Scholar* articles of all time appeared in the May-June 1973 issue. The article, titled, "Children's Books and Racism," capsulated the point that I seek to make as I put forth the following analysis of *The Legend of John Brown.* The author of that article, Bettye I. Latimer wrote, in part,

> … white children are imbued with a progressive sense of superiority from their earliest encounter with the world of literature. Consider the huge, plush world f fun and fantasy which young children delight in. All the loveable characters – the clowns, the fairies, elves and angels. Peter Pan, Little Red Riding Hood, and that grand matriarch, Mother Goose – are invariably white. Even Dr. Seuss's (sic) fantastic characters, who come in a bright array of colors, are seldom black (p. 21).

That's what the general idea is, especially when it comes to appeasing and entertaining white kids. But there is another side, and the picture and images are both literally and figuratively much "darker."

According to an incredible article that appeared in the website Atlanta Blackstar, you all can see what I have known for decades: insulting black kids was quite normal in this society. The article, titled, "). Eight disturbingly racist children's books designed to devalue black people," offers up some of the following titles. If you're from my generation, you may remember hearing or seeing them in your "school library."

How about **Ten Little Nigger Boys. According to the article, "'***Ten Little Nigger Boys*' was one of several nursery books series that taught white children to count in the late 1800s and the early 1900s. Depicted in the book, caricatures of

Black boys are eliminated by a series of events, counting down to the last one. A subtle psychological key was that the black boys were "eliminated until there were none." Is that not what the parents of these white kids were doing and to this day, apparently still have as a goal when it comes to answering the question, "what are we going to do with all these niggers"?

And second one that most of us remember is, **The Story of Little Black Sambo.** *"The Story of Little Black Sambo"* is a children's book written and illustrated by Helen Bannerman, and first published by Grant Richards in October 1899. The name "Sambo" was used as a racist epithet in the United States and although the story was about a Black boy in southern India, the illustrations of the character were similar to demeaning images that plagued Black people during that time. And this bitch Bannerman has the nerve to have a minority fellowship in an attempt to clean up the damage she did. But as far as I'm concerned, it's too little, too late.

The Adventures of Huckleberry Finn is pretty mainstream to this very days. White folks are ashamed of it because it was written by one of their all-time literary heroes, Mark Twain. As the article points out, *"The Adventures of Huckleberry Finn"* is a novel by Mark Twain, first published in the United Kingdom in December 1884, and in the United States in February 1885. This book has been heavily criticized for its racist content, mostly because twain used the devaluing epithet "nigger" over 200 times.

But that's not all. Another book was actually titled, **The Ten Little Niggers.** *"The Ten Little Niggers"* is another counting book for children with the demeaning title that was popular at this time. However, this book was presented as a musical. Young white children sang the words of the lyrics, for example: "Ten Little nigger boys went out to dine; one choked his little self, and then were nine." **The Strange Tale of Ten Little Nigger Boys is an actual title.** *"The Strange Tale of Ten Little Nigger Boys"* is a children's novel published by M. A. Donohue & Company, Chicago and followed the trend. The book, which was released in the early 20th century, was thought to be harmless "fun" and was once common.

Remember the classic, **The Story of Doctor Dolittle?** *"The Story of Doctor Dolittle"* (1920), was written and illustrated by Hugh Lofting, and is the first of his Doctor Dolittle series of children's novels about a man who learns to talk to animals and becomes their champion around the world. According to Atlanta Blackstar staff, "in a subplot of the book, an African man wishes to marry a white princess. After acknowledging the difference of race, Dr. Dolittle bleaches him white, which gave off a 'burning brown paper' smell." Can there be any doubt why white folks, as a collective, from the cradle to the grave, think that they are superior to black people.

And finally, and you may not believe the title of this one. It's called **Let's Hurry or We'll Miss the Public Lynching.** Atlanta Blackstar explains that, in the late 19th and early 20th century, many books were developed in the United States and the United Kingdom to propagate the devaluation of Black people in their relative societies.   Some of the books were so outrageous, comedian Bob Staake's made '*Let's Hurry or We'll Miss the Public Lynching*' parody cover to bring light to the era.

As most of us now know, these few are just a fraction on the hundreds that were made during our early school years, mainly impacting on the pre-Baby Boomers, but nevertheless continuing on to this day. And what would be the purpose? The white kids in those days had no black kids in their neighborhoods. So what would be the goal or intent be for such books aimed at kids? The answer is simple: to program their own children with hate, and to humiliate any black children that might be within earshot of the stories to not only *hate themselves, but to hate all who are like them.* That's what I think.

With context provided, let's get to the book that is the subject of this analysis, *The Legend of John Henry.*

THE LEGEND OF JOHN HENRY: LITERARY TRICKNOLOGY AND STEREOTYPING

As the Black Power movement was about to begin, the same year as the Watts Riots (1965) and a year after Malcolm X was gunned down in New York City, another slam against Black self-esteem was published as a children's book. This book was placed in (purchased by) the libraries of almost every school district in the country and was published by none other than Scholastic Incorporated out of New York.

The book was titled, *John Henry: An American Legend.* It was a story that was heard from generation to generation before the author, Ezra Jack Keats, got it published in 1965. Children had the legend both read and told to them by their teachers, just as Little Black Sambo and other degrading tales were a key part of the elementary level curriculum. There were plenty of pictures, which were also drawn by the author.

The 27-page booklet was published by Scholastic Inc., which also had outlets in Toronto, London, Auckland and Sydney. This booklet was also undoubtedly distributed in these areas. In other words, the harm had an international impact. I shall address that impact later in this paper.

Following is the text of that book, word for word, with my analyses filtering in and out. Hopefully, this analysis will be read and shared with those of us who may think that the "legend" of John Brown is positive and productive when, in reality, both the story and the character were and continue to be poisonous, proudly negative, and downright pitiful.

Finally, an understanding of what constitutes a "legend" is in order. Quite simply, the *Merriam-Webster Dictionary* defines a legend as, "a story from the past that is believed by many people but cannot be proved to be true," or "a famous or important person who is known for doing something extremely well." What does a black man have to do to gain "legendary" status in a racist society? Well, it should be pretty clear. To begin with, the truth of what was accomplished has to be called into question. But more importantly and germane to this analysis is the fact that it has to be a person who is known for doing something "extremely well."

And what did John Henry do? He killed himself trying to impress the white man, that's what he did. But don't just take my word for it: on the following pages I will prove why such a black man would be held up as a "legend" by white people who, for the most part, would hate someone of his ilk.

Like most stories of this kind, you have to consider the impact that it can and will have on the little ones. After all, they are the ones who you are trying to brainwash and bullshit, and they are the ones whose self-esteem you want to manipulate. So you start off with all these descriptors of nature and little animals and that kind of shit. Check it out:

> A hush settled over the hills. The sky swirled soundlessly
> round the moon. The river stopped murmuring. The wind
> stopped whispering, and the frogs and the owls and crickets
> fell silent – All watching and waiting and listening. Then – the
> river roared! The wind whispered and whistled and sang. The
> frogs croaked, the owls hooted, and all the crickets chirped.
> "Welcome, welcome!" echoed through the hills.

All this nature taking place around them and, in a cartoonish and unrealistic way, the stage is set for some of the most racist storytelling in the annals of these kinds of tales. And here it comes:

> And John Henry was born, Born with a hammer in his hand!
> "Bang! Bang! Bang! rang little John Henry's hammer through
> the cabin, as he crawled about. What's that rascal up to now?
> His other chuckled. And before she knew it, he was big
> enough to help her around the house. As he grew up, he did a
> man's work with his father.

Born with a hammer in his hand. As a black studies professor, I have studied racism in children's literature and the impact that it can have on the mind of the child. How do you explain a newborn baby with a hammer in his hand? Is it destiny? Is it a way of showing that this is all that the child will be able to do in with his life? Who will explain it to the black child in this kindergarten or first grade room? How can a white teacher explain the nuances of racism in children's literature when she was probably force-fed it herself?

The Legend of John Brown was not the first or the last, as pointed out earlier in this analysis. After claiming that he was born with a hammer in his hand, the story embellishments continue:

> One day John Henry thought, "I'm taller and stronger than anyone around. It's time I went out into the world." He said goodbye to this mother and father, and off he went. He worked on farms and in cotton fields. But all that was too tame. So he got himself a job on a riverboat.

He ventures out on his own and much like the black college graduates of today strikes out to find a white man to adopt him. To this day, you hear everything that black men talk about has to do with work: "are you workin?," "who you work for?", "I gotta find me a job" and so on. Very rarely do you hear any of them talking about creating a job for themselves.

Moving on:

> One stormy might the ship plowed through the darkness Suddenly the big steel rod that turned the paddle wheel broke. The wheel stopped turning. Smash! Went the rod through the bottom of the ship. "Pump water! shouted the captain. "Get to port before we sink!" John Henry leaped to the paddle wheel crank. He seized it, pushed, grunted, and pulled. Slowly the giant wheel turned. With all his strength he kept it turning. "Lord Almighty, help us," someone whispered in the long, dark night. Day broke. They sighted shore and pulled into port. A thunderous cheer went up for John Henry!

This reminds me of a scene from the movie, "The League of Distinguished Gentlemen" where the heroes are on Captain Nemo's submarine, The Nautilus (also known as "the sword of the sea") and traitor/spy Dorian Gray has placed a bomb on it, causing the gears to freeze. Dr. Jekyll becomes super-strong Mr. Hyde and swims to the bottom of the ship and, just like John Henry, pushes and grunts and gets the giant wheels to turn. '

In this case John Henry has become the white man's hero – for saving his (whitey's) ship. That is a metaphor for far too many of the "black heroes" and "leaders" of today – they are "success stories" because of something they've done to improve, upgrade, salvage or contribute to the white man's system.

Following the "thunderous cheer,"

> John Henry felt a new excitement in the air. Men were talking
> of railroads being built from the Atlantic to the Pacific.
> "They're going to lay those tracks over rivers, across prairies
> and deserts, and right through mountains."

So if the white man is excited, the black man gets excited. Their glory is ours to experience vicariously. As Malcolm X taught long ago in reference to what he called "the house negro, ", "they loved their master more than the master loved himself. They would give their life to save the master's house quicker than the master would. The house Negro, if the master said, "We got a good house here," the house Negro would say, "Yeah, we got a good house here." Whenever the master said "we," he said "we." That's how you can tell a house Negro." And we can see this in John Henry, despite all his strength.

A good "negro" is one who helps his master fight because after all, the master's enemies are the negro's enemies. The story tells us that, "Through Indian lands and stampeding buffalo herds, and badlands," Goodbye, boys," cried John Henry. "I'm going to swing me a hammer on them beautiful new tracks!" So John Henry already has a plan: he's going to go find another white man to adopt him! He's ventured through "Indian lands," which means that they probably had to fight and kill some of them. Then they went through "stampeding buffalo herds," meaning that they killed off the animals that the Indians needed for food and clothing (and in most cases, just left them lying there). Now he's off on another new adventure so he can use all that power to expand the railroads which, in turn, would strengthen an economy that had people who looked like him locked out.

In vintage coon fashion, check out the following:

> "My hands are just itchin' to hold a hammer again," John
> Henry said. He tried one for size, and laughed. "It sure does
> feel fine." How he drove those spikes, singing to the clanging
> of his hammer! The men joined in, their voices singing,
> hammers ringing. John Henry's gang was in the lead. Day
> after day the tracks moved steadily westward.

All of a sudden John Henry has a gang that is following his lead. Just like today when the black ministers rally the congregation to do his bidding which, of course, is the same bidding that the white man has laid out for him the night before. Just like today when the black politician uses his town hall meetings and soap box to mouth the positions of his white master and the gullible throng eats it up and goes wherever that so-called "leader" tells them to go.

When an obstacle gets in the way, the mindless flunky must step to the side and let the white man lay out a plan. The flunky will be called back when it is once again time for physical labor. Take note:

> Rising across their path was a sprawling mountain range. Its snow-capped peaks reached high into the clouds. "We'll have to tunnel through," said his friend, L'il Bill. "It'll be awful dangerous. Could be cave-ins," someone put in. "That suits me fine," said John Henry. "Me, too," added L'il Bill. "Here's how we do it, boys," the foreman called out.

The more danger and the more threats, the happier this "negro" seems to become. And this is the subtle message that gets driven into the minds of all young people, but especially to black kids. They are being programmed to love their jobs, work very hard and to not let any obstacle deter them. In a word, preparing them for wage slavery.

So here is the plan:

> "A couple of men'll drive a hole in the rock. Then the powder men'll put dynamite into the hole and explode it. The others'll cart the loose rock away. We'll do this again and again until we have a tunnel right through this mountain. And it's goin' to be a real big tunnel boys. Big enough for a giant locomotive pullin' one o' them long strings o' trains. All right, boys, blast away!"

This is the story that they tell the little kids who are gullible and naïve enough to believe that such a plan is the way it was done all of the time. But in many cases, when those mountains were very high, do you know what these cold-blooded racist white boys would do? They would tie a rope around the waist of a Chinese worker and get on top of the mountain. They would then lower him down and swing this immigrant into the mountain after lighting the stick of dynamite. He would toss it down and then get swung back out. Sometimes the momentum enabled him to get out before the dynamite exploded. Sometimes it didn't.

An article titled, "Chinese Immigrants and the Building of the Transcontinental Railroad" (http://www.class.uh.edu/gl/china1.htm) we find additional background as it relates to railroad construction and Chinese labor:

To carve out a rail bed from ridges that jutted up 2,000 over the valley below, Chinese immigrants were lowered in baskets to hammer at solid shale and granite and insert dynamite. During the winter of 1865-1866, when the railroad carved passages through the summit of the Sierra Nevadas, 3,000 lived and worked in tunnels dug beneath 40-foot snowdrifts. Accidents, avalanches, and explosions left as estimated 1,200 Chinese immigrant workers dead.

In any case, these images of white boys sweating and doing all this work on the railroad is one small part of the story. Back to *The Legend of John Henry:*

Deep into the mountain they worked. John Henry's singing echoed through the tunnel. The powder men got ready to blast more rock. They filled as hole with dynamite, put in a long fuse, and lit it. Run, men!" cried the foreman. They all scrambled back, ready to dash clear of the blast.

A true prototype of the happy black laborer that these white people have perpetuated about our people for centuries. They want the world to believe that those who were enslaved were content and happy; that those who were working from "can't see in the morning until can't see at night" were walking on air and upbeat about their condition. How else could the beastial treatment of human beings be explained, talked about or written about? So John Henry was being oppressed: he willfully and blissfully went about his business and it was so good to him, that he actually *sang* while he was in those hazardous tunnels!
Then,

 At that instant came a great cracking and rumbling and the entire tunnel trembled around them. "It's a cave-in!" "We're trapped!"

So what do they do in this time of danger? Check it out:

There was no place to run. The fuse burned closer to the dynamite. John Henry was nearest the fuse. He ran to put it out but tripped and fell!

So once again this confused black man is risking his life for these white folks. Again, Malcolm X described these types of "house negroes" when he explained that, "If the master's house caught on fire, the house Negro would fight harder to put the blaze out than the master would. If the master got sick, the house Negro would say, "What's the matter, boss, we sick?" We sick! He identified himself with his master more than his master identified with himself."

John Henry injures himself and pay close attention to the following: "Oooh, I'm hurt bad," he groaned. "I can't get up." The fuse burned farther out of reach. Others rushed toward it, but they were too far away. Suddenly John Henry remembered he still had is hammer in his hand!

Remember that Malcolm taught that, "If the master's house caught on fire, the house Negro would fight harder to put the blaze out than the master would. If the master got sick, the house Negro would say, "What's the matter, boss, we sick?" We sick! He identified himself with his master more than his master identified with himself.

Pay close attention to a central fact; nobody tried to save John Henry! Nobody tried to drag him out of there or otherwise rescue him from the impending explosion. This speaks volumes about the way this white writer views black life. John Henry, after kissing all that ass, had to figure out a way or come up with an idea to save himself. And when it all comes down to it, despite the social worker mentality of these white people, isn't that the way it usually ends up?

Moreover, how you can forget that you have a hammer in your hand is beyond me, but it shows that he is so obsessed with pleasing white folks that he only considers his own safety as an afterthought. It reminds me of that idiotic title of Gale Sayers' autobiography, I Am Third. He says, "God is first, my friends and family are second, and I am third." Ain't that a bitch? In my book, I am first because I have to be first in order to even be able to appreciate God. If I believe in God, then he won't mind me putting my friends second (because I choose them) and family third (because I had no choice in selecting them).

So John Henry picks up his hammer and slams it down on the fuse and puts it out. He saves his own life. After that, "Sighs of relief filled the smoky tunnel. "Whew! Help me up, boys," mumbled John Henry. Clearing their way through the cave-in, the men carried him to safety." It was only after John Henry asked for help that he received it. They did not volunteer it nor did they take it upon themselves to see it as a necessity or priority. That kind of vibration is a metaphor for the way that people view most black people even today in 2015 – as an afterthought, as also-rans, as expendable commodities.

Continuing:

> Some days later they heard an unfamiliar clutter. Down the
> tunnel came a group of men with a strange machine." This is a
> steam drill. It can drill more holes faster than any six men
> combined," a new man bragged. "Who can beat that?"

If you have a brand new steam drill, then why in the hell would you ask a group of men "who can beat that"? I'll tell you why.

When the white man discovers a black man with special physical or athletic ability, the first thing he wants to do is control it and market it. In 1937 after winning the Olympics, these white folks got another Uncle Tom, Jesse Owens, to run a dash against a race horse. Jesse won. In July of 2012, the newly crowned fastest man in the world, Usain Bolt, was paid to run against a horse. The previous fastest man in the world, Ben Johnson (later busted for "doping"), a black Canadian, not only ran against a thoroughbred horse, but also against, get this – a stock car! And in March of 2014, this idiot named Dennis Northcott, an NFL wide receiver, raced an ostrich. The ostrich dusted him.

Are you beginning to see my point? Just by having these races the white man is delivering another one of those subliminal images for people to maintain in their minds: that black men are animals and therefore it is perfectly alright to pit them in races against *other* members of the kingdom of thingdom. This is a reflection and reinforcement of the John Henry image, and recall that Ben Johnson ran against a stock car. White athletes, for the most part, don't measure up in this way, so rather than admit that, they consign black men to the category of "animals" and treat them accordingly. In the case of John Henry, he is not viewed as human, but as a black "machine" of sorts.

Furthermore, the steam machine is there to take the place of those men! That's the purpose of technology: to save the white man money so that he has to hire as few people as possible. This system does its to his own race members and he damn sure does it to people of color, male and female alike.

So here comes technology and up steps a true "coon:" John Henry. Check it out:

> John Henry stepped forward. "Try me!" He and L'il Bill took
> their work places. John Henry gripped his hammer. L'il Bill
> clutched his steel drill. "Check the machine," came an order.
> A nervous hand fell on the switch. In the dark both sides
> waited for the signal to start. A hoarse voice counted, "One,
> two – THREE!"

So this black man who doesn't have a pot to piss in or a window to throw it out of, takes the challenge personally and opts to impress the white man by taking on a damn steam drill. So the stage has been set, and the point that must be made is that the children listening to this story are having their minds prepared for the upcoming "challenge." They all know that John Henry is black and that the people he is working with are presumed to be white. They know that John Henry is a strong black man, but they also know that he's dumb as a bag of hammers. These are the images that these kids will retain in their minds as they grow up and make associations in real life and in future stories, televised or in print.

Moving on:

> The machine shrieked as it started. John Henry swung his hammer. The crash of steel on steel split the air! Clang! Bang! Clang! The drill got red-hot in L'il Bill's hands. He quickly dropped and picked up another. Hiss! Whistle! Rattle! Men frantically heaved coal into the hungry, roaring engine and poured water into the steaming boiler.

So in essence, John Henry is being pitted against, not only the steam machine, but against an entire crew of white boys who are putting coal into the machine! And in the mind of the child, all this is completely fair. And guess what? In the minds of white people in general, that's the way it's always been: them and their technological "advances" against us. They fear and envy the black man, and they always have. Their first observations of us struck at their core on two levels: first, the color our skin and secondly, the sizes of our dicks. That's right: these homoerotic macho white boys always had an attraction for other men's penises, and ours was no exception. Don't take my word for it: read *Sexual Racism* (Charles Herbert Stember, Jr.), *White Racism: A Psycho History* (Joel Kovel) and/or Calvin Hernton's *Sex and Racism in America*.

And here we go:

> Whoop! Clang! Whoop! Bang! John Henry's hammer whistled as he swung it. Chug, Chug! Clatter! Rattled the machine. Hour after hour raced by. The machine was ahead! "Hand me that twenty-pound hammer, L'il Bill. Harder and faster crashed the hammer. Great chunks of rock fell as John Henry ripped hole after hole into the tunnel wall. The machine rattled and whistled and drilled even faster. Friends doused John Henry and L'il Bill with cold water to keep them going.

So this sick competition was being supported by people who doused them with water so that they (read: John Henry) could keep on going. And sitting in judgment, as is the case in real life, is the white man. By increasing competition and sponsoring competitions, his system is the ultimate winner. Small concessions like prizes, awards and honors mean nothing to him. The only thing he cares about is the ceaseless pursuit of profit.

In vintage coon fashion, John Henry sees this is some twisted and tawdry "game." How else to explain the stereotypical "singing" that black people seem to engage in the harder the work gets?

> Then John Henry took a deep breath. He picked up two sledge
> hammers, and sang: "Ain't no hammers strike such fire/Strike
> like lightning, Lawd, And I won't tire!/Hammers like this,
> Lawd, There's never been!/I'll keep swingin' 'em, Lawd,
> Until we win!"

One sledge hammer at a time was not enough for this "boy." He picks up two and then sings a song that is full of bullshit. He's signing to "the Lawd" as if the Lawd doesn't know what is taking place and as if he needs advice. Secondly, why would the "Lawd" put him in such a fucked up situation? After all, he was born with a sledge hammer in his hand, remember? Can you imagine how much that must have stretched Mrs. Henry's pussy? And third, what does he mean, "until WE win"? John Henry still sees himself as a part of a system that has shown him nothing but disdain-and-how-dare-you. This is so typical of far too many black people, even today, who continue to ask, "What's wrong boss – WE sick?"

The story continues:

> John Henry swung both mighty hammers – faster and faster.
> He moved so fast the men could see only a blur and sparks
> from his striking hammers. His strokes rang out like great
> heartbeats.

So John Henry is performing all these incredible feats of strength so that he can do what? So that he can dig a fuckin' tunnel! And when the railroads are built and the trains come through, he won't even be able to get a job as a porter!

> At the other side of the tunnel the machine shrieked, groaned
> and rattled, and drilled. Then all at once it shook and
> shuddered – wheezed – and stopped. Frantically men worked
> to get it going again. But they couldn't. It had collapsed! John
> Henry's hammering still rang and echoed through the tunnel
> with a strong and steady beat.

So John Henry outlasted a machine. This is how stereotypes are perpetuated. The machine broke down and the big, strong black man just kept on going. This is why white people think blacks have a higher pain threshold than "average" people, this is why white women think black men can last longer and are better in bed than white men, this is why black people have always been viewed as "different" when it comes to their physicality, in general. And when it comes to brains we are also viewed as different: in an inferior way, that is.

In fact, the machine is described in such a way that it has more human characteristics than John Brown does. After all, the machine tires out, it shudders, it actually wheezes, and it groans. And while the machine is showing weakness akin to human frailty, the big black buck, like the Eveready Bunny, just keeps on going and going and going.

Finally,

> Suddenly there was a great crash. Light streamed into the dark tunnel. John Henry had broken through! Wild cries of joy burst from the men. Still holding one of his hammers, John Henry stepped out intro the glowing light of a dying day. It was the last step he ever took. Even the great heart of John Henry could not bear the strain of his last task. John Henry died with a hammer in his hand.

So, like so many black veterans in the wars that they fought for this country, like so many black workers who labor for decades and then retire or die on the job, or like so many of the enslaved who were worked to death, John Henry dies, literally, with a hammer in his hand. The kids listening to this story are supposed to feel sad for John Henry, but their pity is for the fact that he had to die; what they should be sad about is the way that he chose to LIVE!

Check out how the story, the "legend" of John Henry concludes:

> If you listen to the locomotives roaring through the tunnels and across the land, you'll hear them singing. Singing of that great steel-driving man--- John Henry. Listen!

And look at how John Henry is remembered: not only as a steel-driving man in an age where steel driving men are obsolete, but he is also (supposedly) remembered when you hear a train whistle, a whistle that simulates singing. And that's one thing black people are given credit for that does not threaten white folks.

On the back of the book is the following statement and overview of "the legend" of John Henry:

> People still tell the story of John Henry. John Henry was the strongest man who ever worked on the railroad. He hammered through rock. He hammered through steel. One day he hammered so hard, he won a contest with a drilling machine!

And these are supposed to be selling points? What black child is going to get a boost in his self-esteem when he hears this kind of bullshit? Is this one of the contributing factors to why so many black kids grow up striving to be big and strong so they can play pro football – since all the steel driving jobs are taken?

In sum, *The Legend of John Brown* is an insulting fable that contributes mightily to the self-esteem of black children and gives white children an undeserved sense of entertained superiority. It also feeds into the concept of detrimental reliance because John Brown worked to his death under a "contract" to help white people push through a railroad. Though treated like shit, he was a "wage slave" whose sense of self became wrapped up in "having a job" and "a days pay for a days work."

On a related note, the people of my generation grew up with these songs that carried a John Henry theme when it came to sex. Songs like "All Night Lover" and "60-Minute Man" immediately come to mind. And there were a ton of songs that attributed super human pussy qualities to women as well. What I'm saying is that all this shit is dangerous to and for a people who have been so lacking in civil rights that they have often doubted their own humanity. Super powers ain't gonna get it. The only way to stop these people from writing about you and brainwashing your children is to remember the fable about the lion and the hunter.

The child is sitting on his father's lap and asks, "Father, each day you tell me that the lion is the king of the jungle and yet at the end of the story, it is the hunter that always wins. Why is that? The father looks at his son and says, "Son, that is the way it is always going to be – until the lion learns how to write."

Feel me?

THE UGLY DUCKLING:
Color-Coded Images and Implications

INTRODUCTION

The key to the story, and the metamorphosis of the bird, can be found in the following excerpt:

> But what did he see in the clear stream below? His own image; *no longer a dark, gray bird, ugly and disagreeable to look at, but a graceful and beautiful swan.* To be born in a duck's nest, in a farmyard, is of no consequence to a bird, if it is hatched from a

swan's egg. He now felt glad at having suffered sorrow and
trouble, because it enabled him to enjoy so much better all the
pleasure and happiness around him; for the great swans swam
round the new-comer, and stroked his neck with their beaks, as a
welcome (emphasis added).

The so-called "ugly duckling" got dogged. And he got dogged because, as
you can see, he was darker than the other ones. This dogging took place within a
context and environment that was a utopia, based on the descriptions of the
author. Attention to detail was paid to the surrounding beauty, from the water
and trees to all the greenery. This is what makes the ugly duckling truly "color-
coded:" anything mentioned in the story that has to do with being "dark" is
either about the oversized duckling or some dark trees that are still as yet
juxtaposed with white clouds and a blue sky. And remember: this is a child's
tale and children, for the most part, are very visual.

Think back, if you will, about those old Tarzan movies. In order for this
white man to look like "Lord of the Jungle," those films had to also deal with
the backwardness, gooniness and "savagery" of the African natives that were the
overwhelming majority. Only in that way could Tarzan, and his "whiteness"
(equated throughout those movies as being universal, all-powerful, and superior)
stand out even more and in doing so, maintain the myth of white superiority.
The story "The Ugly Duckling" operates on the same paradigm.

It's called cultural racism, to be more precise. Indeed, "cultural racism," is
what J.M. Blaut of the University of Illinois at Chicago has written about when
he posits, "Cultural racism needs to prove the superiority of Europeans and
needs to do so without recourse to the older arguments from religion and from
biology …" Further,

> Diffusionism therefore depicts a world in which Europeans are
> permanently the most progressive and advanced people, and non-
> Europeans are permanently backward, *and permanently the
> recipients of the progressive ideas, things, and people from Europe*
> (cited in Armah, 1992: 21 – emphasis added).

There are a number of other variables at work throughout this story that
make it clear that the duckling as not just "ugly" because of its darkness,
although its darkness plays a critical role. Throughout the story, as you will see,
the duck is put down not just because of his darkness, but simply because he was
"different" in a number of ways. The lesson then is that if you are *different* you

are somehow *deficient* when compared with the white, long-necked swans that are idolized throughout the tale.

One can also charge, as I do, that the entire context of this story was one steeped in various forms of "ugliness." As a result, the so-called "ugly duckling" was no more than the context to which he owes his existence: it is impossible to born into a context of ugliness, hatred, vitriol and conflict and as a result, either: (1) assume some of those characteristics yourself, or (2) become emotionally, psychologically and culturally scarred by what is taking place. Evidence of this follows.

DIFFERENCES ARE DEFICITS

Human beings, by nature it seems, are generally fucked up. But those who have the power, no matter what society or culture we are talking about, tend to set the rules for everyone else. As a sociology professor, I teach about values and norms, and these are the areas that provide the basis for discriminating against certain groups or individuals who are deemed "different" from what those in power believe to be the "norm."

For the novices out there, a norm is defined as, "a standard, model or standard for a group" (*Webster's New World Dictionary of the American Language*). Norms are established by people who have the power, and these norms range from laws that must be followed to what constitutes beauty. It is this latter "norm" that serves as the basis for this analysis.

In the book The Ugly Duckling, there are a myriad of examples of how those who have the power to define also have the power to defile. Hints about white being desirable and beautiful and about that which is dark and different being inferior inundate this tale. Following are but a few examples.

The egg that contained the "ugly duckling" is the last one to be hatched. What kind of message does this send? It sends a message that all that is "normal" has become violated and that something is "wrong" with this last egg. Even before the duckling is hatched, the mother is saying, "But just look at all the others, are they not the prettiest little ducklings you ever saw?" And then she adds, "They are the image of their father, who is so unkind, he never comes to see."

So the father of all of the ducklings is what we would call a "deadbeat dad." The attention to personal detail is important to note because what it tells us is that the images that are described are all intentional and are meant to serve a purpose. It is up to us, the readers, to engage in critical analysis and figure out exactly what those purposes could be. So now we know: (1) all of the ducklings thus far are beautiful as far as their mother is concerned and (2) that the father is nowhere around and the mother really doesn't give a shit.

Then comes some early labeling and stigma. Since the mother is curious about why the one egg has not hatched yet, she engages in supposition and conjecture. She tells her friend, the duck and the duck wants to "see the egg that will not break." Then, the duck surmises that it must be a turkey's egg. And since it is only a guess, the duck does what so many human beings do when they come across something they cannot understand or describe: they call for abandonment. The duck recommends that the mother of the unhatched egg that contains the "ugly duckling" simply, "leave it where it is and teach the other children how to swim."

As an educator, I believe this is the way it must have been back in the 18th and 19th century when a child was born with a mental problem and society couldn't define it and teachers had no idea how to deal with it. So they labeled the child in a number of ways, mainly with the stigma of being "mentally retarded." And this shit stuck for centuries. In recent times they've modified it, but the treatment of children with special needs was treated in the same way that the duck recommended the mother treat that egg that was "different:" abandon it and give your attention to the others."

In today's vernacular this would be known as "the triage approach." In wartime, a triage unit is the medical unit that treats soldiers who have been wounded. Their priorities are the ones that they can treat right away, and the ones who are truly fucked up just have to wait. In urban planning circles, the triage approach is used for the ghetto and the barrio when it comes to funding. City planners get the money and since most of them are white, they view low-income areas as "hopeless," so they spend the money where they think it can "do the most good." My point here is that the duck's recommendations to the mother duck are not new or nerve-shattering. They are very typical of people who don't know, and rather than take time to find out what's going on, it's much easier to say "fuck it" and ignore the problem at hand.

But the mother duck doesn't agree and says she'll wait a little while longer for the last egg to hatch. And sure enough the egg did hatch and as the tale teaches those in listening range, a young one crept forth crying, "Peep, peep." It was very large and ugly." Before the newborn can even cut a fart, the mother has her views of its appearance, and that viewpoint can have a major impact on the way that the duckling feels about itself, especially if the mother treats it according to those initial perceptions.

The mother ha hopes and tries to make the best out of what she perceives to be a negative situation. At one point, as you will see later in the analysis, she makes the comment, "He is my own child, and he is not so very ugly after all if you look at him properly." This is so typical of mothers: most of them love their children unconditionally. I said MOST of them. If we place this tale in a human context, we can find abusers in all races who want to deny or refuse to acknowledge a child because it has a giant head or a fucked up mug. But this is one of the few positives in the tale: the mother didn't give up, but at the same time, it doesn't appear as if she really cared all that much. I will provide additional evidence in the analysis section of this book.

The tale includes a reference to an "old duck" that has Spanish blood and as such, *she is well off.* So not only are the implications racist, but they are also classist. Back in the day and even today, the concept of being "Spanish" is usually assumed to refer to Latinos who are white (or whites who are Latino). It's a cover for a lot of Latinos who want to assimilate into the system in one of three ways: culturally, martially or structurally. I will address this Spanish mentality and why this duck would be presumed to be "well off" later in this book.

Violence is also meted out to the poor duckling on several occasions, just because of the way he looked. Things got so bad that at one point in the tale he said to himself, "how thankful I am for being so ugly; even a dog will not bite me." This is the result of the stigma, stereotyping and deep-seated attacks on self-esteem that those who are "different" are forced to have to deal with. Some accept it and respond by just trying to keep a low profile; others seek out someone who has even lower self esteem than they do; and still others just say "fuck it" and commit suicide. And in this tale, the so-called "ugly duckling" does contemplate suicide at one point.

There you have it: a story that you thought was just about physical appearance. But in this case, Hans Christian Andersen, who published this tale in 1844) knew what he was doing with his laser-focused descriptions on the physicality of the environment, the conditions, the various conflicts and most importantly, what constitutes beauty and what should be deemed "ugly."

THE UGLY DUCKING: (by Hans Christian Andersen (1844) – ITS THEME

The fairy tale begins, thusly:

> It was lovely summer weather in the country, and the golden corn, the green oats, and the haystacks piled up in the meadows looked beautiful. The stork walking about on his long red legs chattered *in the Egyptian language, which he had learnt from his mother.* The corn-fields and meadows were surrounded by large forests, in the midst of which were deep pools. It was, indeed, delightful to walk about in the country (emphasis added).

Anne Sexton, in her book, *The Poet's Story*, wrote, "it doesn't matter who my father was; it matters who I *remember* he was. If we want truthful memories of what was, we have to be able to describe what took place in honest terms; we cannot expect our children to grow and become productive if those who are educating them are calling Africa, our ancestral homeland, "The Dark Continent." The same holds true for "The Ugly Duckling."

Hans Christian Andersen had no respect for anything African, and that includes Egypt. Why then, the reference to a stork that is walking about on his long red legs chattered in the Egyptian language, which he had learnt from his mother? In a story where lily-whiteness is the pinnacle of beauty, of what purpose could a reference to Egypt serve? Oh, that's right: when white folks saw the beauty of the pyramids, the Sphinx and other architectural masterpieces that they could never have built, they decided to make the Egyptian culture WHITE.

This was at about the same time that the slave trade was in full swing in America and Europeans were still referring to Africa, as the sister said earlier, as "the dark continent." All except for Egypt, where they even now in 2015 try to say that Cleopatra was a white woman.

And the reference to a stork and Egypt is only one side of the coin – the one that has nothing to do with real beauty. Look at how the summer weather is described ("lovely), the color of the oats ("green") and the meadows ("beautiful"). And even the walk in the country is "delightful." All of this is by design, and Hans Christian Andersen is a professional storyteller and writer. He knows the importance of imagery and as I have quoted many times, "He who controls images controls minds, and he who controls minds has little, if anything, to worry about from bodies" (Chairman Mao).

So we have established intent and the attitude behind these purposeful writings. Now we can continue with the story:

> In a sunny spot stood a pleasant old farm-house close by a deep river, and from the house down to the water side grew great

> burdock leaves, so high, that under the tallest of them a little child
> could stand upright. The spot was as wild as the centre of a thick
> wood. In this snug retreat sat a duck on her nest, watching for her
> young brood to hatch; she was beginning to get tired of her task,
> for the little ones were a long time coming out of their shells, and
> she seldom had any visitors.

More descriptions set the stage for the idyllic life of these creatures. Pay close attention to this exquisite storytelling: "sunny spot," "pleasant old farm-house," "great burdock leaves," and "snug retreat." Doesn't this smack of that which is comfortable and relaxing? And in the middle of it all is this mother duck watching her babies as they are hatched one-by-one. And she did it all by herself.

Do you know who this scenario can be compared to? Today's African-American woman, that's who. I didn't create the situation I'm just delivering the message. When this story was written it was even worse: black people enslaved in the South and deemed "inferior citizens" every place else. But in all those cases you found a few strong families and yet the black woman was the rock. She was the one who gave birth to the children in situations far less comfortable than the one that the mother duck experienced.

Next comes the birth of the "cute little duckies," as the children who are hearing these words would respond:

> The other ducks liked much better to swim about in the river than
> to climb the slippery banks, and sit under a burdock leaf, to have a
> gossip with her. At length one shell cracked, and then another, and
> from each egg came a living creature that lifted its head and cried,
> "Peep, peep." "Quack, quack," said the mother, and then they all
> quacked as well as they could, and looked about them on every
> side at the large green leaves. Their mother allowed them to look
> as much as they liked, because green is good for the eyes.

The author provides vivid detail, to say the least. The young ducks are born and right away the mother knows that since "green is good for the eyes" (it has actually been established that green is relaxing on the eyes, which is why so many lobby areas related to the medical professional are painted light green). She knows all this and she's more than happy to give her new born babies the "freedom" they want to explore the surrounding greenery. The stage has been set for what is about to come (it's always darkest before the dawn):

> "How large the world is," said the young ducks, when they found
> how much more room they now had than while they were inside
> the egg-shell. "Do you imagine this is the whole world?" asked the
> mother; "Wait till you have seen the garden; it stretches far beyond
> that to the parson's field, but I have never ventured to such a
> distance. Are you all out?" she continued, rising; "No, I declare,
> the largest egg lies there still. I wonder how long this is to last, I
> am quite tired of it;" and she seated herself again on the nest.

The hatching of the eggs went just the way she expected – or it *almost* turned out that way. Detail is the key to maintaining power over those who you want to influence. The more detailed the story, the more realistic it will sound (despite the fantasy aspects of it) and the more believable it will be.

The young ducks in the story are curious and inquisitive. They want to know about the world around them. In turn, like a good mother, she informs them that there is much more to see and truthfully admits that she's never ventured far enough to see the garden or the parson's field. Her patience with that last, large egg is weighing thin. But like a devoted mother, a point that lures the children hearing the story can appreciate or at least identify with, the mother duck is determined to stay on the nest until it hatches.

> "Well, how are you getting on?" asked an old duck, who paid her
> a visit. "One egg is not hatched yet," said the duck, "it will not
> break. But just look at all the others, are they not the prettiest little
> ducklings you ever saw? They are the image of their father, who is
> so unkind, he never comes to see."

This tale is dangerous because it is linking animal behavior with the intimate enterprise of marriage. First of all, there is no explanation as to why the daddy duck would ditch the mother. Maybe he caught her fucking another duck behind his back; maybe she fucked up on some bills or was hard to get along with. I know this sounds ludicrous, but if you're going to bring up the issue and them go into detail about how much the kids look like daddy, then daddy deserves some kind of say. This story, written by a man, takes the woman's side. Maybe Hans Christian Andersen was a rump roaster, who knows?

The mother duck's friend is in her business big time, as you can see in the following excerpt:

> "Let me see the egg that will not break," said the duck; "I have no doubt
> it is a turkey's egg. I was persuaded to hatch some once, and after all my
> care and trouble with the young ones, they were afraid of the water. I
> quacked and clucked, but all to no purpose. I could not get them to

> venture in. Let me look at the egg. Yes, that is a turkey's egg; take my
> advice, leave it where it is and teach the other children to swim."

Bad advice from a "close friend." This is another positive point that the tale makes. Other than the color-coded racism and classism, the tale does teach that sometimes people act like they know something that they simply do not know. It also teaches young people to be careful who they trust. These are important lessons, but it is important that you and the reader, understand a basic tenet of "tricknology:" you mix tidbits of the relevant and true with bullshit, and the unwitting listener accepts the whole kit n' caboodle. That's how the snake oil salesmen did it back in the old days of the wild west and that's the way the white man and his doctors, attorneys, health care professionals, educators at all levels, civic leaders, ministers, priests and rabbis do it today.

The mother duck has her own views on the subject – after all, it is *her* baby. So she commits to the following:

> "I think I will sit on it a little while longer," said the duck; "as I
> have sat so long already, a few days will be nothing." "Please
> yourself," said the old duck, and she went away. At last the large
> egg broke, and a young one crept forth crying, "Peep, peep." *It was
> very large and ugly.* The duck stared at it and exclaimed, "It is
> very large and not at all like the others. I wonder if it really is a
> turkey. We shall soon find it out, however when we go to the
> water. It must go in, if I have to push it myself." (emphasis added).

When the large egg breaks the last of her young comes out and guess what? It is described, not by her, but by the writer of the story as "very large and ugly." Now as critical thinkers, we have to ask ourselves, what is the purpose of such a designation? Can anything positive come out of such a description? More importantly are there any present-day characters that white people would describe in such a way? You know, large, and ugly? You guessed it: the black athlete! And the way that the mother duckling reacts to it is so typical of two types of people: (1) the mother of these creatures (athletes) and (2) the white people who see that they can benefit from training, brainwashing and preparing them to dunk, run, tackle and engage in any form of physicality for their (white folks') benefit.

After all, what is her reaction? She is going to have to see for herself whether it is a turkey or a duck. Everyone wants to "test" or "judge" that which is not like the "norm." In that way they can categorize and if need be, better isolate that creature based on how they feel it can or cannot fit in to the "normal state of affairs." The fact that the mother duck has her doubts says a great deal about the degree of real "concern" she has for the last born. But she had to test it just to make sure. And this is what happened:

> "Oh," said the mother, "that is not a turkey; how well he uses his legs, and how upright he holds himself! He is my own child, and he is not so very ugly after all if you look at him properly. Quack, quack! come with me now, I will take you into grand society, and introduce you to the farmyard, but you must keep close to me or you may be trodden upon; and, above all, beware of the cat."

The mother is going to claim a youngster that she gave birth to. She doesn't have to necessarily have to agree with her bias in terms of how it looks, but she is going to do all she can to try to convince herself that she didn't fail. And that is what parenthood is all about: making sure that their youngsters don't fail because if they do it will make them look bad. They won't admit it, but I agree with the sociobiologists one key point: protecting and loving your child is really protecting your own genetic future. I believe that people, men and women – parents – are just that damn self-centered.

The mother duckling is convinced that her young one is not a turkey, but you have to "look at him properly" to see that he's not ugly. If a young one is beautiful, he is going to be beautiful at any angle. If you have to "look at him properly," then you're just fooling yourself. Face the facts: you got an ugly ass kid now deal with it!

Then comes the advice to the young one, because she cares about his well-being. She knows how society is and tells him to stick close to her. And she adds with a special caveat, "beware of the cat." Now see, this is where black parents go wrong. They turn us over to these peckerwoods and most of them don't even know what's going on in the schools, especially pre-school and kindergarten. My parents didn't know shit about what we went through. My mom just knew that we needed mats for nap time and that was about it. They had no idea about the humiliating stories that we had to listen to during "reading time," from "Little Black Sambo" to this bullshit about "The Ugly Duckling." We were being programmed and our parents were confident that it was "education." It was education, alright: an education in oppression. And you wonder why there are so many confused Jemimas and Uncle Toms in our ranks?

Like the mother duckling, our parents needed to "introduce us to the farmyard." We needed to be better prepared. The one thing that kept me from being a brainwashed sellout like the majority of my classmates was that my family moved from lily-white Hastings, Nebraska to the California Bay Area – at the height of the Black Power movement. And I never had any idea whether or not my parents knew what was going on with the Black Nationalist movement or not. But I know this: I was hitch hiking to Oakland every chance I got and I was spending a lot of time with older Black Nationalist bruthas and sisters on Grove, San Pablo and other streets near Black Panther headquarters.

I learned about the "farmyard" from people who wanted to prepare me intellectually for what was waiting. Although I was in high school, I attended school at an all-black institution (or so it seemed to me) when we got to Pittsburg, California and was immediately dubbed "gifted and talented." It is clear to me now that I was smarter than many of my teachers, but one thing I learned; black people were doing some things in nearby Berkeley and Oakland, and they were pissed off about something. And that is how I was introduced to the farmyard; not by my mother or father, but by older people who gave a fuck about the race and were willing to fight the power: "beware of the cat."

Continuing on:

> When they reached the farmyard, there was a great disturbance; two families were fighting for an eel's head, which, after all, was carried off by the cat. "See, children, that is the way of the world," said the mother duck, whetting her beak, for she would have liked the eel's head herself. "Come, now, use your legs, and let me see how well you can behave …

This mother really cares and she's showing her young ones the way the world functions. This shows that she is logical – except when it comes to understanding the concept of "beauty" and "ugly." Like today's intelligent black people, you can be smart and still have unconscious self-hatred. You can have college degrees and still suffer from what psychologist Roderick W. Pugh referred to as, "The-we-ain't-ready-syndrome." Maybe if the mother duck truly wanted her children to know the way of the world, she would have been a little more instructive when it came to treatment of their youngest sibling.

Instead, she falls prey to classism and teaches her kids that elitism calls the shots. Check out the following:

> You must bow your heads *prettily to that old duck yonder*; she is the highest born of them all, *and has Spanish blood*, therefore, *she is well off.* Don't you see she has a red flag tied to her leg, which is something very grand, and a great honor for a duck; it shows that everyone is anxious not to lose her, *as she can be recognized both by man and beast.* Come, now, don't turn your toes, a well-bred

> duckling spreads his feet wide apart, just like his father and
> mother, in this way; now bend your neck, and say 'quack.'"
> (emphasis added).

Let's look at what I call "brainwashing tips" and see the relevance of this lesson to real-life situations.

First, the concept of bowing your heads "prettily to the old duck" who is supposedly some kind of Spanish royalty. Sounds like to me like mama duck is teaching her kids how to kiss ass, how to "kneel before Zod!" These kinds of ass kissing tips have been given out by more than a few black mothers in the name of "keepin' my chile safe." That's one way to look at it. Another way to look at it is to send your kid out there thinking that white people are logical and that they don't "see race as an issue." In my book, to be forewarned is to be forearmed. Teaching kids to "kneel before royalty" has long been the downfall of minority groups and it sends the wrong message of kids who don't learn about merit because they don't believe in it, thinking white folks have all the opportunities "cornered."

Secondly mother duck had a red flag on her leg which to the mother duck, is something "grand" and "a great honor" because "it shows that everyone is anxious not to lose her …" No, the Spanish duck has been "branded" in my book. That red flag on her leg identifies her as "the one" in the same way that white folks put brands on their cattle. When all is said and done, the duck is going to be on somebody's dinner table, I don't care how rich her blood is. So it's a class system where you have those on the lower rung (ducks) thinking that there are those among them who are "better" than the rest of them. Malcolm X once asked, "what does the white man call a black man with a PhD?" The answer: "Nigger, that's what they call him." As Karenga (1967) put it long ago, "There are no exclusive rights to any one black man; either all are free or none are free."

Third, the fact that her loftiness is "recognized by both man and beast." Let me tell you something: mother duckling is right on this one, but for the wrong reason. These are two different forms of "recognition;" this Spanish duckling might be viewed as a member of the elite duck corps to the ducks, but to the human race she's just another meat dish on the menu. Both involve recognition, but at what level of life? This goes back to the Malcolm X quote that I shared earlier: in the black community, for instance, there is no class struggle because there is only one class – the class of the dispossessed.

Fourth, the mother duckling is teaching the young ones how to stand properly, how to bend their necks and how to speak. This is an attempt at assimilation. No matter how they bend their necks or what the caliber of their "quack" is, they are still going to be seen as ducks. This is a lesson that these Uncle Tom negroes, who rode into the system on affirmative action mandates, are going to have to learn. They have keys, but they don't fit anything. No matter how expensive your suit or tie is, in the final analysis you're going to be monitored and you're going to be monitored differently than your white colleagues, and the reason for that is because of one thing: skin color.

Continuing:

> The ducklings did as they were bid, but the other duck stared, and said, "Look, here comes another brood, as if there were not enough of us already! and *what a queer looking object one of them is; we don't want him here,"* and then *one flew out and bit him in the neck.* "Let him alone," said the mother; "he is not doing any harm." *"Yes, but he is so big and ugly,"* said the spiteful duck "and therefore he must be turned out." *"The others are very pretty children,"* said the old duck, with the rag on her leg, "all but that one; *I wish his mother could improve him a little."*

Let me interject here and address a couple of points raised by and within the preceding paragraph.

First of all, the "here comes another brood" syndrome. This is nothing more than group hate, which is an extension of the self-hate that groups who think that they "have it made" show toward newcomers who they think are going to interfere with the imagined progress they've made. Among black people this is known as "the crawdad syndrome," so named because crawdads in a bucket will drag down one who has almost made it to the top of the bucket so that they can elevate themselves.

Sociologists would call this an "in-group versus out group" type of situation, except one thing is very important to know. Those in power, those who made this first group "number one" in the first place, don't give a FUCK about either group! The fact is, the more enervating internecine conflicts, the better those in power feel. The first group says, "here comes the brood," but in reality, all involved are nothing more than a "brood" as far as the shot-callers and power barons are concerned. And ain't none of these decision makers of the duck persuasion.

Secondly, the statement (a product of Hans Christian Andersen's mind), "what a queer looking object one of them is; we don't want him here." Shades of racial segregation in America and the housing conflicts of the 1950s and 1960s. These are the same words that would be used by white folks as they saw black people coming into "their" neighborhoods. We were "queer looking" because we had skin color, something that they spend billions of dollars a year in tanning parlors trying to get. And they didn't want us in their neighborhoods for what many view as sexual reasons. After all, one of their main slogans was, "the key to the classroom is the key to the bedroom."

Third, after the insults came the physical brutality when one of the offended group of ducks "flew out and bit him [the ugly duckling] in the neck." Remember, this story was published in 1844, and bear in mind what was taking place in America at around the same time: white folks were behaving, toward black people, the same way these offended ducks were acting toward "the new brood." In fact, black people were being treated like a "brood" because enslavement was alive and well and segregation was supported by national law! This nation was violent even during the "nonviolent" crap that Martin Luther King, Jr. was espousing. Why? Race hatred, akin to the disdain that the ducks who felt offended were showing to the incoming ducks by resorting to violence.

Fourth, mama ducks defense of her young one: "Let him alone," said the mother; "he is not doing any harm." No, he's not doing any harm. But maybe she should remember that as she continues to deal with the "largeness" and "darkness" of her youngest child. Maybe what she is doing by playing those color games and espousing how "beautiful" her other kids are at the expense of "the ugly duckling" is far worse than the fact that one duck bit the child on the neck. Psychological abuse can be worse than physical abuse.

Fifth, "Yes, but he is so big and ugly," said the spiteful duck "and therefore he must be turned out." These are the lessons that children should be taught and then those lessons have to be linked to race. Hans Christian Andersen more likely than not didn't have the cultural competence to handle this. He was just a racist white boy, probably gay, making the mother duck look good despite the psychological color-coded abuse she was heaping on her son's back. If you're not white, anything else is going to be viewed as "non-white," and the prefix "non" means, "the absence of," or "without," both of which make being white the norm.

Sixth and finally, the others are very pretty children," said the old duck, with the rag on her leg, "all but that one; I wish his mother could improve him a little." The only way to "improve" him would be to make him lighter. I've heard this before. Even now there are creams pawning themselves off as "blemish creams" that will "make your skin clearer," but back in the day they were called what they were: skin bleaching creams. This is what happens when you've been brainwashed by an alien race and programmed to hate anything black or anything that is not "white."

> *"That is impossible, your grace," replied the mother; "he is not pretty; but he has a very good disposition, and swims as well or even better than the others. I think he will grow up pretty, and perhaps be smaller;* he has remained too long in the egg, and therefore his figure is not properly formed;" and then she stroked his neck and smoothed the feathers, saying, "It is a drake, and therefore not of so much consequence. I think he will grow up strong, and able to take care of himself." *"The other ducklings are graceful enough,"* said the old duck. "Now make yourself at home, and if you can find an eel's head, you can bring it to me." (emphasis added).

Now, for analysis of the previous excerpt.

We begin with the first point, which sounds like a mother attempting to explain a child who has a mental disability. "That is impossible, your grace," replied the mother; "he is not pretty; but he has a very good disposition, and swims as well or even better than the others. I think he will grow up pretty, and perhaps be smaller; he has remained too long in the egg, and therefore his figure is not properly formed." It's all about a male being "pretty"? This is why I believe that Hans Christian Andersen was gay: why so much attention on the male of the species when it is clear that the female is the one with all the beauty and males, for the most part – with the exception of the peacock and the tiger, in my opinion - are nothing more than food-gathering stragglers?

Then comes the backhanded compliments which sound more like a "wish and hope" type statement than anything else. She strokes the "ugly duckling's" neck and feels she has to "explain" that, ""It is a drake, and therefore not of so much consequence. I think he will grow up strong, and able to take care of himself." Mothers of all races are strange; they seem to think that their kids can do no wrong. In this case, as is the case with too many mothers in modern-day America, they think they can raise boys to be men, they think they can "fix" anything that is wrong with any male and they tend to believe that their male children "were good boys and would never do anything like that."

The mother duckling is doing her son a disservice with all this bullshit. He is what he is and as we would later find out, nature would take its course. The only thing she can do with this on-going defense "by any means necessary" is turn him into a homoerotic recluse that will rise up with gender confusion. In the case of single parent families in today's black community, the rise of the wannabe thug and the closet homosexual are what happens when you defend your son "by any means necessary" and give him the belief that he has "carte blanche" when it comes to doing anything he wants to do.

Then, in vintage "hater" style (long before the term became fashionable), the older duck suggests, "The other ducklings are graceful enough … Now make yourself at home, and if you can find an eel's head, you can bring it to me." When she sees that the mother duckling is going to stick by her son (while ignoring her unsolicited advice), she turns to the rest of the brood. Again, Hans Christian Andersen seems to have an insight on the female psyche, almost as if he IS a female. Get it?

Moving right along with the tale:

> *And so they made themselves comfortable; but the poor duckling, who had crept out of his shell last of all, and looked so ugly, was bitten and pushed and made fun of, not only by the ducks, but by all the poultry.* "He is too big," they all said, and the turkey cock, who had been born into the world with spurs, and fancied himself really an emperor, puffed himself out like a vessel in full sail, *and flew at the duckling, and became quite red in the head with passion, so that the poor little thing did not know where to go, and was quite miserable because he was so ugly and laughed at by the whole farmyard.* (emphasis added)

The poor "ugly duckling" was the subject of ridicule. He was out of his shell, but as you can see, people felt he "looked so ugly," that he was bitten and pushed and made fun of – not only by other ducks, but by all poultry. That includes chickens. Now when a chicken makes fun of yo' ass, you must *really* be fucked up! All joking aside, even the turkey cock attacked the poor duck and the duck felt badly because he was laughed at by the whole farmyard.

Sound familiar? This is the kind of "degradation campaign" that black men and women had to undergo at the workplace in the Northern part of the United States. The south had enslavement practices, of course, and while northern states often talked about how wrong it was, the fact is that racial segregation was still the law of the land. And that meant that white people opposed interacting with black people. To see a black person at the work front was an insult to white folks, who believed that this black person was taking a job that a white man should have. And one need only glean the books addressing the history of the American worker to see that the ugly duckling's treatment and that of a man perceived as an "ugly duckling" – and African-American male – were quite similar.

What do you think "Amos n' Andy" was all about? What do you think those minstrel shows were aimed at? Why do you think that posters showing black kids eating huge slices of watermelon and black men "coonin' it up" were so popular? Even to this day "the farmyard" – American society – remains hostile to black people and is not above ridicule, scorn and yes, violence. Remember the Imus radio show, when this peckerwood had the gall to refer to a team of black women as being "nappy headed"? The comparisons are endless.

The tale of "The Ugly Duckling" teaches us more:

> So it went on from day to day till it got worse and worse. The poor duckling was driven about by everyone; even his brothers and sisters were unkind to him, and would say, "Ah, you ugly creature, I wish the cat would get you," and his mother said she wished he'd never been born … The ducks pecked him, the chickens beat him, and the girl who fed the poultry kicked him with her feet. So at last he ran away, frightening the little birds in the hedge as he flew over the palings (emphasis added).

On-going harassment and getting "dogged" at every turn. Even his brothers and sisters joined in. They seemed to wish he was dead. Now as black people in 2015, don't most of us know families like this? Because so many black men have fathered children with more than one women, isn't it typical that there would be animosity in some of these "extended" or "mixed" families? The duckling had it hard, but we should be able to relate. And those black kids sitting in class listening to these stories had to be torn up outside. The key to the brainwash is to strike some chords that the listener can relate to. Black kids, for the most part, were taught to hate themselves and those like them. They might not have known why, but it was planted in their little minds with fucked up stories like the ones written by Hans Christian Andersen.

And next the ultimate insult: the mother duck who was defending this little bird throughout the story – now we find out her inner feelings. According to the storyteller, in addition to his brothers and sisters hating his guts, his own dear mother said she wished he was dead. My how this must have impacted black children to hear this. And those of you who are reading this, who might be parents or might know someone who has kids in kindergarten, check with the Curriculum Department because the white people of today are not above sneaking shit like this into the curriculum in the name of "political correctness" (by their standards).

Let us continue:

> "They are afraid of me because I am ugly," he said. So he closed his
> eyes, and flew still farther, until he came out on a large moor, inhabited
> by wild ducks. Here he remained the whole night, feeling very tired and
> sorrowful. In the morning, when the wild ducks rose in the air, they
> stared at their new comrade. "What sort of a duck are you?" they all said,
> coming round him.

This is a very sad story, and it shows that it was not really the duckling who was "ugly;" it was the reactions of the people around him, and their heaped their collective "ugliness" upon this young bird. This is the mob mentality and work and is akin to what Oliver C. Cox referred to in his book *Caste, Class and Race* as "the manhunt tradition." In this case the "ugliness" and all the teaming up destroyed the self-esteem of this young duckling, so much to the point he didn't even have the confidence or willpower to seek out a mate:

> He bowed to them, and was as polite as he could be, but he did not
> reply to their question. *"You are exceedingly ugly,"* said the wild
> ducks, "but that will not matter if you do not want to marry one of
> our family." (emphasis added). Poor thing! he had no thoughts of
> marriage; all he wanted was permission to lie among the rushes,
> and drink some of the water on the moor.

These stories have a way of legitimizing the mores and norms of a system, whether those norms and mores are legitimate or not. In this case, the concept of marriage which in 1844, was considered the goal of anyone especially females. The man was not a real man unless he "had a family" and that meant a wife and kids. Females were treated like shit and this was also part of the way things were done; the concept of the wife-beater t-shirt, which is so popular with rednecks and Latinos today, is named after the abusive norms established by men all over the world, and mastered by the white man.

In the case of the so-called "ugly duckling," I make the point that what was ugly was the imposition of these bullshit marriage norms. Such norms put pressure on people to enter into relationships that they may or may not be ready for. The concept of shacking up didn't make things any better once the white man countered it with "palimony" lawsuits. But remember this is 1844 and even the ugliest duckling was supposed to view marriage with sacred observance.

The tale continues, thusly:

> After he had been on the moor two days, there came two wild
> geese, or rather goslings, for they had not been out of the egg long,
> and were very saucy. *"Listen, friend,"* said one of them to the
> *duckling, "you are so ugly, that we like you very well. Will you go*

with us, and become a bird of passage? Not far from here is another moor, in which there are some pretty wild geese, all unmarried. It is a chance for you to get a wife; you may be lucky, ugly as you are." (emphasis added)

Do you see how precise Hans Christian Andersen seeks to be when teaching the correct terms for things? No, it's not "geese, but "goslings." And that is why I know this man was a color-conscious racist: he knows that the concept of being "dark" is also linked to being "dark" or, more definitely, to being "non-white."

Insults are hurled even while upholding societal norms: ""Listen, friend," said one of them to the duckling, "you are so ugly, that we like you very well. Will you go with us, and become a bird of passage? Not far from here is another moor, in which there are some pretty wild geese, all unmarried. It is a chance for you to get a wife; you may be lucky, ugly as you are." Getting a wife will make everything alright – looks may not matter. And guess what? That's the way it's always been in cultures where marriages are "arranged," and that is what we are talking about here: hook up permanently with someone so you can be accepted by the majority.

Later, the birds come under attack by some hunters:

"Pop, pop," sounded in the air, and the two wild geese fell dead among the rushes, and the water was tinged with blood. "Pop, pop," echoed far and wide in the distance, and whole flocks of wild geese rose up from the rushes. The sound continued from every direction, for the sportsmen surrounded the moor, and some were even seated on branches of trees, overlooking the rushes …

Look at the attention to detail: gunshots being described, situations being outlined and even the placement of the hunters being clearly delineated. So once again, we see that purposeful intent of this story, and such detailed descriptions lend more credence to the overall theme of "ugliness" and how being different is not something that you should be proud of. Another message is that kids should always strive to be one of the "beautiful people" and to pay close attention to what is said about them. This flies directly in the face of the "sticks and stones may break my bones but words will never harm me" bullshit that is being force-fed to these young people by their parents, even as far back as 1844 when this tail was originally published.

More descriptions follow:

> … The blue smoke from the guns rose like clouds over the dark trees, and as it floated away across the water, a number of sporting dogs bounded in among the rushes, which bent beneath them wherever they went. *How they terrified the poor duckling! He turned away his head to hide it under his wing, and at the same moment a large terrible dog passed quite near him. His jaws were open, his tongue hung from his mouth, and his eyes glared fearfully. He thrust his nose close to the duckling, showing his sharp teeth, and then, "splash, splash," he went into the water without touching him, "Oh," sighed the duckling, "how thankful I am for being so ugly; even a dog will not bite me."* (emphasis added).

More fear engulfs the poor duckling, who surely has enough problems as it is. Let's look at some of the repercussions of some of the violence that surrounds this poor duckling.

For one thing, there was the use of those dogs. Sound familiar? That is what they used to chase down what they called "runaway slaves," remember? And don't forget that this was taking place during the same time that this story was published and being read to school-aged children. And then when black people started fighting for human and civil rights, the hound dog was replaced with the police dog (German Shepherd) and "sicced" on black protesters. The "ugly duckling" was being victimized, as were black people during the periods I suggest, simply because he was "different" from the American norm.

The dog missed biting and perhaps killing the duckling after it fell into the water. But when you've low self-esteem, you blame everything that happens on yourself. Despite the dog's ineptness and clumsiness, the duckling nevertheless concludes, "Oh, how thankful I am for being so ugly; even a dog will not bite me." This has to strike at the core of the young listener's psyche: in fact, the statement is the foundation for suicidal considerations. This story is dangerous, and what is "ugly" about it is not the duckling; it is the conditions that give rise to the kind of anti-life and pro-aggression tendencies exhibited by both humans and their animal counterparts.

Continuing on:

> And so he lay quite still, while the shot rattled through the rushes, and gun after gun was fired over him. It was late in the day before all became quiet, *but even then the poor young thing did not dare to move.* He waited quietly for several hours, and then, after looking carefully around him, hastened away from the moor as fast

> as he could. He ran over field and meadow till a storm arose, and
> he could hardly struggle against it. (emphasis added).

The young duckling had survival skills and out of fear, did what he had to do to get past the threats to his life. But as a young duck he had no defense against the psychological violence that was being waged against and imposed upon him. The hunters and their guns were one thing, but on-going harassment and threats from his peers and other members of the kingdom of thingdom were too much to bear. His sense of self had been severely impaired – much like the subconscious minds of the kids who had to listen to this bullshit. The concept of "The Ugly Duckling" had such a profound impact that references are made to the story and metaphors are used regarding the theme of the book to this very day, some 170 years later.

Moving on:

> Towards evening, he reached a poor little cottage that seemed
> ready to fall, and only remained standing because it could not
> decide on which side to fall first. The storm continued so violent,
> that the duckling could go no farther; he sat down by the cottage,
> and then he noticed that the door was not quite closed in
> consequence of one of the hinges having given way. There was
> therefore a narrow opening near the bottom large enough for him
> to slip through, which he did very quietly, and got a shelter for the
> night.

So now out of desperation we have criminal trespass and invasion of privacy committed by the duckling. Regardless of the storm and the fact that the door to the cottage was slightly ajar, he had no right to enter. Despite the poor condition of the hinges, he had no right to take advantage of the situation. In this case, "the ends justifies the means," which seems to be a recurring theme in this story (along with, "if it feels good, do it").

He now had shelter for the night. There is no long-term planning for this desperate young duck. He thinks only about the immediate. This is a good time to teach the young people who are listening to this tale that, "short term pleasure yields long term pain." But that's not the case: "if you see someone you don't like, insult them;" "people who are different are inherently inferior and deficient"; "always strive and give priority to that which is beautiful." These are the unspoken lessons that are inculcated into the minds of these children in addition to the obvious themes of value judgments and class issues.

More descriptions and character introductions follow:

A woman, a tom cat, and a hen lived in this cottage. The tom cat,
whom the mistress called, "My little son," was a great favorite; he
could raise his back, and purr, and could even throw out sparks
from his fur if it were stroked the wrong way. The hen had very
short legs, so she was called "Chickie short legs." She laid good
eggs, and her mistress loved her as if she had been her own child.
In the morning, the strange visitor was discovered, and the tom cat
began to purr, and the hen to cluck.

What we have here are introductions of three character types as they relate to the incursion of this young duckling.

Take notice that in all of these scenarios, there is no male figure that the duck can identify with. Females dominate the setting in terms of main characters. Where is this woman's husband or male companion? There is no attempt at an explanation. To this juncture, the only description we have in reference to the duckling's father is that he didn't care enough to even come around. Such a negative characterization is something that children during 1844 may not have been able to relate to, but as the story continues to get handed down from generation to generation, such a male bias could possibly play a role in the subsequent debasement of the black child and the "attitude" that he (or she) takes back home to his (or her) mother.

The "tom cat" is a male figure, but since the woman refers to him as her "little son," this still makes him inferior to her, rather she defers her power or not. He kissed her ass and entertained her for the most part (" … was a great favorite; he could raise his back, and purr, and could even throw out sparks from his fur if it were stroked the wrong way"). The role of the minstrel for the most part; a role that black males would be assigned to in the years ahead (except that any "stroking" that was done was done at the end of a whip).

And what about the hen? Just as the tom cat was around for the amusement of the woman, the same can be said for the hen. But she also served more of a utilitarian purpose: she laid eggs. The kind of "love" that this woman had for the hen and the cat is akin to the love that a farmer has for his mule or horse; it is based on the relationship of master-slave for the most part. Although the story says that the hen was treated as if she was the woman's "own child," let us not forget that child abuse was alive and well in 1844, and just because bearing a child (in this case owning a hen) takes place, doesn't mean that the relationship is either real or rock strong.

The duckling had snuck into the cottage and was discovered by the inhabitants described above:

> "What is that noise about?" said the old woman, looking round the room, but her sight was not very good; therefore, when she saw the duckling she thought *it must be a fat duck, that had strayed from home.* "Oh what a prize!" she exclaimed, "I hope it is not a drake, for then I shall have some duck's eggs. I must wait and see." So the duckling was allowed to remain on trial for three weeks, but there were no eggs. (emphasis added).

In vintage slave master fashion the old woman views the duckling as a creature who can be exploited (pimped). After finding out what the noise was about and spotting the duckling, the first thing that comes to this woman's mind is that she could get some eggs out of the deal. And because of that exploiter mentality, the duckling was allowed to stay.

After three weeks no eggs came and it appears that egomania permeated the old woman's house:

> Now the tom cat was the master of the house, and the hen was mistress, and they always said, "We and the world," for they believed themselves to be half the world, and the better half too. The duckling thought that others might hold a different opinion on the subject, but the hen would not listen to such doubts. "Can you lay eggs?" she asked. "No." "Then have the goodness to hold your tongue." "Can you raise your back, or purr, or throw out sparks?" said the tom cat. "No." "Then you have no right to express an opinion when sensible people are speaking."

How is a house that obviously belongs to the old woman going to have a tom cat as the master of the house and a hen as the mistress? The point I'm making here is the importance of rank and stratification. Andersen (the author) knows of how important social status is, and this is what makes the subsequent insulting of the duckling even more abominable. The more characters the duckling meets, the further down the social ladder he descends!

Because of the presumed "statuses" that the old woman, the tom cat and the hen believed they were deserving of, their egos were out of line with their abilities, in my opinion. "We and the world"? They felt they were the better halves of the world despite their lowly status? This reminds me of the white rednecks in the south and their views of black people. No matter how low class these white people were, no matter how poor, they always felt that they were better than any black person, even those who had superior social status in the northern part of the United States. White privilege trumps all, or so it seems, and it is still in operation to this very day.

Because the duckling could not produce eggs, purr or raise its back, it had no rights in the eyes of the cat or the hen. Shades of the *Dred Scott* decision of 1857 (passed just 13 years after this story was published), where Chief Justice Roger Taney ruled, "A black man has no rights a white man is bound to respect." Are you beginning to see the class prejudice in play here? If Andersen could effectively describe such class distinctions and prejudices between animals and humans, then he damn sure knew something about the American white man's enslavement of fellow black human beings. And what did he do about it? Not a damn thing.

So the duckling as really nothing but a pariah:

> So the duckling sat in a corner, *feeling very low spirited,* till the sunshine and the fresh air came into the room through the open door, and then he began to feel such a great longing for a swim on the water, that he could not help telling the hen. "What an absurd idea," said the hen. "You have nothing else to do, therefore you have foolish fancies. If you could purr or lay eggs, they would pass away." (emphasis added)

Like a true slave driver, the hen tells the duckling to lay eggs or purr and he would feel better. In other words, work for the benefit of our "master," jump through hoops, scratch when don't nothin' itch and laugh when ain't nothin' funny and if you do these things you will feel better. Why? Because you are contributing to the social and economic wherewithal of this house – which, by the way, doesn't belong to any of us. Sound familiar? This is the typical thinking of black people in this country. The harder you work and the more you do to accommodate, entertain and buttress this system, the better you'll feel – no matter how degrading the things are that you do. You'll own or control nothing, but you'll feel better.

Malcolm X taught us as much in his speech, "The Black Revolution:"

> It's like when you go to the dentist, and the man's going to take your tooth. You're going to fight him when he starts pulling. So he squirts some stuff in your jaw called Novocain, to make you think they're not doing anything to you. So you sit there and 'cause you've got all of that Novocain in your jaw, you suffer peacefully. Blood running all down your jaw, and you don't know what's happening. 'Cause someone has taught you to suffer -- peacefully.

Suffer peacefully. Earlier the duckling was told that he had no rights that anyone was bound to respect. How much more like the plight of today's black man and woman can this duckling's life be?! And there are other similarities:

> "But it is so delightful to swim about on the water," said the
> duckling, "and so refreshing to feel it close over your head, while
> you dive down to the bottom."

This duckling isn't getting the message. His descriptions of good times and ecstatic experiences don't mean shit to those who don't respect or give a shit about him! He's wasting his time in the same way these "protesters," "marchers," "sign carriers, "prayer vigil attendees" and others are wasting their time making moral appeals to a system that has no morals! If this society's violations and crimes against white people were a matter of morality that they respected, there would be no violations or crimes in the first place! As the song "Where Have All the Flowers Gone" so emphatically asks, "when will they ever learn?"

The utopian descriptions of the duckling fall on deaf ears and uncaring individuals:

> "Delightful, indeed!" said the hen, "why you must be crazy! Ask
> the cat, he is the cleverest animal I know, ask him how he would
> like to swim about on the water, or to dive under it, for I will not
> speak of my own opinion; ask our mistress, the old woman—there
> is no one in the world more clever than she is. Do you think she
> would like to swim, or to let the water close over her head?"

When push comes to shove the "overseers" can always rely on "the master" to back them up. And so it is in this case. If they can't relate to it or do it, then they debunk the activity all together. If they can't do it, then the fact that you can means nothing to them. They then heap hagiographic praise on the head of the old woman and make her the ultimate authority. The fact is, if she was so damn "cleaver," why does she have a house where a cat is the "master" and the hen is the "mistress?"

The hen continues her diatribe:

> "You don't understand me," said the duckling. "We don't
> understand you? *Who can understand you, I wonder?* Do you

<blockquote>
consider yourself more clever than the cat, or the old woman? I will say nothing of myself. Don't imagine such nonsense, child, and thank your good fortune that you have been received here …
</blockquote>

It is the duckling who is lacking in understanding! He doesn't understand his situation, his relationship to the decision makers in the house he is staying or that he is wasting his time trying to be logical with illogical creatures! They believe that they are cleverer than he (the duckling) is, and as a result, they have made it clear that they don't have to respect his rights because he has none. Their belief, like the whites who owned the plantations and provided shacks out back for those they enslaved, is that the duckling was "lucky" to "have been received here."

Here is the hen's logic:

<blockquote>
Are you not in a warm room, and in society from which you may learn something? But you are a chatterer, and your company is not very agreeable. Believe me; I speak only for your own good. I may tell you unpleasant truths, but that is a proof of my friendship. I advise you, therefore, to lay eggs, and learn to purr as quickly as possible." (Emphasis added)
</blockquote>

These are the kinds of paternalistic insults that white people use against people of color on a regular basis. They have been programmed to believe that their very presence and interaction with people, even on a master-slave level, should be appreciated. This kind of elitist thinking and condescension is not being lost on the little ones who are listening to this story being read to them. They are so angry at the hen and the way she was treating the ugly duckling. But they cannot see that the ugly duckling is partially responsible: to be so ignorant and submissive in the face of this kind of demeaning treatment is, at least in my view, a crime in and of itself.

The hen calls her statements acts of "friendship" and tells the duckling that she's making her statements for his own good. In fact, she refers to her insults as "unpleasant truths." This has to be written by someone who is aware of the history of his fellow whites. This is the exact same type of bullshit that they pull on those who they oppress, with emphasis on black people. From the Hamitic Myth (the descendants of Ham were cursed to be black according to this bullshit) to pseudo-scientific studies of black inferiority, it was all supposed to be about doing black people a favor by "separating the races" and as a result, preventing racial conflict. The history books are replete with examples of this type of tricknology: these white men did the same thing when it came to inferiorizing women, those with special needs, various white ethnic groups, Latinos, Asians, people from the Middle East, Jews (who are guilty of using it themselves) and so many others.

There are two general responses in the nature of "things." The choices are "fight or flight." In a response pattern typical of the rejected, the duckling decides that "flight" is his best option. So he vacates the premises:

> "I believe I must go out into the world again," said the duckling.
> "Yes, do," said the hen. So the duckling left the cottage, and soon found water on which it could swim and dive, but was *avoided* by all other animals, *because of its ugly appearance.* (emphasis added).

When you leave only after being disrespected, dogged out and given no choice, then it's not only a departure from the premises, it is a forced departure; in other words, an *eviction.*

But the key to the preceding paragraph is that even though the duckling left the cottage and had all these dreams about finding some water, he didn't know one thing: pleasure is an indispensable part of pain. He found good vibes in the water, but the social isolation and stigma trumped all that leisure. As the story makes clear, he found water on which he could swim and dive, "but was avoided by all other animals, because of its ugly appearance."

And this is the message that the kids are picking up on: no matter how personally satisfied or happy you are, if people think you're ugly, then life isn't worth living. Another lesson prioritizes what people think as opposed to what you think about yourself. This is what Hans Christian Andersen was imparting to young people who read or listened to his bullshit fairy tales. The moral is not a positive one because it opens up the door for being defined by other people.

And that is one of the things that is wrong with oppressed people today: allowing alien outsiders to tell them what does or does not "look good." As a quick example, even now a skin cream called Proactive is telling people that this cream can "eliminate blemishes" and make your skin "clear." This is a fancy, roundabout way of promoting skin bleaching creams and skin lightener. How about Stelara, with blonde, pale model Carrie English telling viewers, as she promenades across the set that, "Stelara makes my skin much clearer" (translation: more pale). And what about

And who falls prey to this shit? People with dark skin who want to lighten their skin. Former Chicago Cub Sammy Sosa did it. Magazines do it to black women's complexions, including Beyonce, all the time. But let me give you an international example to show how people place premiums not only on "beauty" but on a certain kind of beauty message that says that the lighter you are, the more attractive you are.

An article on the Not the Nation website (March 23, 2010) was titled, "Thailand Donates 50,000 Bottles of "Whitening Skin Cream to Haiti." The sub-headline adds that, "Abhisit hopes earthquake survivors will feel "more confident" with lighter, more radiant skin." Remember that what made the ugly duckling so despicable in the minds of other people was the fact that he was dark. Now, the article about the Haitian people. Following is the gist of the article, and the comments made in it offer a learning lesson that should be juxtaposed with the messages inherent in "The Ugly Duckling":

> Responding to international criticism that its initial donation of $20,000 was insufficient, the Thai government has generously added 50,000 bottles of whitening skin cream to its aid shipment to earthquake-stricken Haiti. "Thailand is a compassionate nation," said Foreign Minister Kasit Piromya. "We noticed in the news that the Haitians are all very dark-skinned. This is surely one of the reasons they are living in poverty. With lighter skin they could be more successful."

The aversion to dark skin (while Europeans spend billions every year trying to tan their pale skin) is international, and it's because of the white man and his mythmaking machinery. How can someone from Thailand, loaded down with brown people, have the gall to associate dark skin with poverty? Where is the data that shows that lighter skin makes a person more successful? Look at their poverty-laden nation: they're not "light skinned" and yet they live on the fringes of barbarism. But it gets worse as what could be called "the ugly duckling syndrome" continues:

> The donation is co-sponsored by Unilever Thailand Ltd., which has agreed to provide the 50,000 bottles of Citra Ultra White if the government provides shipping. Along with the whitening cream, there will also be 50,000 copies of Citra's new brochure, explaining the power of Citra's double-action anti-aging and brightening formula …

The next time you hear somebody talking about issues of race and/or racism somehow diminishing, you remember the previous quote and the article being cited from. Unilever's products like various bathroom soaps and washes can be found all over the United States, but you can see what their real moral motives are based on. Just referring to the product as "Citra Ultra White" is a statement about race and skin color. And the circulation of brochures "explaining the power" of the formula is putting that racism into print – just like Hans Christian Andersen did with "The Ugly Duckling."

It gets worse – check out the following:

> … "Citra Ultra White lets you look and feel your best," said
> Marlene Van Houten, Unilever's regional marketing director.
> "Whether you're standing in line for UN food shipments, or just
> sorting through the rubble of your devastated village, Citra Ultra
> White provides whiter skin and all-day UV protection."

Remember that old racist saying, "If you're white, you're right; if you're black, get back; if you're brown, stick around"? It appears to be alive and well on an international level because people in Thailand are brown and they appear to hate the concept of "blackness" as much as the people who are white. And look at that racist statement by some white bitch, a major official for the Unilever Company, who says, "… "Citra Ultra White lets you look and feel your best," said Marlene Van Houten, Unilever's regional marketing director. "Whether you're standing in line for UN food shipments, or just sorting through the rubble of your devastated village, Citra Ultra White provides whiter skin and all-day UV protection."

How can whiter skin protect you against ultra-violet rays when white people and that recessive gene and pale skin are getting skin cancer all over the world? If whiteness was so wonderful, why are white people a worldwide minority and why are their ranks shrinking? Now let's fast forward from this incident to March of 2013 and the case of supposedly "conscious" India Arie. As was reported by the *Huffington Post*,

> The 37-year-old star is almost unrecognizable in the cover image
> from her which is causing a lot of backlash and many to believe
> that she has been lightening her skin. This is quite a shock
> considering the afro-centric R&B singer is known for promoting
> black beauty-- most notably expressed in her hit songs "Brown
> Skin" and "I Am Not My Hair."

So she's a hypocrite. At least Beyonce wears her hair blonde and apparently doesn't give a shit what people think. But this bitch India Arie is supposed to be so down to earth, grass roots-oriented and "africentric" - right? Check out the following:

> Sources close to India told TMZ that her "lightened" skin tone is the result of the camera flash and angle. And added that the singer never asked to be lightened. Nevertheless, the celebrity website makes the valid point that India approved the photo without correcting the color of her skin.

She approved it, so fuck all the excuses. These people are suffering from the same psychic sickness that so many people of color are suffering from because of the power of the global "if it ain't white, it ain't right" standards, the same ones that apparently inflicted the thinking of Hans Christian Andersen and his classic tale of "The Ugly Duckling."

Black people share another similarity with the ugly duckling: there's nobody that seems to be willing to help us deal with these negative perceptions of us. For instance,

> The whitening cream represents the single-largest shipment of its kind ever to a disaster-zone. Prime Minister Abhisit Vejjajiva said that the generosity of Thais was evident because so many people had encouraged the donation. "Everyone kept talking about how black-skinned the Haitians are," he said …

Note the extremes. In "The Ugly Duckling," every animal in the farmyard turned against that young duck. In like manner, these people are talking about "so many people" and "everyone kept talking" about "black skinned Haitians." Where is the evidence? Where are their studies? What has the white race done that is so great without the use of bombs, bullets and beast-like men? This racism permeates the world in the same way that pathological observations and actions permeated the farmyard in "The Ugly Duckling" story. Furthermore, the article notes that,

> … "At every discussion about aid, the skin color kept coming up. I see now that the initial pledge of USD20,000 was very low because in the back of our minds we knew that these black people needed something more than just money."

Say what? "These black people needed more than just money"? So in other words, skin color is something to be pitied and "helped"? The ugly duckling was made to feel that nothing he could do could make him white. Now do you see the similarities between his plight and the situation of black people, not only here in the United States, but all over the world?

And it's not just in Thailand. According to the article,

> Many people interviewed for the story seemed to agree with the PM. "I donated some money to help the Chinese after the Sichuan earthquake," said office worker Vasana Prasarnmit. "But these Haiti people are so dark I don't want to give them anything. Maybe if they were lighter, like Obama" …

The thing is, Obama is half-white, which is probably why he's acceptable to so many of the Thai people. This says more about their "anglophilia" than it does about whether or not black skin is abominable. But now you know how the Thai people feel about skin color, especially dark-colored skin. It doesn't seem to bother their women when they're sucking black dick and having sex with dark skinned military personnel.

At any rate,

> … It is believed that the whitening cream can make the homeless, starving survivors of the earthquake look whiter and brighter in just 14 days, according to the Unilever brochure. It is hoped that by looking whiter, the Haitians might be able to secure more aid.

So now you can see the relevance of the story about the ugly duckling. Essential to that story is the hue or color of that young duck, and you have seen how this duckling, who did nothing to harm anyone, was treated. You can see how, despite being humble to a fault, he was treated like shit. And why? Because he wasn't "white" the way his brothers and sisters grew to be.

Now fast forward to 2010 when this situation with the skin lightening creams came up – more than 170 years later:

> "White skin is the key to success in life, whether it's job interviews, finding a mate, or being elected to office," said Chulalongkorn sociology professor Urmkit Srisomwattanathip. "There's no reason to believe this is any different."

A sociology professor making such statements. As a sociology professor myself and someone who taught it for four years, I know that it is "the study of human interaction." Even though most of the better known theorists – C. Wright Mills, Emile Durkheim and Max Weber among them – were more likely than not racists, they never offered up anything that linked skin color to success in life. This might be the case in European countries, but it is clear that brown people like the professor just quoted still suffer from a subliminal Tarzan mentality and apparently believe that the white man's ice is colder than their ice. Dark skinned people, according to Thai values it appears, are the ugly ducklings of the human race.

Back to the story. The seasons are beginning to change and the weather was growing cold:

> Autumn came, and the leaves in the forest turned to orange and gold. then, as winter approached, the wind caught them as they fell and whirled them in the cold air. The clouds, heavy with hail and snow-flakes, hung low in the sky, and the raven stood on the ferns crying, "Croak, croak." It made one shiver with cold to look at him. All this was very sad for the poor little duckling.

Again, Andersen's attention to detail, and as such, evidence that the images that he is painting in his fairy tale are images that are meant to impact the listener and the reader. So when he chooses to write a story about a duck deemed "ugly" by all the other characters in the farmyard and beyond, he had choices that he made. He consciously chose to associate the fact that the duck was dark and the "beautiful" ducks were white. In doing so he helped promote a value system that has impacted and supported the racists all over the world.

Evidence can be found in the following excerpt:

> One evening, just as the sun set amid radiant clouds, there came a large flock of beautiful birds out of the bushes. The duckling had never seen any like them before. They were swans, and they *curved their graceful necks,* while their *soft plumage* shown with *dazzling whiteness*. They uttered a singular cry, as they spread their *glorious wings* and flew away from those cold regions to warmer countries across the sea. (emphasis added).

Just look at the previous quote: inundated with pro-white descriptions, straight from the mind of Hans Christian Andersen. Let us take time to look at and analyze a few of them.

The flock of "beautiful birds" and the duckling's reaction to them remind me of those bruthas who used to see a bunch of white bitches walking into the mall or a restaurant. To them, this was something to behold. I remember the response of rap group PM Dawn when they saw Christina Applegate ("Married With Children") and said that she was "the most beautiful woman" they ever saw. And these are the words that Hans Christian Anderson uses to describe the birds – who were replete with "dazzling whiteness."

Where the birds were flying to or why is secondary. The key is the description of them. And their "beauty" came at the consequent self-debasement of the duckling. Moving on:

> As they mounted higher and higher in the air, the ugly little duckling felt quite a strange sensation as he watched them. He whirled himself in the water like a wheel, stretched out his neck towards them, and uttered a cry so strange that it frightened himself. Could he ever forget those beautiful, happy birds; and when at last they were out of his sight, he dived under the water, and rose again almost beside himself with excitement.

The on-going reference to the "ugly little duckling" is a part of one of the most successful learning strategies on record: reinforcement through repetition. Keep saying something often enough to children, keep telling them what you feel you want them to know or think they *should* know, and they will inevitably retain the information (unless of course they have some kind of learning disability). Then, juxtapose this "ugliness" with the wonderment that he feels when he sees the "beautiful, happy birds," and it is clear that to be dark is to be inferior, and to be white is to not only be beautiful, but to also be in a perpetual state of euphoria. This is psychological warfare at its most diabolical and deadly because it is aimed at the vulnerable and open minds of children in a school setting.

The emotions that the duckling feels are shared with a great deal of focus and specificity:

> He knew not the names of these birds, nor where they had flown, but he felt towards them as he had never felt for any other bird in the world. He was not envious of these beautiful creatures, *but wished to be as lovely as they. Poor ugly creature,* how gladly he would have lived even with the ducks *had they only given him encouragement*. (emphasis added).

The mere appearance of the birds has impacted on the duckling's emotional state meaning that he has been affected psychologically. Anderson teaches that the duckling, "he towards them as he had never felt for any other bird in the world." In other words the duckling was "aroused" by the way these birds looked. He didn't know anything else but their appearance. And this is exactly the affect that white women seem to have on black men, and that African men had on the white man when he first saw our nudity and penises. Arousal. And what takes after that is a reaction formation that leads you to act, in some way, as a product of that arousal.

The excerpt claims that the duckling "was not envious of these beautiful creatures, but wished to be as lovely as they." That is what envy is, asshole! He wants what they have – that is envy. He wishes he could be as they are. That is a combination of envy, self-denial and deflated self-esteem.

In reference to the latter (deflated self-esteem and self-denial), Andersen writes that, "Poor ugly creature, how gladly he would have lived even with the ducks had they only given him encouragement." And this is a lesson that these kids need to always remember. And for kids of color, they should also remember that there are different types and degrees of encouragement.

During the time that this book was published black kids were not allowed to go to school. But when enslavement supposedly ended, they attended black segregated schools. But stories like "The Ugly Duckling" persisted, and probably hurt even more since the teachers in those schools didn't want their kids growing up hating the white man. So these black teachers imparted the same bullshit, pro-white morals as their white counterparts were doing.

What does this have to do with "encouragement"? You can encourage a kid with lies and bullshit so that they can be "accepted" by white folks, or you can tell them the truth about the system and the white-oriented value system. I am afraid that far too many black teachers prefer the former approach. And that's why when these white school systems today go out "recruiting," they head to the Deep South and those black colleges because most of the students have been "pre-brainwashed" and "encouraged" to be "good niggas." Just what the "white doctor" ordered.

The weather was changing and the ugly duckling apparently wasn't paying attention to his own physicality:

> The winter grew colder and colder; he was obliged to swim about on the water to keep it from freezing, but every night the space on which he swam became smaller and smaller. At length it froze so hard that the ice in the water crackled as he moved, and the duckling had to paddle with his legs as well as he could, to keep the space from closing up. He became exhausted at last, and lay still and helpless, frozen fast in the ice.

So he's about to die, but as fate would have it, his life was saved:

> Early in the morning, a peasant, who was passing by, saw what had
> happened. He broke the ice in pieces with his wooden shoe, and
> carried the duckling home to his wife. The warmth revived the poor
> little creature; but when the children wanted to play with him, the
> duckling thought they would do him some harm; so he started up in
> terror, fluttered into the milk-pan, and splashed the milk about the
> room. Then the woman clapped her hands, which frightened him
> still more.

The duckling's life was saved by a man who was poor, but as Anglo norms make clear, even though he was poor he was still a peasant. Not only that, but he had children. The duck was afraid of these humans, as well he should have been (since most of his contact with humans was negative). And at that point, the poor duckling became just another victim of hijinks and human (children's) frolic:

> He flew first into the butter-cask, then into the meal-tub, and out
> again. What a condition he was in! The woman screamed, *and
> struck at him with the tongs*; the children laughed and screamed,
> and tumbled over each other, in their efforts to catch him; *but
> luckily he escaped.* The door stood open; the poor creature could
> just manage to slip out among the bushes, and lie down quite
> exhausted in the newly fallen snow (emphasis added).

What an asshole! The duck was all over the place in what was obviously a desperate attempt to get the hell out of Dodge! The woman was striking at him with some tongs – more violence against a duck that never did anything to harm anyone (but who also never did anything to defend himself). The kids were poking fun at him and were so desperate to catch up to him the tripped all over themselves. But the duck got away.

Hans Christian Anderson has issues. Check out what he writes next:\

> It would be very sad, were I to relate *all the misery and privations
> which the poor little duckling endured during the hard winter;* but
> when it had passed, he found himself lying one morning in a moor,
> amongst the rushes. He felt the warm sun shining, and heard the
> lark singing, and saw that all around was *beautiful spring.*
> (emphasis added).

Anderson, probably running out of ideas and time, personalizes the story and claims that it would be "very said" if he was to relate to all the misery and privations that the duckling went through during the winter. Why? He spend enough time outlining and describing, in vivid detail, the insults, the acts of violence, the harassment and the negative behaviors aimed at the duck. And why would he involve the reader in the story (whoever is reading this story to children is the one who is representing the previous views espoused by Andersen). The seasons had changed once again, and the duckling had survived.

The story continues:

> Then the young bird felt that his wings were strong, as he flapped them against his sides, and rose high into the air. They bore him onwards, until he found himself in a large garden, *before he well knew how it had happened.* The apple-trees were in full blossom, and the fragrant elders bent their long green branches down to the stream which wound round a smooth lawn. Everything looked beautiful, in the freshness of early spring. (emphasis added)

This duck was so young that he didn't realize that he was maturing. His perspective of his environment was changing as was his physiological and behavioral responses to that environment. The old adage teaches us that, "through struggle we become strengthened." This applies to black people who persevered the worst form of enslavement in American history, and came out of it as strong as nails. White people want to limit that strength to athletic prowess, but we know the truth: we also became strong mentally and psychologically (despite having never been "de-briefed" following enslavement and despite vestiges of self-hate and low self-esteem), because we now better understand the oppressive conditions of this country, from the overt (which we had already experienced from enslavement, segregation, lynchings, castrations, rapes, etc.) to the more subtle and overt forms of oppression against us which rage on to this day.

The duckling was in a most similar position. But he still had a subliminal Tarzan mentality when it came to his "color-coded" perceptions of what constituted beauty and ugliness:

> From a thicket close by came *three beautiful white swans,* rustling their feathers, and swimming lightly over the smooth water. *The duckling remembered the lovely birds, and felt more strangely unhappy than ever.*

Again, we see the swans described as "beautiful" and by now we realize that the thing that makes then beautiful is their whiteness. And we also know by now the impact of how those swans looked in the ugly duckling's mind, and we learn that, "the duckling remembered the lovely birds, and felt more strangely unhappy than ever." A low sense of self, a deflated ego and unconscious self-hate would have a tendency to make one feel "strange." That is – unless – he was beginning to identify WITH the swans instead of merely being envious OF them. Could it be?

Not quite yet it would seem:

> "I will fly to those *royal birds,*" he exclaimed, "and they will kill me, *because I am so ugly*, and dare to approach them; but it does not matter: *better be killed by them than pecked by the ducks, beaten by the hens, pushed about by the maiden who feeds the poultry, or starved with hunger in the winter"* (emphasis added).

Still a slave, mentally speaking. Still wanting to associate with those who have only shown him disdain and rejection. Just like Black people in America; continuing with what I call "one-way integration" efforts when it is clear that white folks in general, do not like black folks, in general.

In the previous excerpt how deep low-self esteem can go – almost to the level of self-mutilation and suicide. That's what the duckling is implying when he says that even if the swans wanted to kill him, it wouldn't matter because it is "better to be killed by them than pecked by the ducks, beaten by the hens, pushed about by the maiden who feeds the poultry, or starved with hunger in the winter." The lesser of the evils is tantamount to no choice at all. Karenga (1969) once wrote that the only difference between a liberal and a conservative is that one will shoot you with an M-16 and the other will use a Stoner gun."

Continuing:

> Then he flew to the water, and swam towards *the beautiful swans.* The moment they espied the stranger, they rushed to meet him with outstretched wings. *"Kill me,"* said the poor bird; and he bent his *head down to the surface of the water, and awaited death* (emphasis added).

So steeped in his own self-loathing, and so in love with "whiteness," the so-called "ugly duckling" is not even aware of the change in his own physical makeup. Waiting to die is so typical of those who have been oppressed. Hans Christian Andersen is describing all the symptoms, but leaves out the details regarding what oppressed people tend to do when backed into a corner. Acceptance is but one phase of dealing with an oppressed status.

Black people, even while enslaved, didn't wholeheartedly "accept" their status. White folks wouldn't report the numerous "slave insurrections" (although 1,500 were recorded) because they didn't want to scare off their fellow whites. The myth that is circulated is that of the "happy darkey." Were this the case, slavery would still exist. The ugly duckling, throughout the story, is a story of acceptance of his feelings of inferiority and not taking a chance on confronting your oppressor. And now look at him: head bowed and ready to take the final ass whipping because he feels bad.

But then comes awareness:

> But what did he see in the clear stream below? *His own image; no longer a dark, gray bird, ugly and disagreeable to look at, but a graceful and beautiful swan.* To be born in a duck's nest, in a farmyard, is of no consequence to a bird, if it is hatched from a swan's egg. He now felt glad at having suffered sorrow and trouble, because it enabled him to enjoy so much better all the pleasure and happiness around him; for the great swans swam round the new-comer, and stroked his neck with their beaks, as a welcome (emphasis added).

You can see that a part of the "ugly duckling's" problem was one of color and hue. Look at how Hans Christian Andersen describes it: " … no longer a dark, gray bird, ugly and disagreeable to look at, but a graceful and beautiful swan." Look at the rank order: dark, gray – and then ugly and disagreeable to look at.

So now the duckling had matured and grown into a swan. Andersen writes that the duckling saw its image and it was a "graceful and beautiful swan." How can you see "grace" in a reflection? The point he is making is that the transformation was not only physical but also psychological. The lesson learned is that, "To be born in a duck's nest, in a farmyard, is of no consequence to a bird, if it is hatched from a swan's egg." So socially, the duckling was born in one place but genetically, it was a swan and now it had matured.

The emphasis on physical appearance continues, not only based on the reaction from the duckling itself, but also from young children and from there, the word and the reaction to physical appearance spread like wildfire. As Andersen described it:

> Into the garden presently came some little children, and threw bread and cake into the water. "See," cried the youngest, "there is a new one;" and the rest were delighted, and ran to their father and mother, dancing and clapping their hands, and shouting joyously,

> "There is another swan come; a new one has arrived." Then they
> threw more bread and cake into the water, and said, *"The new one*
> *is the most beautiful of all; he is so young and pretty."* And the old
> swans bowed their heads before him (emphasis added).

The duckling was no being treated like a swan and as a result, the response to its presence was totally different. The response include happiness all around, an acknowledgement that there was a "new swan," and bread and cake crumbs. But the key point is the pettiness on the part of those who were making the observations: it was still all about the fact that the swan had turned white, and was no longer dark in color. This is the message that Andersen wants to convey, but it has much deeper psycho-social implications than one would initially think. Along with the observations came respect and reverence, or, as Andersen put it, "… the old swans bowed their heads before him."

Even the elder swans who one would think would be wiser based on their maturity, were obsessed with physical appearance which, as we now know, comes down to having long necks and being white. That's what this story is all about: to be white is to be right, and if you're black – get back!

Moving right along:

> Then he felt quite ashamed, and hid his head under his wing; for he
> did not know what to do, he was so happy, and yet not at all proud.
> *He had been persecuted and despised for his ugliness, and now he*
> *heard them say he was the most beautiful of all the birds.* Even the
> elder-tree bent down its bows into the water before him, and the
> *sun shone warm and bright* (emphasis added).

When black people released from enslavement, what were they supposed to do? They were still hated in a nation that despised black skin. Many of them went into sharecropping, working for the same white man on his plantation and supposedly "splitting the profits" once the crops were harvested and sold. That rarely happened once the work was done because, as the Dred Scott decision of 1857 made clear, "a white man has no rights that a white man is bound to respect."

And so it was with the duckling. His first response after being "freed" from his "ugliness" was shame because, as the story says, "he he did not know what to do, he was so happy, and yet not at all proud. He had been persecuted and despised for his ugliness, and now he heard them say he was the most beautiful of all the birds. He may have been physically attractive but because of his low self-esteem, his persecution complex, his unconscious self-hatred and a plethora of other psychological shortcomings, this duckling is still "damaged goods" in the areas that are most important. Others may deem or judge him as "beautiful," but he is like the fine, but crazy bitch you meet in a bar. Once you get her home, her true nuttiness and bipolar symptoms become apparent!

CONCLUSION

Hans Christian Andersen makes it clear that it doesn't pay to be "ugly." Check out the closing statement:

> Then he rustled his feathers, curved his slender neck, and cried joyfully, from the depths of his heart, *"I never dreamed of such happiness as this, while I was an ugly duckling"* (emphasis added).

And now the happy ending that the tales written by Hans Christian Andersen are known for. Of course, one child's happiness, as in this case, should be an astute parents' major concern. After all, look at the final sentence of the story where the duckling " … cried joyfully, from the depths of his heart, "I never dreamed of such happiness as this, while I was an ugly duckling."

So what does the child learn? (1) it doesn't pay to be ugly; (2) the people around you are the ones you should listen to and believe in; (3) fathers often leave their children and the mother has to raise them alone; (4) it's alright to ridicule someone who is different; (5) to be dark in color is the same thing as being ugly; (6) that which is white is not only more beautiful, but also more graceful and deserves more respect, and (7) if you don't purr or lay eggs, you ain't worth a shit.

That which was "ugly" really had nothing to do with the duckling. It was the conditions that he was raised in and the attitudes of those around him that represented the *true* "ugliness" in this story. But that is a lesson lost when those doing the reading and who are in front of the classroom buy into the belief that "white is good and black is bad."

What does this have to do with detrimental reliance? Young children grow up to associate that which is true with what the teacher tells them. The instruction is clear: be honest and never talk back to authority figures. That trust creates "reliance" and "dependence" on the power of instruction so when the teacher tells you that being ugly is the equivalent of being "non-white," this goes directly into the mind of the black child. Add to that the "flesh colored" crayon and band-aid, and all that is white is right, and that which is "not white" is somehow as "ugly" as this young duckling. Only when the duckling turned white was it acceptable.

THE STORY OF LITTLE BLACK SAMBO
(and Friends):
Psychological Warfare Aimed at Youthful Minds

ABOUT THE AUTHOR

What motivates a white woman from Scotland to write a book about a child of color. Sure, the story was originally about a child from India but it evolved into the stereotypical and racist bullshit that hit American library shelves by the tens of thousands. Following is some background information about Helen Bannerman and perhaps we can glean some psycho-sociological insights into why this woman thought that a book like this, read to children, would make some kind of contribution to humankind's own understanding of itself.

> Helen Bannerman (born Brodie Cowan Watson) was the Scottish author of a number of children's books, the most famous being *Little Black Sambo*. She was born in Edinburgh and, because women were not admitted as students into British Universities, she sat external examinations set by the University of St. Andrews and attained the qualification of LLA. She lived for a good proportion of her life in India, where her husband was an officer in the Indian Medical Service.

As we can see, she changed her name. When people do that, it's either because they think they are famous and want to be anonymous or because they're Jews and are trying to hide from the gentile. Whatever the reason, a name change is indicative of a mindset that is rooted in shame. She then writes a bunch of books and almost every single one of them (several analyzed in this book) is about a child of color. As scholars, the question we want answered is why her choice of subjects revolves around these ethnic and racial themes.

In addition to my allegations about the shame associated with the name change, note that she was an early victim of discrimination (gender bias) herself.

She was not allowed to even apply for a British University because women weren't being admitted. You would think that this reality would make her more sensitive to the plight of the children she wrote about. But as I will show, it appears that the opposite – discrimination as intense as that which she was victimized by – was the case.

I could not locate any photos of her husband, the guy who was an officer in the Indian Medical Service. But I doubt if he was a man of color or of very dark complexion. India has a serious caste system and they don't like dark skin. She may have taken exams at the University of St. Andrews, and may have attained the qualification of an LLA, but that doesn't mean that she has valid degrees that would be recognized here in the United States. If she lived "a good portion of her life in India," then what would make her write stereotype-laden stories about Indian children?

Did she have any children of her own? Was her husband someone who could see what she was doing? He was a professional man and one has to assume that he was white or else a brown sell-out. At any rate this woman had issues on some level and was definitely lacking in what we would today refer to as "cultural competency."

The background information continues:

> The heroes of many of her books are recognizably south Indian or Tamil children from the illustrations. However, despite the plots having no really racist overtones and usually celebrating the intelligence and ingenuity of the children, the name Sambo has become a slur against people of colour and the books have often been banned or censored. As a result of this controversy, a politically correct version co-authored by Fred Marcellino, *The Story of Little Babaji*, changed the names of the main characters …

Such bullshit and bias is inherent in the previous excerpt. As a scholar and a critical thinker and writer, I have an obligation to clarify these inaccurate before moving on.

To begin with, what "heroes" are you talking about? These kids in these stories were victims who had to respond to adverse conditions, conditions that in some cases were created by their own mistakes and ineptitude. How are they heroes when their "adventures" revolve around basic sustenance and peripheral issues involving animals? They are "recognizable" because they all have brown skin, which brings us to the second point made in the previous paragraph.

It is stated that, " … despite the plots having no really racist overtones and usually celebrating the intelligence and ingenuity of the children, the name Sambo has become a slur against people of colour and the books have often been banned or censored."

First of all, what makes whoever wrote this think that there were "no really racist overtones" to the books that Bannerman wrote? Calling "Little Black Sambo" "black" means something negative once you describe his life, his spate of bad luck, and the fucked up parents he had! And as we know, in white culture, prefacing any phrase or term with the word "black" is always going to mean or imply a negative ("blackmail," "blacklist," "black cat brings bad luck," "blackheart," etc.). Therefore, since Bannerman wrote books with titles like, "Little Black Mingo," "Little Black Quasha," "Little Black Quibba" as well as "Little Black Sambo," then there is something about "blackness" that this white bitch doesn't have much respect for. Although raised in India she was also raised in a culture that had a caste system and that means the darker you are, the fewer rights you have. Not racist? Don't make me laugh.

I'm surely not the first one to notice what I have coined as "linguistic racism" in some of my other writings. My main point here is that my extensive research on the white man's (woman's) use of the term "black" as it relates to the English language, and application of the term before a name, a slogan or an image, is always negative. In simpler terms, even fiction literature such as that penned by Bannerman is a reflection of the attitudes, values and beliefs of those who create it, program it and empower it. What is "acceptable," "beautiful," "good" and "desirable" is defined by those who control the literature.

It is evident, then, that associating "blackness" with all that is evil, impure or backward is widely accepted and associating "whiteness" with that which is good, universal and clean is acceptable society-wide in white and white-thinking caste cultures, and that includes India.

As an example, look at Holland and their Sinter Klaus mythical character who brings presents during Christmas for the kids who have behaved: white horse, white pope's hat and white skin. Who's his sidekick? A dark character named "Black Pete" whose job it is to punish the children if they've been bad. You think these color-coded characterizations are a quirk? Sinter Klaus is white and good; Black Pete is black and bad. To this day in America, the good guys wear white hat and the bad guys wear black hats. Most titles that include the word "Black" (check out the summer 2015 movie "Black Mass" (about a contract killer - played by Johnny Depp - and the upcoming TV show, "Code Black") to see that this dichotomy still exists.

Thus goes the vicious cycle, and it can impact on the long-term health of our kids. The website Your Black World carried an insightful article titled, "Experiencing racism as a Child Can Result in Heart Problems, Diabetes in

Adulthood." According to the article, a study out of Northwestern University showed that adolescents can suffer the effects of discrimination years after the event. Continuing:

> According to Mother Jones, "researchers found that adults who had reported higher levels of discrimination when they were young had disrupted stress hormone levels 20 years later – and that African Americans experienced the effects at greater levels than their white counterparts." According to developmental psychologist Emma Adam, who was also head researcher for the study, kids don't always bounce back from negative experiences. "There's always a tendency to say, 'Oh, they are just kids – they will get over it,'" said Adam. "But it turns out there can be lasting impact."

The information offers up scientific explanations:

> The two decades long study looked at kids from various economic backgrounds and compared levels of the stress hormone cortisol in adults to the responses they gave as 12-year old children. Usually cortisol levels are high upon waking in the morning, increase for about half an hour, then level off. "The high morning levels are there to active you for the day, giving you the energy and focus, and stimulate your appetite to basically rev you up to face the demands of your day," Adam explains.

And,

> Those who had experienced discrimination when they were 12 years old showed differences in their cortisol levels. Their levels were flatter, something Adam attributed to changes in the cortisol levels due to a loss in that "important cycle." "You get a drop of those morning levels, you wake up groggier, and it is harder to sleep at night," Adam explained. Those flat rhythms result in negative health outcomes such as cardiovascular disease, diabetes and depression.

What impact do you think humiliation and ridicule played in so many black kids lives as they listened to these stories being read in front of an entire classroom? Even if the classroom was all-black, the teacher needed her ass kicked for reading it (that pertains to the black teachers as well). But in a classroom that was mostly white kids and only a few black kids (as mine was), the degradation campaign had to be unbearable. Remember then that these stories not only did potential psychological damage, but as the study indicates, also had long-term physiological effects.

Realizing this, and with this brief analysis of Bannerman's background out of the way, we can continue with other important and pertinent information regarding Bannerman, her thinking, her writings and her characters – of which Little Black Sambo was only one.

BLACK SAMBO AS 'TIP OF THE ICEBERG'

The claim is made that the books by Bannerman were "usually celebrating the intelligence and ingenuity of the children." First of all, "usually" doesn't mean all the time. And since the celebrating of intelligence and ingenuity wasn't done all the time, then explain why that was the case. The fact of the matter is Bannerman's version of black intelligence and ingenuity is based on a racist paradigm: it's like the same kind of intelligence that you attribute to a dog that can roll over on command or to a kid with a mental disorder who can read or write. Not only that, but these kids always get themselves into trouble by being in the wrong place at the wrong time – poor decision making. Their parents are usually idiots and the animals they interact with are creatures that these kids should not even be associating with. "Intelligence" and "ingenuity" under circumstances such as these basically give these black kids the same type of acknowledgement that you would give a well-trained circus monkey.

Then there is the claim that, "the name Sambo has become a slur against people of colour and the books have often been banned or censored." A "claim"? It's a fact and a matter of historical record! And furthermore, it's not just the "name" Sambo that is the slur – it is what the name came to represent, thanks to the imagery provided by Bannerman! Sambo wasn't a brain surgeon, an astronaut or a super spy: he was a child that kept fucking up because he wanted some food. His parents were equally as fucked up and, in fact, he ended up providing for *them!* There negative connotations associated with the word "black" and then the imagery of Sambo combine to make the entire book and image a "slur."

The books were only "banned" after the people who were the same color or ethnicity as Sambo started talking shit, kicking ass and challenging the educational system for even offering up such crap. Bannerman didn't see anything wrong with it and neither did her publishers, did they? What goes in is what comes out, and you can't run from the wolf to the fox and expect justice.

Next, check out the claim that, "as a result of this controversy, a politically correct version co-authored by Fred Marcellino, *The Story of Little Babaji*, changed the names of the main characters …" The damage has been done; no "politically correct" version can offset the decades of degradation inflicted upon the hearts and minds of black children and their parents, parents who also had to undergo the same "listening sessions" that involved Sambo's black ass. It's like these assholes who go around thinking that saying "the 'n' word" is somehow better than saying "nigger." How could it be when everybody knows what the letter "n" stands for?

What many people don't know is that Bannerman wrote numerous books, which in my view were little more than clones of either other. In my analysis of Little Black Sambo, I would be remiss without some mention of the other books that this white women wrote, all of them dealing with the lives and what I see as "mis-adventures" of kids of color.

First, I will look at the story of "Little Black Mingo." In this story the writer Bannerman once again puts a young child in jeopardy. In this one, it's a little black girl (they claim Indian, but trust me, she's black) makes friends with a mongoose, but this is only after she's kidnapped by a mugger. What is a mugger, you ask? I'll tell you in the analysis. Let it suffice to say here that the story is about how the little girl avoids being eaten in her quest to escape an island that she has been kept at by this mugger.

Then there is the story of "Little Back Quasha." Again, another child of color (again, a little girl) is under attack, this time by hungry tigers. She loves to read and help people, but the tigers get in the way and she has to be rescued from them.

The third story to be viewed is that of "Little Black Quibba." This young child has a mother who is sick and goes out to try to find help and aid and like Black Sambo, runs into a number of creatures who try to impede the task at hand. After you read it, you'll see why it may be almost as racist as "Little Black Sambo."

And last, and the most famous of all as far as this analysis is concerned, is the story of "Little Black Sambo." We already know: gone to get food and ends up having to give up a lot in order to stay alive. He brings food back to his mother and father and all is well. Or so Bannerman evidently believes.

If a black man or woman wrote a series of books and the title included the words, "Little White ….", I don't care if it was a positive book about lions and lambs falling in love and posing for pictures, the first thing that peckerwoods would say is, "why do you have to mention skin color?" "Why do you have to mention race"? "What qualifies you to write a story about a person of another race that you are not a member of?" It would be like that and the critics would be in an uproar. That person would receive mail from all over the nation, prefaced with the words, "Dear nigger"!

But the white man and woman think they are experts on and can therefore write about anyone or anything, fiction or non-fiction. Even today they are co-opting words from black people, continuing to use terms like "cool," "funky" and "get go" after we've long discarded them. Just recently I heard some white woman in a TV-movie called, "The Perfect Roommate" tell another one that she'll be "S.O.L," a term created by black people which stands for "shit outta luck." At the same time, recall that the 1950s and 60s were filled with these white people claiming to be "race relations experts" who were getting published. Still on the reading lists of many colleges are books like Elliot Liebow's *Tally's Corner*, books like *Cool Pose*, Charles Silberman's *Crisis in Black and White*, John Howard Griffin's *Black Like Me*, Grace Halsell's *Soul Sister*, and many others.

But none of those books pawned themselves off as being flattering to children of color while leveling some of the most dangerous and racist scenarios ever concocted. Even *Black Like Me* had some redeeming qualities (basically a white man repeating what black people had been saying for decades). But as you will see, with the benefit of critical thinking and hindsight, Bannerman paints a negative portrait of innocent children of color, jeopardizing their lives at almost every turn, and then because they are alive and breathing at the end, she (and those of her misguided ilk) consider these stories positive tales.

Finally, I could not locate the full text of some of these tales, but at very least I provided an overview and synopsis of each one. With that in mind, let the critique and commentary beginning with the story of a young black girl makes friends with a mongoose and spends most of her time trying to escape the grotesque grasp of a crocodile (referred to as a Mugger). It is the story of "Little Black Mingo."

LITTLE BLACK MINGO

In one of the reviews I was able to locate, the following overview about Little Black Mingo was provided. Before getting into the guts of the review, the writer offers the following biased viewpoint:

> A story of adventure, creativity, and luck, Little Black Mingo
> has been treasured by children everywhere since it was first

> written in 1901, and this delightfully illustrated edition brings
> the tale to life once more for the enjoyment of readers of all
> ages.

When you see a statement like "treasured by children everywhere," you know that the writer means white kids and kids who have been brainwashed by white people No sane white parent who heard these tales would not be alarmed unless those parents, like the kids in these classrooms, was also "whitenized." Written in 1901, we know that in the United States black people were still legally segregated. Why then, would a black child with an active brain cell, buy into a story about a black female getting rescued from a crocodile by a mongoose? How many of them raised their hands and then received an inadequate response from their teacher, who was more likely than note either white or a black person who was trained to think white?

The description also makes the claim that the story, "edition brings the tale to life once more for the enjoyment of readers of all ages." And there it is: even if the writer of the statement didn't believe it, his/her views still remain in writing as an inducement to read the story. Is the story really for the "enjoyment" of readers? How can you enjoy a story that distorts reality and forces a black child to be dependent on animals and to not give any mention to the parents of that child at all? Isn't this the problem: parental neglect and too many kids (especially of the latchkey variety) taking care of and fending for themselves?

You might argue, "That was in 1901, and it was a different time." Let me tell you something: today in the year 2015, some 114 years later, we still have the same problems, with the main one being the racism that continues to permeate children's books, high school books, college texts, television, film and newspapers. Furthermore, the vulnerability of black children is still being exploited by a majority white decision making system, which cuts aid and assistance to the parents of those kids, whose banks redline, steer and otherwise segregate the housing that those kids live in and whose churches continue to bullshit entire communities by telling them that an invisible man is the head of the household and that the woman should "submit."

The overview continues:

> Story of Little Black Mingo is the exciting tale of a little girl
> who befriends a Mongoose after being kidnapped by a horrible
> Mugger. With the help of the Mongoose, Little Black Mingo
> must avoid being eaten as she tries to escape the island where
> the old Mugger is keeping her.

A little colored girl. Once again Bannerman has placed a child at risk for the sake of a "fairy tale." Why doesn't she use one of her own people? She's about as white as they come, from her race to her early childhood environment. What is it about putting these kids in harm's way that gets her off? Let's delve further.

For those of you who don't know (I for one, did not) what a "Mugger" is, it is a large, relatively timid crocodile of India and Malaysia, with a broad, wrinkled snoot" (*Webster's New World Dictionary of the American Language*, p. 934). So this is no small creature we're talking about.

Also of note is that once again, a black child has been kidnapped. So not only is she jeopardizing the child with a creature that is a danger, but she then totally shows that the child is not protected. This is not the only time that this white woman took swipes at the parents of a black child; she gives those parents degrading names and either the parents are sick, lazy or as in this case, inattentive. In any case, the child is kidnapped by a Mugger that Bannerman describes as being "horrible."

Another syndrome that Bannerman seems to suffer from is that she doesn't appear to want the children killed, but she wants them tortured. Throughout her stories these children are approached, attacked or confronted by these creatures and then, rather than being eaten and having it end there, they are kidnapped, cajoled, bribed and threatened. This is psychological child abuse at its most extreme.

The child has to be rescued, again not by a parent who cares enough to go looking for the lost youth, but by another animal. This is yet another theme that appears in the books by Bannerman. In the case of "Little Black Mingo," that animal is a Mongoose, and this raises another question: why is this child so willing to trust these animals? Why are these kids so gullible? Surely the Mongoose offered no proof that he was going to "rescue" her and take her back home. Her choices, in such a situation, is choosing the lesser of two evils: get eaten by a Mugger or run off with a Mongoose, a creature that can be deadly in its own right, especially when it comes to a defenseless little child.

With the Mongoose, Mingo is able to escape the island where she was held captive by the Mugger.

Now let us move to the next "roast" by Bannerman, this one the story of a little black girl who loves to read and help others. It is the story of "Little Black Quasha."

LITTLE BLACK QUASHA

Admittedly, not that much could be found on this story, and I wasn't going to pay for a copy of it from Amazon. What I did learn was the following nugget of information from a review by someone going by the name "Bachelier 1004." On October 6, 2005, he wrote:

> Her classic story of "Little Black Sambo" is improved upon here, this time our heroine is Little Quasha, a kind, intelligent girl who loves to read and whose unselfish assistance to an unfortunate person is rewarded. Hungry tigers disrupt our scholar while she reads her books, but with the help of a friend she devises a way to escape.

Before my analysis let me add that this guy, "Bachelier 1004" is as confused as most white people who read these kinds of book. What he writes is nevertheless fodder for analysis because he knows very little about race, about what his people call "miscegenation" and therefore his conclusions could hardly be considered scholarly. Offering up far too much personal information about his family life, he spills his guts as follows:

> My mixed-race daughter loves this book. This is an excellent book. Cretins have deprived children of the works of Helen Bannerman for too long. The illustrations are charming and simplistic, with bright high-contrast colors, like a child' view of the world.

"Mixed-race daughter" – his referring to her in this way is mistake number one. He's obviously either white or a brain-washed negro. At any rate he chose to marry someone out of his own race, which is his choice, but it still says something about his psyche. I have always believed that, "You are what you sleep with."

Secondly, if he had a brain, if that little sistah has a black or brown mother, she's black or brown – not white. The only thing white genes do in an interracial relationship is water down the color and dilute it. They may contribute funny-colored eyes and straight hair, but when it comes to skin color, that baby is not going to be pale. So he's got a daughter and he reads this book to her about a little dark-skinned girl whose life is continually imperiled even though she has done nothing to anyone but help and be nice. He sees this shit as entertaining; if this little girl ever years her parents screaming or arguing, or if she gets into it with someone at school, this diabolically threatening story is going to come back to haunt her. It might even traumatize her in later years.

I have three daughters. If this book was in the house (for some strange reason), the only way that I would have them turn the pages is if we ran out of toilet paper and one of them had to wipe their ass. Other than that, I don't dig stories about little black girls who are figuratively being sexually harassed. The father continues his comments on the book:

> I suppose the US government and the Census would classify
> us as a mixed race household, but my children, wife, and I
> are only reminded of it (and offended by it) when we come
> across the increasingly rare person who can't get past
> thinking of people first and foremost as colors, rather than
> using color only to help in a person's description, as is the
> case with the characters and narrative in this book.

This man cannot be wrong. Thinking of people in terms of colors is something even HE is doing. Why are they called "mixed race," then? Why can't he just see them as his fellow peckerwoods that just happen to be darker? This sounds like that "I'm colorblind" bullshit, and that stuff is nothing but a lie and an insult. To be "colorblind" to the white man is to say that they don't see you as a black person, an Asian or a Latino, but as an extension of their own white value system! If they're color blind, then they're also culture blind and view you as an "American" and that's why so many of them cannot understand civil rights, social protest or charges of racism. "Gee minitly, man, can't we all just get along?"

He makes the statement, "when we come across the increasingly rare person who can't get past thinking of people first and foremost as colors, rather than using color only to help in a person's description, as is the case with the characters and narrative in this book." Who is he to define what is appropriate when it comes to race? This is the same kind of paternalistic pontification that some of those people I mentioned earlier were getting away with back in the 1950s and 1960s, disguised as self proclaimed "race relations experts." Just because he got some pussy, got married and had some kids doesn't make him any less racist than any other peckerwood.

Bannerman's books are about both color and the characters. The characters are accident-prone because they are black. They need to be rescued because they are black. Their parents are negligent because they are black. This is no accident because Bannerman has the same type of plot and method in all of her books. She doesn't pick on Swedes, Brits, Scandinavians or her fellow Scotsman. She targets brown people and the "characters" that she offers up continually have to negotiate or make deals in order to survive.

Still as yet, this ignorant white man concludes his "review" as follows:

> And our children love it, this is a top pick when they choose
> a book themselves. We've never had any "black" or "white"

> questions from any of our kids from reading it, they simply
> want Quasah to get her book and beat those tigers and make a
> new friend. Our whole family could not be more charmed by
> this delightful world.

A brown child that loves to read is stopped by some tigers. If it is true that she wants to "beat those tigers" (rather than simply try to escape from them), then this is even more racist on Bannerman's part: why should a young black girl be pitted against killer beasts? What is there to gain? Is she a delegate from the sheriff's office? No. She's a child whose parents evidently don't give a fuck because Bannerman never shows a grown black adult doing a damn thing. This omission, when added to what I just charged, makes the book all the more racist.

On to the next racist book, this one titled, *Little Black Quibba.* I am going to analyze the entire story for the purpose not only of critique, but also for purposes of clarity and correction.

LITTLE BLACK QUIBBA

How Bannerman got away with this racist shit is beyond me, but then again most of her supporters and readers were white people and even the brown ones who read it from India should have been pissed. But remember: whiteness is a mentality and because so many people of color suffer from a subliminal Tarzan mentality, they see what the white man sees, worship what the white man worships and, like the white man, they hate themselves.

The story begins, thusly with tragedy and insults galore:

> Once upon a time there was a little black boy, and his name was
> Little Black Quibba. And his/ Mother was called Black Flumbo. But
> she was very ill, and had to lie in bed.

Let us begin with a basic question: why does he have to be a little *black* boy? What is the relevance of his race? I think I have the answer. If he's a black boy, then the dumb shit that he is about to get involved in can be more readily explained. But this opening statement is about more than the skin color of the boy. Look at what this white woman, Bannerman, has to say about this child's mother.

Her name is "Black Flumbo." What is the relevance of this name? Now if you recall, Little Black Sambo's mother's name was "Black Mumbo." Are we to assume that their first name is "Black," and if so, why? The answer is because Bannerman wants us to know that it is the "black" in them that keeps them in positions of poverty and danger. Why would she insult these women with these names unless she had not contemplated the importance of promoting something negative or otherwise fucked up? Describing her characters by prefacing the names she gave them with "Black" sets the stage for the racism that permeates every single one of Bannerman's stories.

Back-to-back insults because following the laughable name (and you can believe that the children were cracking up when they heard this woman's name) is the fact that "she was very ill, and had to lie in bed." So again, a story that was written for children chooses to make the story one focused on a child of color and the child, once again, has to care for the parent and take care of the family needs (just as Little Black Sambo had to do).

But the stage is not set – we need a professional diagnosis so that the raw tragedy of the situation can be shared with readers and listeners:

> The Doctor came to see her every day, And gave her nice medicine. And nasty medicine, But she got worse and worse, till at last the Doctor said she must die, unless she could get twenty mangoes to eat every day.

So many mixed messages for young children to have to devour and digest and then, since most of the people in front of the classroom are idiots who were, in turn, trained by morons, the kids are going to get a lopsided, prejudicial and anti-black view of the world. Let me point out a few of the issues I have with the previous paragraph.

To begin with, the doctor was visiting her every day. What doctor, in his right mind, needs to visit a patient every day? And if he made all these home visits, were they free? How did she pay for this personalized care? If he was seeing her every day, then wasn't that a waste of time since she ended up being diagnosed as someone who was going to die anyway? Bannerman may be a published author, but she is *non compos mentis* when it comes to understanding medicine and the legal profession!

Secondly, what is meant by "nice medicine" and "nasty medicine"? And of what relevance is the distinction between the two? Were the medicines helping the woman or not? And why were there so many if the woman was, indeed, on her death bed? Third, if she was taking all this medicine, why was she getting "worse and worse"? Perhaps it was the combination of all these meds. At any rate, to continue giving someone medicine in a state like the one that Black Flambo was in is contributing to whatever it is that is killing her.

Fourth, why the death sentence unless she ate twenty mangoes every day? And if the doctor knew about the "mango cure," why didn't he tell her that from the outset? Why did he continue visiting her and giving her meds on a regular basis? This kind of bedside manner and medical protocol makes even less sense than Bannerman's bullshit stories do.

Moving on:

> This made poor Little Black Quibba very sad, for he did not know
> where to find even one mango. However, he took the bluest basket
> in the house, and set out to see what he could find.

The child was distraught, and for good reason. And of what possible relevance is the fact that the basket was blue have? Bannerman has issues with color, from the skin of the children she writes about to the color of baskets, the latter making no sense at all.

The child strikes out to find the mangoes:

> He asked everybody he met, but nobody could tell him where to find
> any. At last he met a great big Elephant. "Oh, Mr. Elephant," said
> he, "do you know any place where mangoes grow? " Now this bad
> Elephant knew quite well, but he wanted to keep them all to himself,
> so he answered: " No, no, no. I don't; I don't. There is none this
> way."

So here's Quibba, this young child, out seeking mangoes so that he can save his sick mother. Who would paint a picture like this but someone with a mental disorder and trust me, racism is indeed a mental disorder. What does this small child do? Quibba walks up on the largest land mammal on earth and asks for help. He walks upon one of the greediest creatures ever created and asks that creature about food. In reality, the child would have been mauled. But not on the sick planet from which Bannerman hails. Quibba asks the elephant for help and the animal is made out to be the bad guy. He turns the child down claiming not to know where any mangoes can be found.

So the story teaches the listeners about rejection and disappointment. The following passage bears this out:

> So poor Little Black Ouibba turned round and went sorrowfully
> back. And the Elephant stood and watched him out of sight. And
> Little Black Quibba went along a very long weary road, but he could
> not find any mangoes ...

This poor child is doing all he can to save his mother. Bannerman is not above painting black people in her stories as failures and otherwise desperate individuals. Do you think this is by coincidence when you consider the detail that she gives to animals, the descriptions of shrubbery and other aspects of the environment and so on? No. She is intentionally painting these pictures of black human beings in such a way that they can be pitied and on occasion, laughed at.

Moving right along:

> At last he met a Snake, and he asked it. "Oh yes," said the Snake, " I'll show you where there are lots of mangoes." But he thought to himself: " When I get this nice fat little boy into the jungle, I'll eat him up." So he made him turn back again, and led him along the long weary road, till they left all the houses behind, and the jungle began to get thick.

Here is a child out by himself (no adults to call upon, and certainly no black male role models – does Quibba even have a father at home?) and he befriends a creature that is almost universally known as being a creature that you don't fool with. Some culture consider a snake evil and a spawn of Satan and others deem it good luck, but still a creature to respect and avoid. At any rate, the snake has bad intentions and dupes the Quibba into turning around and takes him out of his way. This is the story of a pedophile if I ever heard one. Now because of the snake the child is even more lost than he was before.

Deception. Near mutilation. Is there no bottom?

> Presently they met three frogs, and they croaked out: " Oh, Little Black Quibba, don't go with that Snake; he eats people' -Oh no, I don't," said the Snake; "I only eat grass." But as soon as they had passed, the Snake made a dart back, and when Little Black Quibba looked back he could not see the Frogs, and he began to suspect that the Snake had eaten them. This made him rather more watchful.

Throughout the story the child is never just "Quibba," but is incessantly referred to as "Little Black Quibba." Again, we have to ask ourselves what the purpose could be. As an educator, as I've stated before, I understand most of the educational theories and models. One of the earliest and still most reliable is the concept of "reinforcement through repetition." The child listening to this story may not remember the various creatures, may not recall the environment or what the jungle looked like, but one thing will stick in his/her mind: that the lead child's name was "Little Black Quibba." And can there be any doubt that when this story came to the United States, more than a few white kids got their asses kicked by calling a black classmate by this name (as a goof) and that even more black kids felt the sting of shame and embarrassment each and every time this name was uttered throughout the reading of this story.

Accompanied by the two-faced snake, Quibba and the snake come across three frogs. How did the frogs know who Quibba was? He has never met them before. Bannerman's stories are illogical in almost every respect except for her descriptions and her insults of black people. The snake lies and says that he only eats grass, but after Quibba and the snake left, the snake doubles back and Quibba can only "suspect" that he ate the three frogs. This belief supposedly, "made him "rather more watchful."

Rather more watchful? Why is Quibba second-guessing one of the few intuitions that he had that actually makes sense? He trusts every creature he comes into contact with, takes the word and diagnosis of a doctor who is obviously a quack, but when it comes to a life or death determination, he decides to give a snake the benefit of the doubt. Yet another slap in the face of this black child.

The story moves on:

> So they went on together, and at last Little Black Quibba found himself in a splendid mango grove, with hundreds of trees, and thousands of ripe mangoes. Oh, how he jumped for joy.

So he finds the mango grove, and he's happy but were it not for the snake, he may have never found the mangos. But as the song by The Undisputed Truth teaches us, "Beware of the handshake – it hides a snake." And in this case, these words are the literal truth. Check it out:

> When suddenly the Snake darted at him, hissing: " Ha, ha! Little Black Quibba, now I can eat you safely! Little Black Quibba had just time to jump into the big basket, as the Snake dashed at him, and to pull the lid down. Then the Snake tried to open the lid; but there was a loop of string inside, and Little Black Quibba held it firmly shut.

Now this black child who hasn't seen a black adult all day and who has no father figure of mention, is wandering through the jungle with a creature that has no moral compass. He is now in a life-and-death struggle with that creature and is hoping to be able to keep a snake away from him as he hides in a basket. How much hate can you show toward this child? Bannerman is writing a story that shows on-going hazardous situations and jeopardizes a black child's life. She has no cultural competency whatsoever, and other than protection by the First Amendment (which only applies to her books and literary rights here in the United

States), this bitch should not even be allowed to share her viewpoints. She is the female literary version of George Wallace, David Duke, Bull Connor and Donald Trump all rolled into one.

This snake is full of hate for this black child, and it appears to be about more than the fact that the snake was hungry. Most creatures from the kingdom of thingdom do get frustrated and perturbed and if they can't get their prey where and when they want it, they move on to greener pastures. Remember the tale of the fox and the overhanging grapes; he tried and tried for them but when he couldn't reach them he finally said, "Fuck it, they were probably sour anyway."

This hatred for this black child might make the kids who are hearing the story feel worried about him, but in the final analysis is was the child's own poor judgment that got him into trouble. On an even deeper level it was his mother's fault for allowing that child to venture out looking for mangos. It was also his mother's fault for having a child by a man that is so worthless that he is not even given an afterthought in the entire story. This latter image is a recurring theme in the Bannerman books: the parents are fucked up, the father is lazy, worthless and invisible, and the mother is neglectful on some level.

Check out the changes this sneaky snake is willing to endure in order to get his fangs into this African child:

> Then it tried to swallow basket and all; but, though it gaped horribly,
> it could not open its mouth wide enough to take the handle in. So at
> last it climbed up on one of the mango trees, and hung the basket on
> a branch, and, curling itself round the stem, it pretended to go to
> sleep, hoping that soon Little Black Quibba would tire of the basket,
> and would try to get out.

This snake is doing more plotting and planning than anyone else in the story. He is taking advantage of a black child's naiveté and hopes to feed on him – just like Europeans took advantage of Africans who trusted them and then, when that trust was won over, here came the European with the missionary, the mercenary and the militant. And the European-American did the same thing on these shores when it came to the conquest of the Natives. Therefore a "snake" is a fitting metaphor.

Moving right along:

> Presently Little Black Quibba peeped out and was just going to try
> to get away, when up came the Elephant and said, " Oh! you are
> stealing my mangoes. I will throw you over the precipice. "No, no,"
> screamed the Snake;" I am going to eat him up. Take him out of the

basket and give him to me." "No, I won't," said the Elephant; "you're
his friend, and seizing the basket he swung it over his head.

Two animals fighting over a little black boy. The mangoes didn't belong to
anyone, but the elephant, being bigger, wanted them for himself. This is akin to
Britain and the United States both fighting over slices of Africa, who would kidnap
the most black people, get the most gold, mine the most diamonds and bauxite and
so on. This is just like that situation, but the kids listening to this story wouldn't
know anything about that. All they know is that the little black boy was powerless
in a situation where power was obviously valued above all else. And when those
white kids left the classroom and got a look at black kids and black adults, they
could see the powerlessness reinforced in their social reality. And this bitch
Bannerman was a part of that institutional arrangement.

But the fight was on:

> But the snake twined round his leg and tried to drag him back. The
> Elephant gave a great tug and fell over the precipice himself, and the
> basket, with Little Black Quibba in it, caught in a bush on the very
> edge, and Little Black Quibba scrambled out. Then the Snake tried
> to let go, and the Elephant tried to hold on to him, and they
> wriggled and twisted, and struggled and screamed till you would
> have thought there were twenty snakes and a hundred elephants
> fighting.

Here are two animals fighting and a black child literally being caught in
the middle. What is on Bannerman's mind as she pens these words? What is her
motivation? What does she expect to get out of having teachers in schools read this
bullshit to impressionable students? What about the young children in India who
have to listen to and relate to this drivel? Does she think she is making a positive
contribution to humankind's own understanding of itself? There can be no reason
other than the fact that she knows she is promoting racial animosity by promoting
stereotypical images of people of color being inferior to whites. This is the
unspoken message in every single one of Bannerman's tales.

Moving on:

> And at last they got themselves tied into such a tight knot that
> neither of them could do anything more. And the Elephant seemed
> to get heavier and heavier, and he pulled the Snake out longer and
> longer, and thinner and thinner, till at last The snake broke with
> a Snap! into three pieces, and out jumped the little Frogs all alive
> and well, saying: " Didn't we tell you he ate people?"

So let me get this straight. The snake is snapped in half and the frogs, still in his gut, are freed? The snake is dead, mutilated by the elephant. Is this the kind of bullshit that young children are suppose to learn something from? All they are learning about is how to justify killing a living creature and as long as a human being is saved in the process, the ends therefore justify the means. The frogs, while barely escaping annihilation themselves, nevertheless have the temerity to utter with an "I-told-you-so" attitude, "Didn't we tell you he ate people"? Again, Quibba is made to look like a dumb, gullible asshole while every member of the animal kingdom is made to appear as if no matter how bad things get, they can still outsmart a black child.

More mutilation continues:

> Meantime the Elephant was dashed to pieces on the rocks, far away below. Then Little Black Quibba bravely scrambled over the Snake's tail and climbed up the tree, which he shook with all his might, and Down came dozens of lovely ripe mangoes, all red and yellow, till the ground was perfectly covered with them.

Does the reader explain to the children who are listening what "dashed to pieces" means. Do these kids know that the elephant's brains, guts, eyes and other parts of his anatomy are torn asunder? Do they care? How will this affect them when they leave that classroom? This story is not only racist, but it is deadly on a number of levels and explains, at least in some small part, why children of all races grow up to be so desensitized when it comes to death and dying. Add to stories like these the proliferation of these violent video games and the violence that is shown even in movies rated PG and PGl-13, and there should be no surprise why pathology, mass murdering, serial killings, terrorism and overall hatred based on race are increasingly prevalent.

In an attempt to camouflage the murder of the elephant, Bannerman is quick to use an "ends justifies the means" doctrine when, even as the elephant's brains are bashed open on rocks, mangoes become readily available! Again, thanks to the snake's tail, Quibba climbs the tail, scales the tree down comes "dozens of lovely ripe mangoes, all red and yellow, till the ground was perfectly covered with them." Now there are mangoes galore. The snake is dead but his tail proved to be effective. The elephant has been destroyed and despite all this death surrounding this young boy, he still has the wherewithal and commitment to gather the mangoes. A positive story, right?

Wrong .

The late John F. Kennedy once said, "The time to repair the roof is when the sun is shining." This story is about responsive or reactive behavior. The mother was sick, but why? Why didn't she prepare when she knew she was getting sick? She had been ill a long time and knew that she had a child to think about. Where were Quibba's aunts and uncles? And again, where was his father? Why was she laying up there on her fat ass dying and bringing a doctor to help her when her own child was basically taking care of himself? The time to address the illness was to act proactively and even when the illness comes, Quibba could have been cared for and would not have had to walk through the jungle interacting with elephants and snakes.

At any rate,

> How quickly Little Black Quibba filled his basket! Then putting it
> on his head he hurried home, smiling for joy. As soon as he got
> home, he ran to his Mother, with a big mango in each hand.
> Even the sight of them made her feel better.

So the little boy saves his mother and again, the inference or insinuation of gluttony and greed is heaped upon a black woman. In Bannerman's stories they are usually fat and out of control when it comes to food and the consumption of good. This woman was no exception – just seeing the mangoes made her feel better. And now comes the final insult:

> And before the basket was empty, she was just as fat and just as able
> to jump for joy as Little Black Quibba himself.

This big, fat greasy supposedly "sick" bitch sat up there on her Kentucky Fried Chicken eatin' ass and ate all those mangoes – and didn't offer Quibba shit! After this tub of lard finished them off, she was fatter than she already was, got up out of her sick bed, and had the nerve to jump for joy. Maybe if this sidewalk cruncher had jumped a little bit more, on a more regular basis, she wouldn't have gotten sick in the first place! Or maybe she would have been strong enough to at least roll through the jungle and find her own mangoes!

All of Bannerman's stories have a similarly insulting thematic pattern, but none of them is better known that that classic, racist tale of none other than "Little Black Sambo." My analyses of that story follow.

THE STORY OF LITTLE BLACK SAMBO – COLOR- AND RACE-CODED STORYTELLING

And … here we go:

> Once upon a time there was a little black boy, and his name was
> Little Black Sambo. And his mother was called Black Mumbo. And
> his mother was called Black Mumbo …

As the most popular of all of Bannerman's books, this one does follow a pattern of the others. There is a little black boy and his mother is insultingly greedy (as you will see later). Her name is also an insult, and this is by design. She was called "Black Mumbo" but that doesn't mean that it was her name. In the same way that black people are called "nigger" or "boy" by the white man who doesn't have time to ask our proper names. This is just par for the course and it reminds me of a story that Richard Pryor shared on one of his albums. Two rednecks come down to the ghetto looking for pussy, and here's what happens:

> **Rednecks:** Hey boy, you know where we can get us a
> couple of nigger gals?
> **Pryor:** Why don't you muthafuckas bring some white
> bitches with you when you come down here?
> **Rednecks:** Now, now – ain't no need ta talk dirty!

There is nothing wrong with the reference to "nigger gals," but when they are countered with "white bitches," they feel offended. This has to be the way Bannerman would feel if she or one of her precious daughters were referred to as white bitches or, more germane to this story, if they were named "White Mumbo."

The stereotype of black people being turned on by bright colors and baubles permeate the stories of Bannerman. For instance, note the following:

> … And Black Mumbo made him a beautiful little Red Coat, and a
> pair of beautiful little blue trousers. And Black Jumbo went to the
> Bazaar, and bought him a beautiful Green Umbrella, and a lovely
> little Pair of Purple Shoes with Crimson Soles and Crimson Linings.
> And then wasn't Little Black Sambo grand?

The reason for the color descriptions is to affirm the stereotype and to teach children the lesson of black inferiority by filling their little imaginations with the concept of "color." And just as that red coat, the green umbrella, the purple shoes (with crimson linings and soles) and those blue trousers titillate their minds, so does the color black – which pales (no pun intended) by comparison. All that is associated with black is slow-witted, irresponsible and silly. And this brings us to another point.

His father, Black Jumbo, is the one who dolled his son up in all this bullshit. This inter-generational form of conspicuous consumption is one reason why black people continue to believe that dressing nice is going to somehow set them free. And why is the father's name Black Jumbo? We all know that the word "jumbo" is a synonym for "big," right? And we know that this white woman holds stereotypical views of black people, right? But there is one belief that the white race holds about black men that is almost universal: that being that black men have big dicks. Why else would he be called Jumbo? Was he tall? This was never mentioned. Think about it.

After describing the previously mentioned colorful attire given to him by his father (who should have known better), the previous passage poses the question, "And then wasn't Little Black Sambo grand?" The answer to the question is, "hell no!" but the explanation requires a comparison so that a learning experience can be extracted from this racist foolishness.

Do clothes make the man? That is what the American popular culture establishment will tell us. And this bullshit is reinforced by minorities who seem to out dress and "out flash" their white counterparts. The only difference is that in America, because of white privilege and skin color, you can dress as slouchy as hell and still be associated with the people who have the power. Look at Warren Buffett; supposedly the richest man in the world and about as slouchy as they come. Black men have always out dressed white men and black students out dress white students. And the reason for that is that white people understand the importance of essence over appearance. While we spend our money on shoes, "gear," jewelry and hair extensions, whites go about the business of studying, sucking dick and doing whatever it is they do to establish contacts and connections with the power barons of the world.

So the question is asked, " … wasn't Little Black Sambo grand? No he wasn't. He may have had on bright colors and appeared to be grand, but we should all remember that grandiosity is not greatness and all this regalia doesn't in any way minimize the fact that in the eyes of the white kids who are listening to this story, Little Black Sambo is just that: little and black.

The story continues:

> So he put on all his Fine Clothes, and went out for a walk in the
> Jungle. And by and by he met a Tiger. And the Tiger said to him,
> "Little Black Sambo, I'm going to eat you up!"

So we have to ask ourselves, why is this little boy getting all dolled up so that he can go for a stroll in the jungle? The answer is that both the father and the mother were idiots and didn't give a shit about the child's welfare; they just wanted to make sure that no matter what happened to him, he looked good when it happened. As you can see, all those "fine clothes" that Bannerman keeps reminding people about didn't do any good when Sambo got his ass in a sling, did it? Simply watch an episode of "Cops" or "Cops Reloaded." These cops pull over some black kids who are wearing $200 and $300 gym shoes and jewelry up the ying-yang. But they're busted and going to jail and maybe prison. What good did those shiny rims, the expensive paint job and that clothing do for them? Not a damn thing.

So then, when Sambo was met by the tiger, and the tiger said to him, "Little Black Sambo, I'm going to eat you up!" what good did those shoes and that coat do his little black ass? None of that shit impressed the tiger because the tiger knew that underneath all those fine garments as human flesh. And it's the same way in the Personnel Departments around the United States in 2015: you've got on a suit, a tie and you just got a haircut. You may even have a degree. But guess what: you're just another version of Little Black Sambo to these peckerwoods. As Malcolm X asked more than four decades ago, "What does the white man call a black man with a PhD?" Answer: "Nigger," that's what they call him." Sambo, nigger – in the total scheme of things, what's the damn difference?

Now comes the transition to the role of Uncle Tom:

> And Little Black Sambo said, "Oh! Please Mr. Tiger, don't eat me
> up, and I'll give you my beautiful little Red Coat." So the Tiger said,
> "Very well, I won't eat you this time, but you must give me your
> beautiful little Red Coat." So the Tiger got poor Little Black
> Sambo's beautiful little Red Coat, and went away saying, "Now I'm
> the grandest Tiger in the Jungle."

The tiger was just as materialistic as Sambo was. That coat and its color seem to have a priority with both of these individuals, but the tiger was even more fucked up. Why? Because if he used his head he would have realized that he could have eaten Sambo and then also had the red coat, the shoes, and everything else! But this is what conspicuous consumption oriented behavior does to you; like money, it is the ultimate confounding of things. In this case, it makes silly things seem important. Thinking he was the "grandest tiger" in the jungle just because of a man-made coat (which is unnatural for his species) shows how assimilated this tiger was and how warped his priorities came to be due to his ignorance.

Little Black Sambo got out of that scrape, but no sooner did he overcome one obstacle then came, as is the case with many black males in any society, yet another problem standing in the way:

> And Little Black Sambo went on, and by and by he met another Tiger, and it said to him, "Little Black Sambo, I'm going to eat you up!" And Little Black Sambo said, "Oh! Please Mr. Tiger, don't eat me up, and I'll give you my beautiful little Purple Shoes with Crimson Soles and Crimson Linings."

This tiger was not as clueless as the first one. Sambo describes the shoes down to the detail but this tiger knows that there are not enough shoes to fit all four of his feet. In reality, both tigers are going against their nature just so they can be like or look like the very humans who hunt him on a regular basis. Like today's corporate negroes who want to dress and act like their master so that they can gain some semblance of "acceptability" and "respectability," the tiger thinks that the shoes will somehow make him "better" than the other tigers. What the shoes do is make him look like as much of a freak as a necktie (symbolizing a lynch rope from days gone by) makes a black man look today in 2015.

But Sambo's offer is not enough.

> But the Tiger said, "What use would your shoes be to me? I've got four feet, and you've got only two; you haven't got enough shoes for me." But Little Black Sambo said, "You could wear them on your ears." "So I could," said the Tiger: "that's a very good idea. Give them to me, and I won't eat you this time."

So now the tiger looks even more ridiculous. Not only that, but the shoes that are on his ears are going to impede his hearing. But does he care? No. So along comes another tiger (this part appears to be missing from this version of the story and this one wants Sambo's trousers

> And Little Black Sambo said, "Oh! Please Mr. Tiger, don't eat me up, and I'll give you my beautiful little Blue Trousers." So the Tiger said, "Very well, I won't eat you this time, but you must give me your beautiful little Blue Trousers." So the Tiger got poor Little Black Sambo's beautiful little Blue Trousers, and went away saying, "Now I'm the grandest Tiger in the Jungle."

Sambo readily submits to these creatures without even having to be threatened, or so it seems. So he has to strip down like some bitch being punked for his gym shoes and give up his pants. The animals of the jungle, in this case the tigers, are as hung up on material things as Sambo's family. And like Sambo's family, all these nice clothes serve no functional purpose as it relates to control of one's life or destiny. They were still broke, still unstable and had no access to anything that would guarantee them access to power. As Woody Harrelson (Caucasian) told Wesley Snipes (African-American) in the movie, "White Men Can't Jump," "You'd rather lose and look good than to win and look bad." And so it seems to be with the "Sambo syndrome" and the apparent obsession with giving clothing a near sacred relevance in his life.

Moving on:

> And Little Black Sambo went on, and by and by he met another Tiger, and it said to him, "Little Black Sambo, I'm going to eat you up!" And Little Black Sambo said, "Oh! Please Mr. Tiger, don't eat me up, and I'll give you my beautiful Green Umbrella." But the Tiger said, "How can I carry an umbrella, when I need all my paws for walking with?" "You could tie a knot on your tail and carry it that way," said Little Black Sambo.

It seems to me that if Sambo was innovative enough to get a tiger to put shoes on its ears and to get this particular tiger to tie a knot in his own tail in order to carry an umbrella, he (Sambo) should have been smart enough to know that all the stuff he was bargaining with did not make him "grand." The fact that he had no power to deal with his own situation in terms of having access to food, the fact that his parents didn't either, clearly shows that the father's priorities were fucked up and were being imposed on his young son.

At any rate the tiger fell for it:

> "So I could, "said the Tiger. "Give it to me, and I won't eat you this time." So he got poor Little Black Sambo's beautiful Green Umbrella, and went away saying, "Now I'm the grandest Tiger in the Jungle."

So all three tigers were as dumb as Sambo. In fact, they were as dumb as these black gang members who shoot one another over turf, over bitches or over the colors they wear. Wanna see? Check it out:

> And poor Little Black Sambo went away crying, because the cruel Tigers had taken all his fine clothes. Presently he heard a horrible noise that sounded like "Gr-r-r-r-rrrrrr," and it got louder and louder."Oh! dear!" said Little Black Sambo, "there are all the Tigers coming back to eat me up! What shall I do?" So he ran quickly to a palm-tree, and peeped round it to see what the matter was. And there

he saw all the Tigers fighting, and disputing which of them was the
grandest.

Fighting over false perceptions – just like black people in America do.
Believing in fraternity affiliations, sorority linkages, who goes to which church,
gang ties and what neighborhood you live in – all this kind of foolishness. And
these tigers fighting over "which of them was the grandest" is as stupid as all this.
In both cases, the white man stands back and laughs because neither the tigers in
"The Story of Little Black Sambo" or the black people with the cliques and
struggles that I've named have any power and don't own a damn thing.

All they have are enervating, internecine struggles that lead to death:

> And at last they all got so angry that they jumped up and took off all
> the fine clothes, and began to tear each other with their claws, and
> bite each other with their great big white teeth. And they came,
> rolling and tumbling right to the foot of the very tree where Little
> Black Sambo was hiding, but he jumped quickly in behind the
> umbrella.

Just like gang members: fighting and doing battle to the death over shit that
they don't own or control. And because they have low self-esteem and unconscious
self-hate due to centuries of brainwashing from the days of slavery, they fight one
another the way they would fight total strangers. And the tigers, also apparently
brainwashed (as they fight over apparel) are doing the same thing:

> And the Tigers all caught hold of each other's tails, as they wrangled
> and scrambled, and so they found themselves in a ring round the
> tree. And the Tigers were very, very angry, but still they would not
> let go of each other's tails. And they were so angry, that they ran
> round the tree, trying to eat each other up, and they ran faster and
> faster, till they were whirling round so fast that you couldn't see their
> legs at all. Then, when the Tigers were very wee and very far away,
> Little Black Sambo jumped up, and called out, "Oh! Tigers! Why
> have you taken off all your nice clothes? Don't you want them
> anymore?"

The hatred makes these tigers go insane it seems. Literally chasing their
tails, these animals are only concerned about "eating each other up," comparable to
what gang members are committed to in the name of "payback" or "vengeance."
They don't appear to see much more than the fact that they have to defend their
turf or their colors. More recently, the word that is used is that they were
"disrespected." And to them, that is grounds to kill another black person.

Bannerman's tale of Sambo moves on:

> But the Tigers only answered, "Gr-r-rrrr!" And they still ran faster
> and faster and faster, till they all just melted away, and there was
> nothing left but a great big pool of melted butter (or "ghi," as it is
> called in India) round the foot of the tree. Then Little Black Sambo
> said, "If you want them, say so, or I'll take them away." But the
> Tigers would not let go of each other's tails, and so they could only
> say "Gr-r-r-rrrrrr!"

The tigers are yellow in hue so they ran so fast that they melted into butter. This is the part of the story that enthralls children because when I first heard it, I got past the "black Sambo" part and began to actually get hungry! At any rate these tigers made utter asses out of themselves. And to show that the racist name-calling by Bannerman is by design, take note that in the story, in parentheses, she "explains" that the pool of melted butter is known as "ghi" in India. She knows the culture and she knows the people, but she degrades them nonetheless. This is the quintessential definition of the term, "white racism."

> So Little Black Sambo put on all his fine clothes again and walked
> off. Now Black Jumbo was just coming home from his work, with a
> great big brass pot in his arms, and when he saw what was left of all
> the Tigers he said, "Oh! what lovely melted butter! I'll take that
> home to Black Mumbo for her to cook with."

So the tigers melted but before that, ran totally out of the clothes that they had craved so much. Sambo put the clothes back on again. So Black Jumbo, who had a job, comes across the tigers and sees the "lovely melted butter." So the father stumbles across a windfall and immediately takes it home for Black Mumbo to cook. There is no mention that she is his wife – but she is Sambo's mother. This is vintage white thinking when it comes to black male-female relationships. So what we can deduce from this omission is that Sambo was born out of wedlock and Mumbo and Jumbo are simply "shacking up." What an image to paint for the child of color!

Again, greed and gluttony raise their ugly head when it comes to the food-crazed black woman:

> So he put it all into the great big brass pot, and took it home to Black
> Mumbo to cook with. When Black Mumbo saw the melted butter,
> wasn't she pleased! "Now," said she, "we'll all have pancakes for

> supper!" So she got flour and eggs and milk and sugar and butter,
> and she made a huge big plate of most lovely pancakes.

What this deadbeat muthafucka was doing walking around with a brass pot is never explained. The point is that he had one, and then in vintage traditional sexist fashion, he hands everything over to Black Mumbo to cook. Why didn't he take his sperm donating ass in the kitchen and fire up the grill? Sure, this is the early 1900s, but even back then these white assholes knew that what they were doing to women with that "your place is in the kitchen and the bedroom" stuff was bullshit. And that Bible talk about "the man is the head of the household" is equally ludicrous. How are you going to be the head of the household when you ain't got a pot to piss in or a window to throw it out of?

So he hands it over and his wife is so "pleased" to see the butter. The first thing that comes to this fat bitch's (we have to assume she's a tubster) is "pancakes," and she starts cooking. Oddly, she has all the ingredients that are necessary for the pancakes but she is lacking in the ingredients that it takes to be a good and responsible mother. This, in turn, leads one to wonder just what in the FUCK Sambo was doing taking long walks in the jungle without parental permission, missing meals and doing intellectual battle with tigers? Black Mumbo has enough wherewithals to keep a supply of pancake batter at the ready, but she lets her kid wander off into the jungle. What an irresponsible slag!

This may sound petty, but as a critical thinker I have to ask: why is this woman making a "huge big (redundant) plate" of pancakes? There is only the three of them. Of course, such a preparation of feast-like dimensions feeds into the gluttony image. And here in the 21st century in America it is true that those born and raised in poverty do grow up to have eating disorders in an attempt to compensate for the lack of grub they had as children. And a big plate of pancakes are the last thing that Sambo's fat ass parents (again, I am assuming) need. They are the ones who need to be taking "long walks" in the jungle so they can take off some of that weight!

As we near the so called "happy ending" of the Bannerman tale, the following insights are shared:

> And she fried them in the melted butter which the Tigers had made,
> and they were just as yellow and brown as little Tigers. And then
> they all sat down to supper. And Black Mumbo ate Twenty-seven
> pancakes, and Black Jumbo ate Fifty-five but Little Black Sambo ate
> a Hundred and Sixty-nine, because he was so hungry.

So, even though this story was written at a time when health conscious eating as probably never heard of, just pay close attention to the message that is imparted because this story still exists and the book will still be gleaned or heard by some young person; probably as a goof, but nevertheless taken in as a source of entertainment.

My point is that the pancakes, loaded with carbohydrates are in plentiful supply. And to top it all off they now had "butter" from the tigers. In reality, that was eating the DNA of the tigers which may have been infected with who knows what. On top of all that there is the sheer volume of what was eaten: the deadbeat dad, Black Jumbo, ate 55 pancakes and the mother ate almost half that number, clocking in at a whopping 27. And to add further insult to Sambo's psychological injuries, this little black child at 169 pancakes, more than three times more than his father and just over six times more than his mother. And why? "Because he was so hungry." And that's how it ends.

Why was he hungry? Because he had been out cheating death all day with tigers breathing down his neck. He hadn't eaten before he left home, another sign of parental neglect. And then he comes home and pigs out, imitating his parental role models, which is still neglect on their part. No sane parent would allow a little boy to eat that many pancakes. All I can say is that they better have a helluva lot of toilet paper!

Well that's the story of one of the most racist depictions of a black child ever written. And it remains popular, as I will prove in the following section.

POPULARITY OF LITTLE BLACK SAMBO

I add this section to the analysis to show that black pain means nothing if white people are being entertained. They just don't seem to give a shit when it comes to black people, including black children. Following are some responses that I got off the Little Black Sambo blog in August of 2015. These responses show you, for the most part, how lightly these white people take the issue of racism and mis-educating of not only black kids, but their own kids.

Why do I say that? Because children imitate what they see. If a white child hears *The Story of Little Black Sambo*, he is going to assume that it's alright to use that word around some of his black classmates. And when he does, he is going to get his ass kicked. Then he runs home to mommy and daddy, who apparently also see nothing wrong with a "fairy tale," and come to the school demanding that the black kids who fucked their son (or daughter) up be suspended or punished in some way, they will have to deal with the parents of that black child. That could lead to more vitriol and in turn, more ass whippings for someone. This creates a race problem where there need not have been one: dump the fuckin' story about "black Sambo" and a small part of the problem of mis-education will be resolved (temporarily).

Malcolm X once called racism "the cancer that is destroying America." And this is where it begins: in the mind and behaviors or the white teacher, the white school teacher, the white publisher and the white family system. None of these groups wants to acknowledge or give overdue respect to the descendants of those that their ancestors enslaved. They are still in denial about it or, at very least, they want to talk about "that was the past" – as if their entire present-day culture is not an on-going tribute to their fucked up history.

My responses to people of this ilk appear in between each one of their responses.

> DONRHOLLOWAY 1 month ago
> I used to eat at Sambo's all the time when I was stationed in San
> Diego in the Navy. I still have the book "Little Black Sambo" in my
> library at home.

White folks and black folks differ in so many ways.

What you just read is why I wrote this book. They don't give a shit. The fact that the book is in his library isn't going to become a teaching lesson for his children. When they pick the book up and ask daddy what's "Little Black Sambo"? what is he going to say. "Oh it's a book about some niggers"? He can't admit the racism in that book without confessing to his own role (perhaps indirect, perhaps covert but racism nonetheless) in promoting or believing in such images. When he laughs at J.J. Walker on reruns of "Good Times," when he cracks up at George Jefferson on "The Jeffersons," when he shouts out, "run, nigga run" during a football game, he is endorsing the Black Sambo character.

But these black "millennials" are almost as ignorant as white folks are. The following response has to be a black person because the first name is one of those fucked up names that only a black mother could come up with. Check it out:

> Tyrion Lannister 8 months ago
> I remember going to Sambo's as a kid whenever we went to
> Disneyland. Good memories, amazing food. I still remember the
> murals on the wall from the story of "Little Black Sambo" heh

Tyrion? He's got the situation twisted. He's talking about the restaurants and the name was so fucked up and got protested so much that the owners changed it. But this black muthafucka is talking about "good memories" and "amazing food" because he most likely didn't see anything wrong with it. Just like those black "toms" in Dallas, Texas don't see anything wrong with eating at The Cracker Barrel or The Cotton Patch. Then he sees the murals of Sambo on some wall, but does he give a shit? No. And you wonder why white people laugh at us and don't take the "protests" and "prayer vigils" seriously.

Another similar response follows:

> eyeseer1 3 months ago
> The last existing Sambo's can be found only in Santa Barbara, CA.

These assholes don't get it. If there was a restaurant called "Little Cracker Peckerwood," every white person in the known universe would be protesting. Not only that, but the peckerwoods who give out the business licenses wouldn't even approve it. But it's alright to name a restaurant "Sambo's" because if you're white, and the bankers are white and the business certifiers are white, then they don't give a shit if you insult a few niggas.

Here's proof:

> 38yofrmut 9 months ago
> It sucks this restaurant chain went defunct. Too politically incorrect.

See? Racism comes in all forms and has all kinds of supporters. Many of them don't think there is anything wrong with the name "Sambo" and will tell you as much. And in my book that makes this kind of person as racist as somebody with a lynch rope in his hand telling his pals, "Let's go round up some niggers."

More evidence follows:

> Bozo onthebus 6 months ago
> No. I think it was the foot high burger that was impossible to eat.

How can society get past the black Sambo image of black people when peckerwoods and negroes do not take it seriously? This is why I continue to tell people that America is about as good as it's ever going to get as far as race relations are concerned: the races are divided and, if anything, it will only get worse as the nation becomes increasingly brown and black. And the concept of Little Black Sambo is one reason why white people are not trusted and in many cases, they are not even liked.

For instance, check out the following response to Little Black Sambo, placed on line a year ago:

Georgiacatcrimson 1 year ago
Sambo's looks almost like Denny's!

Denny's had their share of discrimination lawsuits and allegations of racism as well. For instance, in 1994, New York Times reporter Stephen Labaton wrote that, that Denny's had to settle a $54 million lawsuit, paying off more than 4,300 clients who had been refused service or had been forced to wait longer or pay more than white customers. And in 1999, in Racine, Wisconsin where I used to live, the Denny's was sued for allowing offensive material to be posted on their bulletin boards. Research reveals that in 1998, the restaurant was sued by a family in East St. Louis for ignoring them and using racial slurs. Remember: some of those Denny's were purchased from closed down Sambo's restaurants.

And the link could be established as the following statements bears out:

amy beth lee 6 months ago
Actually many Sambo's restaurants in the Philadelphia suburbs
became Denny's when Sambo's shut down

In my book it was a situation where a tradition of racism was continued. Sambo's was founded in 1957 by two white boys, Sam Battistone and Nevell Bonette. They claimed that "Sambo" was a conjunction of their two names: "Sam" from Battison's first name and "Bo" from Bonnette's surname. Yeah, I'll bet. White people want to do dirt but when they're caught they always have a lie handy. And even if that was the truth, as soon as they found out about Bannerman's Little Black Sambo story and how controversial it was, they should have immediately changed the name. But did they? No.

Do you know why? Because an issue isn't "controversial" until peckerwoods say it is. Just because you insult millions of black people that doesn't make it controversial because black people lack power. Now when those class action lawsuits started coming in, only then did Battison and Bonnette start making moves to change some names. First they changed a few of them co "Cocos." Then the northeastern stores changed their name to "No Place Like Sams." A few carried the name "Jolly Tiger" which in my view is a direct slap in the face of black people again because we know the role that tigers played in the Little Black Sambo story. Today most of them are named Seasons Friendly Eating.

There were 1,117 Sambo's restaurants in the United States. Some of them underwent the name changes I shared with you and others were sold to Denny's (and we know how that went) and also to Godfather's Pizzas. You remember that Uncle Tom named Herman Cain who was a Republican Presidential candidate? He was the president of that company for a long time. So the Uncle Tom tradition, right in line with the parents of Little Black Sambo, was maintained.

There is only one original Sambo's left, and that is in Santa Barbara, California where, by the way, the two former owners live. According to one website one of these owners was also the mayor of Santa Barbara for a short time. Who voted for this asshole knowing that he owned a restaurant called "Sambo's." But Battistone was also an original owner of the NBA's New Orleans Jazz, which later moved to Utah and became the Utah Jazz.

See how a children's tale can spread and evolve into a racist reality in a nation that is half a world away from India, where Bannerman was writing her racist stories?

One of the responses on the Little Black Sambo site provides an interesting but related tidbit:

> iamunderground 3 months ago
> This is almost as good as the Coon Chicken Inn.

At first I thought this blurb was a goof. But as a scholar I am obligated to check out anything that could be an insult to black people, whether it was written by white folks or blacks. And guess what? There really was a Coon Chicken Inn.

According to my research, the Coon Chicken Inn was founded in 1925 and stayed open until the late 1950s. It was very popular in those times, but then again, America was racially segregated and white folks didn't have to worry about running into black people, especially not racially conscious ones. The logo was a giant smiling blackface caricature – the white version of a minstrel or "coon." Some people say the face was that of a porter. The first establishment was in Salt Lake City, Utah and later, expanded to Seattle, Washington.

After a lawsuit and protests, the owner agreed to drop the name "Coon" from the title and changed the color of the caricature from black to blue. That was about it until the outlets (there were four of them nationally) eventually closed down in around 1957.

Now you can see that white people, as a collective, have no problem with Little Black Sambo because they have no problem with any caricature that insults black people.

The next review shows the ignorance of the writer as he tries to make some racial distinctions:

> joseph bloseph 1 year ago
> the story was of an East Indian Boy I believe, not an African
> American.

When it comes to people of color, does it really matter what the nationality or ethnicity is: white folks go by *race*, and an Indian child and a black child in America share a common hue, make no mistake about it. Once you understand that Bannerman is a white woman writing about black male and female children, and then you can arrive at the obvious fact that some type of psychosis is involved. Out of that psychosis comes a reaction to skin color which is based on negative images of what that color represents in European and Euroamerican culture. In short white = all that is good, universal, clean and normal and black = all that is bad, parochial, dirty and abnormal.

Another email review read, as follows:

> Robert Bischoff 1 year ago
> Though "Sambo" is said to be an insult to Africans, early ads for this chain depicted an Indian boy and a tiger....later, they used a chef named Family Sam, with a voice by Arnold Stang (he looked nerdy, too)...but it didn't help. (BTW - did anyone notice that Sambo's logo looks like Denny's?)

What does he that Sambo "is said to be an insult to Africans"? I believe that even the most weak-minded and ignorant of people can read the story and see that it is an insult to black people. They don't have to agree, but they at least should have the intellectual wherewithal to *see* it! An "Indian boy and a tiger" is the key to the racism: the whole story of Little Black Sambo is about his fear and being able to "give the clothes off of his back" to these creatures who had no business even accepting them! The chain's images of an Indian boy and a tiger is therefore a visual reminder of a story that is an insult to black people.

He's talking about the restaurant chain and then adds that " … they used a chef named Family Sam, with a voice by Arnold Stang (he looked nerdy, too)...but it didn't help." I did the research and didn't see anything about "Family Sam," and if it was used it was in response to lawsuits that were condemning the original Sambo's name! This guy must have seen a television commercial that used a voice and an image of some white man in order not to scare away white customers. But that's a marketing ploy, a diversion from the original racist imagery that the owners were charged with.

The final point made by this particular individual is, "by the way – did anyone notice that Sambo's logo looks like Denny's?" I'm not so sure that it does any more, but I know this: the original Sambo's logo looks nothing like Denny's because the negative caricatures are no longer there! But there is one thing that

Denny's continued even after many of the Sambo's outlets were purchased by them: the racist neglect and abuse of black patrons. That seems to be a constant.

Now comes a defender, a former employee, who shares her sentiments:

> Theresa Kessler 1 year ago
> I used to work for Sambo's..then it switched to No Place Like Sam's..I was there when they closed the door..however, one comment I would like to make..the name Sambo was NOT named because of the black Sambo, but by the owner's names... SAM Battistone, Sr. and Newell Bohnett. They took the SAM from one name and the BO for the beginning of the last name of the other owner...and thus came up with the name Sambo's. The name was changed years later as it was heading toward bankruptcy to No Place Like Sam's...but just 5 months after the name change, we were closed down. I was working the shift when the owners came through and said to serve the patrons in the place at the time but not to let any more people in.

She says she was there when Sambo's closed the doors. Some of them switched over to No Place Like Sams and others chose other names. But she forgets to mention the reasons and motives behind the changes. She instead wants to go back to the discussion of how the two owners combined their names and used the joint name "Sambo" as their restaurant name. I don't give a shit if that's the case or not. It's what a manager or owner does in response to the concerns of his customers that is the real testament of character. If I have a friend named Hosea and my last name was Cronky, and we joined together and named a restaurant "Honky," every peckerwood and his mama would be talking shit, writing newspaper articles and probably setting the place on fire.

She writes that "the name was changed years later as it was heading toward bankruptcy to No Place Like Sam's..." She skips the key facts that white people tend to omit when they're praising their own: Sambo's was dogged out by black people and it became a national movement. It was out of that protest that they lost customers, lost revenue and it was only then that bankruptcy HAD to be filed!

In her own personal case, the writer adds that five months later, her store was closed down. She recalls that, "I was working the shift when the owners came through and said to serve the patrons in the place at the time but not to let any more people in." The concept of "not letting any more people in" was similar to the racist vibe that both Sambo's and Denny's gave to more than a few black people who ventured in for a meal. And because of that, maybe this person knows how such rejection and neglect feels.

Another respondent is obviously both young and naïve and believes he is sharing the story of Little Black Sambo as if he's breaking a major news story:

> Darick Robertson 1 year ago
> This was Sambo's menu and restaurant art from the 70's
> http://www.tommcmahon.net/images/sambosfull2.jpg it's based on a
> story from 1899 about a South Indian boy who tricks four tigers and
> ends up with pancakes.

This is something that most people already know. He came across a photo which anyone can access. The so-called "South Indian boy" was dark skinned meaning that genetically speaking, he was black. The concept of "south Indian" is not a racial designation, it is a nationality. Sambo and others that Bannerman wrote about – Mingo, Quasha and Quidda – are all children of color. And that is why the writer disrespected them so and why white listeners sat by and viewed their degradation as being "acceptable."

The next "reviewer" writes:

> Raymond Clark 1 year ago
> it used to be a SAMBO'S in warner robins ga on Watson blvd in 70's
> and 80's, Now it's a doctor office across the street from HOUSTON
> MEDICAL CENTER.,Warner robins is an air force town of
> ROBINS AFB.

This is excellent geographical information. But Sambo's was accepted by white folks all over America, not only in the Deep South. Do not forget that there were more than 1,100 restaurants – somebody was disregarding the name and just seeing it as "business as usual." And why did they disregard it? Because it didn't affect or insult their racial group. Once black people started dealing with it and the "reasoning" about the name being a conjunction of the names of the two owners, the walls came tumbling down.

The next one takes a stab at Rev. Al Sharpton and Rev. Jesse Jackson:

> Phillip Jackson 11 months ago
> Sambo's is a great place to eat.....what you think AL, and Jessie??
> Who cares if it was considered racist? Get over that thought process!

This writer has a black name, but he sounds like a white boy. First of all references to Sharpton and Jackson neither of whom, admittedly, does much. Secondly, the question "who cares if it was considered racist"? Evidently this asshole doesn't. Finally, "getting over that thought process" is why and how racism is maintained and perpetuated. People want to put racist activity behind them because "ignorance is bliss." The less you know, the less responsibility you have to assume in doing something about what you know. This is the mindset of people like Phillip Jackson and millions of white people and their complicit negro lackeys around the world.

On the same day, the same guy – Phillip Jackson -- offers more stupidity-riddled "insights":

> Phillip Jackson 11 months ago
> fool4singing 1 year ago
> I never even knew that "Sambo" was a racist term until someone (an
> elder) told me. Just proves that some things will go away, but
> overly sensitive people keep the negativity going forever.

Overly sensitive people? You stupid muthafucka! Do you think Jews are "overly sensitive" when they continue to teach their children and grandchildren, "never again"? Do you think peckerwoods in the South are "overly sensitive" when they can't forget that ass whipping they took from the North and still fly their confederate flags? When it comes to issues like white racism, you keep that shit going by reminding the racists that you know what they're up to. If it was up to them they would paint their heinous actions an entirely different shade and find a way to flip it onto black people. But to this point, it hasn't worked. But that doesn't mean that they won't keep trying.

A final website comment and review follows:

> tefachead09 2 years ago
> You all know "Sambo" is a slang name for a black person and there
> was uproar over their name at that time.

Yeah. Heavy concepts. Anyway, there you have it. Sambo is as popular as ever for the right and wrong reasons. You know where I stand. But now let's look at the "collective mind" of black people and how such an image may or may not have affected them and what the majority population (in this country, for now) would have to benefit from circulating a book like this, one that they know will be shared with young children from all racial backgrounds.,

THE MINDS OF BLACK FOLK

How much psychological damage did Bannerman do (and those of her ilk, including but not limited to Sir Arthur Conan Doyle, Agatha Christie, Robert Louis

Stevenson, Rudyard Kipling, Edgar Rice Burrows, to name but a few), not only to the minds of black, Indian and other children of color, but to white kids as well? And what about the on-going psychological damage down to white and black adults who went through this era of "fairy tales" and "stories" that impugned the human worth of people of color? Those white kids had a good hearty laugh at the expense of black people, would go back home and share this good time with their parents. In turn, those parents would also find it humorous and the racist imagery continued on and on, legitimized by some of the assholes who I quoted earlier. The impact and effects, as you can see, continue to linger on and on.

What did this do to the black psyche one would ask? Let me modify an essay that I wrote as an introduction to my 1993 Nebraska Humanities Council-funded, "Black Is the Color of Society's Fears." The basic importance of images and the impact on the black mind and as a support for a white supremacist system still makes the point regarding Helen Bannerman's image-oriented racism. The opening part of the book that I wrote, with updated modifications relative to this book on Bannerman's stories, appears as follows:

In 1993 in Albany, New York, during a budget meeting, a 60-year-old white city councilman, Joseph Kover, referred to New York State Comptroller M. Carl McCall as "a nigger from Harlem." When questioned about the apparent racial slur, Kover said he did not think he had done anything wrong because "the definition of a nigger … is a black man." Kover, a Republican from Deepark, N.Y., refused to resign. (November 25, 1993).

The preceding situation that was just outlined in the newspaper excerpt is, in my view, the logical and inevitable outgrowth of a culture whose very core is stapled to racist beliefs. The very essence of Anglo-American culture is anti-black and pro-white. My contention is that any talk of race relations "improving" is nothing more than sheer hypocrisy, loaded with conjecture and bullshit. No culture is more than the sum total of its language and the symbols that that language creates. American society – and societies beyond its boundaries which use the English language and the images that the language promotes and describes – are inextricably tied to racism because of the biases in that language and those images.

Frantz Fanon wrote that, "a man who has a language consequently possesses the world expressed and implied by that language (1967: 18). And it can be further explained by Afrocentric scholar Molefi Asante, who posited,

An ideology for liberation must find its existence in ourselves, it cannot be external to us, and it cannot be imposed by those other than ourselves; it must be derived from our particular historical and cultural experience. Our liberation from captivity of racist language

is the first order of the intellectual. There can be no freedom until
there is freedom of the mind (Asante, 1988: 31).

These two irrefutable points work hand in hand to explain why the world of the African-American in this country is so constructed and limited, narrow and Neanderthal. The American educational system uses a racist language and racist imagery and pawns these off as being "normal," "acceptable" and the memorization of them oftentimes "mandatory." The battle for the black mind was already won during slavery, and then after enslavement ended, there was no "de-briefing" to eliminate that 400 year brainwashing.

We have mocked and been dominated by an individual whose ethos and belief systems created a set of word systems which consigns our very skin color to a category of inferiority (e.g., Little Black Sambo, Little Black Mingo, Little Black Quasha, etc.) As Dr. Frances Cress Welsing explained in her theory of "color confrontation,"

> … The initial psychological defense maneuver was the "repression" of the initially felt thought or sense of inadequacy – being without color and, of secondary importance, being in deficient numbers, both of which were apparently painful awarenesses. This primary ego defense of repression, was then reinforced by a host of other defensive mechanisms. One of the most important was a "reaction formation" response whose aim it was to convert (at the psychological level) something that was desired and envied (skin color) into something that is discredited and despised … (Welsing, 1974: p. 35).

And,

> … The whites desiring to have skin color but being unable to achieve this end on their own, said in effect, consciously or unconsciously, that skin color was disgusting to them and began attributing negative qualities to color and especially to the most skin color – blackness (Welsing, pp. 35-36).

Though heavily Freudian in its interpretation and analysis, Welsing's thesis is one excellent starting point to figure out just why these white people act the way they do and why they have to use their institutional arrangements (Bannerman used storytelling) to consign anything that is not white to a category of inferiority. White folks, always willing to play the victim in matters of race and rarely willing to admit to anything even remotely racist, what other explanation could there be?

Therefore the key is to "disarm" those you fear or envy the most, and do all you can to keep them hating themselves and worshipping you – a tactic that, even to this day, has worked wonders for the white supremacy mechanism, not only here in the United States, but all over the world. And Bannerman may have been raised in India and born in Scotland, but she knew the color symbols and she knew how to promote white supremacy by way of degrading black folks. As I've written elsewhere, "How can a kid who sees Bojangles beside Batman or Stepin Fetchit next to Superman going to have a positive self-image?" (Stelly, 1977: 5).

Essentially however, the racist inclination inherent in the English language are examples of "cultural racism," which is what J.M. Blaut of the University of Illinois at Chicago has written about:

> Diffusionism therefore depicts a world in which Europeans are permanently the most progressive and advanced people, and non-Europeans are permanently backward, and permanently the recipients of the progressive ideas, things, and people from Europe (cited in Armah, 1992: 21).

We can cite no better example than the language that the Euroamerican speaks, which he forces his "citizens" to learn, memorize and "master," and it is a language that promotes "whiteness" as being the ultimate in goodness and purity, and "blackness" and "darkness" as being something dirty, evil, inferior or negative. Thus, linguistic racism is being circulated in line with the technology that is used to disseminate it.

One article cited as far back as 1983 that,

> … [T]he volume of words flowing through such media as publishing, broadcasting, mail and telecommunications can reveal some of the fine structure of the much-talked about "information explosion" and how people are reacting to it … In 1960, an estimated 58 percent of the words that Americans actually heard or read through the measured media came to them by television or radio … by 1977, the figure was 69 percent, or the equivalent of 19,500 words daily … (Omaha World Herald, 1983: 13-A).

If that was the case 32 years ago, then can you imagine what must be taking place in this, the era of the Internet, Worldwide Web and global communications?

So although the white majority has control over our lives, we give them even more when we use word symbols and accept the kind of negative imagery (such as that conveyed in *The Story of Little Black Sambo*) that disempower us and refuse to use the power that is within us to deal with our situation. It should be no surprise then that so many of our people feel that they have been left to weak to do anything but wander and why many young black people reject education because of images and messages that have nothing positive or productive to offer them.

The issue then, is human dignity, which we are continually being robbed of each and every time we view negative images and allow the use words like "blackmail," "blacklist, or each time we accept a myth that a "black cat brings bad luck" or a "white lie is just a tiny one." And if individuals who subscribe to using these words understood the potential long-term negative impact, they would not use them. If, on the other hand, they choose to use such words, then they are subtly impugning our skin color, our culture and disregarding our dignity as human beings. And, these kinds of people should be corrected or dealt with – by any means necessary.

CONCLUSION

The issue then, is human dignity, which we, as Black people, are continually being robbed of each and every time we use words like "blackmail," "blacklist, or each time we accept a myth that a "black cat brings bad luck" or a "white lie is just a tiny one." And furthermore, every time we allow a classroom of children to sit at the feet of some kindergarten teacher who reads this bullshit, complete with exclamations and nature descriptions, we destroy the mindset of yet another generation of young people.

Furthermore, if individuals who subscribe to using these words understood the potential long-term negative impact, they would not use them. If, on the other hand, they choose to use such words, then they are subtly impugning our skin color, our culture and disregarding our dignity as human beings. And, these kinds of people should be corrected or dealt with – by any means necessary.

So let's recap:

> Born in Edinburgh, Scottish author Helen Bannerman (1862-1946) spent more than thirty years of her life in India, *where she started writing illustrated letters to her two daughters, who were being educated in Scotland.* Those letters became the basis for Bannerman's first and most famous book, The Story of Little Black Sambo, as well as nine more tales of clever children overcoming the odds, including Story of Little Black Mingo and Story of Little Black Quibba.

Here's my question: what were these white bitches "communicating" about in those letters? Why is the elder writing stories about black boys and girls and sending them to her daughters who were going to school in lily-white Scotland? Was she trying to make sure that her racist views and values would be perpetuated? In sum, what in the FUCK is wrong with this family?

Had I note cared enough about overturning the racism inherent in *The Story of Little Black Sambo*, I would not have learned about these other three Bannerman stories that I have shared with you. And that is why work, research and study are so important. Not the kind of research that the white man "assigns" to you in the guise of "homework" (because the bulk of my writings and analyses have come during times when most of you would consider "leisure"). The fact is, it is through study that we become strengthened, which is why I can out-debate any white boy (or black person for that matter) on the face of the earth.

As has been written, show me a true nationalist and I'll show you somebody who studies. White boys don't have to be told to write policy designed to keep people of color under control; *it has become second nature.* Even a white woman from Scotland like Helen Bannerman knows what time it is and is writing stories that she has to know are going to do damage to the black psyche. Does that stop her? Of course not. And why?

Because, as Karenga (1967) once wrote, "White doesn't represent a color; it represents a mentality that is anti-black." He is correct in that white is not a color at all, it is the absence of color. But can there be any doubt that as you study and see racist drivel from Scotland, India and countries all over Europe that the white supremacy mechanism is in full effect, not only among white contemporaries, but also in the minds of subsequent generations?

Psychological warfare being aimed at people of color at all levels, and it dominates our lives from the womb to the tomb. The Story of Little Black Sambo and the other stories that I've analyzed in this book should make it clear that the white supremacy mechanism and all of its attendant elements are in full effect, and have been throughout historical memory. This short book is aimed at providing information and insights so that none of us *ever* forget.

TEN LITTLE NIGGERS: A CRITICAL ANALYSIS

INTRODUCTION

The philosophical question might best be summed up in the words of Curtis Mayfield and the Impressions who posed the question in 1968 in their hit, "Choice of Colors:" The lyrics, in part, are these:

> If you had a choice of colors,
> Which one would you choose, my brothers?
> If there was no day or night
> Which would you prefer to be right?

The people with the power use that power to both define and defile. The "great" Agatha Christie was no different. She wrote suspense novels and most of them were filled with intrigue and yes, murder. According to Wikipedia, her novel, *And Then There Were None* is considered by many to be her masterpiece. But how many of you Agatha Christie fans know that this novel was originally published in 1939 under the title, *Ten Little Niggers*. You heard me: the research says that she got the title from a "British blackface song," and that is what serves as a major part of the plot.

You know what "blackface" is, right? It's where peckerwoods use charcoal to paint their faces black, their lips white and then do that minstrel type shit that they find so hilarious. The concept was highlighted in the Spike Lee movie, "Bamboozled." And even though the charcoal is gone today in the United States, there are still black minstrels today masquerading as civic leaders, ministers, political officials and Republican Presidential candidates. And today, white boys continue to be fascinated with black popular culture and rip if off, many times as a goof. Hearing people like David Spader say, "Gotsta have it" or their urban detectives using terms like "From the get-go,," "super cool" and so on is more evidence of the white fascination with that which is black and urban.

But let's get back to *And Then There Were None* (previously titled, *Ten Little Niggers*). This was Christie's best selling novel, "with over 100 million copies sold" according to Wikipedia. So this means that there are people all over the world who hold certain views of "niggers" (a revised version refers to the poem as "Ten Little Indian Boys") and Indian (from India) and those views are insultingly negative.

The plot of the book mimics the contents of the poem. According to one of the overviews of the book,

> In the novel, ten people are enticed into coming to an island
> under different pretexts, e.g., offers of employment or to
> enjoy a late summer holiday, or to meet with old friends. All
> have been complicit in the death(s) of other human beings

but either escaped justice or committed an act that was not
subject to legal sanction. The guests are charged with their
respective" crimes" by a gramophone recording after dinner
the first night and informed that they have been brought to
the island to pay for their actions …

Over the years this plot seems to have been used time and time again on television and a few movies. The concept of being brought to an island, the idea of people being taken out one by one – these are themes that we still see. But it is Agatha Christie's book that is known worldwide, and the racist insinuations and descriptions of the deaths of those poor black kids (whom she called "niggers") or the "Indian boys" is still a reflection of this bitch's racist mentality.

The plot overview continues:

They are the only people on the island, and cannot escape
due to the distance from the mainland and the inclement
weather, yet gradually all ten are killed in turn, in a manner
that seems to parallel the ten deaths in the nursery rhyme.
Nobody else seems to be left alive on the island by the time
of the apparent last death. A confession, in the form of a
postscript to the novel, unveils how the killings took place
and who was responsible.

White people knew this shit was going to be insulting. One of the reviewers on line attempts an explanation:

This is included not from racism, but because of Agathe
Christie's detective story of the same name, and this rhyme
not being in print anywhere, a lot of people in Austria have
asked me about it. If you are offended about the text please
accept my apologies.

Why accept an apology from someone who wrote a poem and a book based on how she felt about certain people? She tells the truth about her racist views and therefore has nothing to apologize for. Do you think the publishers who helped make it a best seller feel "sorry" for the use of the word "niggers"? Of course not. White people tend to apologize for shit that they have no power in changing. President Bill Clinton apologized for slavery, although he had not direct role in it. At the same time he was apologizing he was paving the way for the most arrests of black youth with his Minimum Federal Sentencing Guidelines in the history of this nation. White folks apologize because of fear of retribution, not because they really mean it.

Following then, is the poem in its entirety. I will break it down later in this book. Again, the title of the poem is, "Ten Little Niggers:"

Ten little nigger boys went out to dine;
One choked his little self and then there were Nine.
Nine little nigger boys sat up very late;
One overslept himself and then there were Eight.
Eight little nigger boys travelling in Devon;
One said he'd stay there and then there were Seven.
Seven little nigger boys chopping up sticks;
One chopped himself in halves and then there were Six.
Six little nigger boys playing with a hive;
A bumble bee stung one and then there were Five.
Five little nigger boys going in for law;
One got into Chancery and then there were Four.
Four little nigger boys going out to sea;
A red herring swallowed one and then there were Three.
Three little nigger boys walking in the Zoo;
A big bear hugged one and then there were Two.
Two little nigger boys sitting in the sun;
One got frizzled up and then there was One.
One little nigger boy left all alone;
He went out and hanged himself and then there were None.

So the last five words – "and then there were none" – is the focus and fulcrum of Agatha Christie's book, which was later changed to those very words. But the precursor was "Ten Little Niggers" and this should never be forgotten and in my view, can never be forgiven.

TEN LITTLE NIGGERS: A CRITICAL ANALYSIS

This poem, titled, "Ten Little Niggers," is about genocide, about infanticide and about the wanton and willful elimination of black children. It has been memorized and has served as the butt of jokes for multiple decades, and the bitch who wrote it is regarded as one of the truly great novelists of all time. But let's look at this poem and get an idea of how this white woman views black people in general, and the low regard she has for black children – "niggers," as she calls them – in particular.

The first two lines read, as follows:

Ten little nigger boys went out to dine;

One choked his little self and then there were Nine …

So these kids went out to eat. But let's be clear: since black men are considered "boys" in the white lexicon, they could be teenagers or for that matter, young adults. The concept of the black man as "boy" has even become a part of the millennial argot, as in "I gotta go see my boys," or "me and my boys are gonna head downtown." No one seems to notice because too many people are pointing their fingers at the word "nigger" and can't see that the black community, as a whole, has already been "niggerized." This poem by Agatha Christie is but one small example.

So these kids are going out to eat and what happens? One of them chokes "his little self" and dies. He chokes? With nine of his comrades around? What was on Christie's mind to have a young man die because of his own lack of knowledge and in front of those who knew nothing of the Heimlich maneuver? So not only are the "little nigger boys" prone toward group behavior, but they are ignorant of the strategy and tactics of self-preservation. And this is what makes them "boys" in the eyes of the writer: their collective stupidity.

Moving onward (but not necessarily upward):

… Nine little nigger boys sat up very late;
One overslept himself and then there were Eight …

How do you "oversleep" yourself? Obviously the child had some kind of disease that he didn't know about and ended up dying in his sleep. But the important thing here is that the myth of the lazy black man can be perpetuated because no one dies from "oversleeping." This was probably written at a time before issues like Sudden Infant Death Syndrome (SIDS) became a convenient way to explain crib deaths. But to simply "oversleep" is a racist knock against these black kids and again, the death is self-inflicted (akin to choking to death).

Continuing:

… Eight little nigger boys travelling in Devon;
One said he'd stay there and then there were Seven …

This is the first black child who has decided to drop out of the group. But because he is black, there is no reason to explain by – leaving the listener or reader to assume that he just abandoned his pals and, since he was black, it probably had something to do with pussy or money.

But never fear: death is right around the corner as we learn,

>   … Seven little nigger boys chopping up sticks;
>   One chopped himself in halves and then there were Six …

Self-mutilation, or was it suicide? Why all the negatives? Why is this white bitch writing about black youth in such a way? Why couldn't it be "ten little peckerwoods"? How about "ten little honkies"? No. Although there is another version called "Ten Little Indians," what difference does it make? They are people of color as well. So these poems are all aimed at degrading people who are not white. And the motive is clear.

The poem continues:

>   … Six little nigger boys playing with a hive;
>   A bumble bee stung one and then there were Five …

In the previous case one of the kids is killed because the group was fucking off. Playing with a hive means playing with bees, and a bee sting kills one of them. All the bases are being covered, from self-mutilation and suicide to outright poor decision making. Children listening to this poem are developing a lack of respect for these "nigger boys" and may assume that any black kids they see are as careless as the ones in this poem. All this assumption can reap is an ass whipping or a cracked jaw.

The next stanza offers the following:

>   … Five little nigger boys going in for law;
>   One got into Chancery and then there were Four …

The first semblance of success where one gets into law school leaving four more behind. But remember, only one of the five made it even though they all applied. So even in regard to this supposed "accomplishment," there is still an insult that only one of five black people is capable of making it into a system that calls for intelligence. There is no doubt that Christie knew what she was doing. Even while killing off each of the black kids, she makes it a point that not only do they leave the group, but they leave it through death or, as in the previous case, by being "selected" by the system. But as the movie "Highlander" bears out, "there can be but one …"

Moving right along:

>   … Four little nigger boys going out to sea;
>   A red herring swallowed one and then there were Three …

A red herring? How is a fish that is never more than two feet long, usually less than one foot, going to swallow a little boy? Couldn't this bitch think of anything else? Of course she could: there's sharks, piranhas, and so on. But in order to truly humiliate these kids, she has a fish that normally feeds on copepoids, zooplankton and arrow worms actually swallow whole a human being. What kind of misinformation is being fed to the young people listening to or reading this story? A little boy that can't fight off a fish? One more slap in the face of black kids. Not only are they destroyed, but they usually bring about their own destruction or they leave the group for selfish and personal reasons.

Interestingly, a "red herring" is a term, a figurative expression that, according to Wikipedia, "refers to a logical fallacy in which a clue or piece of information is or is not intended to be misleading, or districting from the actually question." So in a way, the entire scenario regarding a child being swallowed by a fish is a "red herring" of sorts.

Continuing on:

> … Three little nigger boys walking in the Zoo;
> A big bear hugged one and then there were Two …

More indecision and negligence. The one that got "hugged" apparently got too close to the cage. The bear killed him immediately. Again, I have to ask: what good are poems like these? The only purpose would be to ridicule black youth. After all, they start off ten strong and then proceed through a series of fuckups and mishaps, meaning that the concept of "strength in numbers" means nothing to them. They are being divided and decimated and seem not to mind. This, in my view, is not only the goal of white folks (to divide and destroy us), but it is also an indicator of their belief that, "if you give 'em enough rope, they'll hang themselves."

And does this not hold true in ghettoes around the country? Gangs, who hang together based on their colors and turf, can be torn apart if you add one scrawny white bitch to the equation. Groups like the National Urban League, the NAACP and even the Department of Housing and Urban Development experience lapses in their long histories because black men (and Latino males) can't keep their dicks in their pants. The word is out: the higher the position and the longer the job title, the greater the likelihood of us fucking up.

The numbers dwindle as the poem continues:

> … Two little nigger boys sitting in the sun;
> One got frizzled up and then there was One …

How is the sun going to "frizzle" a black child when we are the people of the Sun? It's the white man and his genetically recessive gene that makes the sun his enemy! He is the one who suffers from sun burns and various forms of skin cancer as a result of exposure to the sun! Seems to me that Agatha's got her niggas mixed up! A black child sitting in the sun and frying is about as likely as lions and lambs falling in love and posing for pictures!

And now, the grand (racist) finale:

> One little nigger boy left all alone;
> He went out and hanged himself and then there were None.

The most diabolically fiendish "death" of them all. This shit was written in the United Kingdom, but also at a time (1939) when black men in the United States were actually being lynched in the South, and when the country was legally segregated. Why would this bitch write a poem about a black child hanging himself? When it comes to these ten black kids she's described everything from fratricide and homicide to infanticide. She has no respect for black people and the poem makes that quite clear.

A HISTORY AND ANALYSIS OF SINTER KLAUS, SANTA CLAUSE AND "BLACK PETE": Documentation and Discussion

INTRODUCTION

There are far too many white people in the world who see humiliating black people as a part of their mythology as a "goof." There is no other way to explain why Sinter Klaus, a white man catering to white kids over in the Netherlands should have to have a black assistant named "Black Pete" who has horns and is the one who must beat the children with a birth rod if they are bad. If they are good, Klaus – riding a white horse and wearing a Pope's hat – gets to provide the gifts. Translation is universal: all that is white is good and all that is ugly, inferior and evil is bad.

Also known as "Zwarte Piet", one resource reminds us of the general amusement that such a character represents among the lily-white nations that acknowledge Sinter Klaus:

> The Zwarte Piet character is part of the annual feast of St. Nicholas, celebrated on the **evening of 5 December** (Sinterklaasavond, that is, St. Nicholas' Eve) in the Netherlands, Curaçao and Aruba and on 6 December in Belgium and Luxembourg, when **sweets** and **presents** are distributed to children. The characters of Zwarte Pieten appear only in the weeks before Saint Nicholas's feast … The tasks of the Zwarte Pieten are mostly to amuse children, and to scatter **pepernoten, kruidnoten** and **strooigoed** (special sinterklaas candies) for those who come to meet the saint as he visits stores, schools, and other places. (Wikipedia, 2016).

This shit is passed out in elementary schools all over America. Because of my work, the Omaha Public Schools and the Milwaukee Public Schools have taken it out. This brief essay is evidence and a warning to other educators to get rid of it. The black child has enough issues with low self-esteem and Uncle Tom role models without having to see this black caricature (who is a white man in blackface in real life presentations) being paraded around and featured in packets that are sent home, packets on "how Christmas is Celebrated Around the World."

Read and learn.

MY INTRODUCTION TO "BLACK PETE"

Cartoons are fictional characters much like Santa Claus, although some would prefer the word "mythical" to "fictional" since in many cultures, there really was someone similar to this man known as Kris Kringle or St. Nicholas. At any rate, Santa Claus also exists in a nation where his very presence is a racist one, and that nation is Holland. In that nation, a man named Sinter Klaus gives children gifts to children if they are good; but if they are bad, he calls upon his assistant to punish the children. And guess that assistant's name is?   BLACK Pete!

Although this author spearheaded movements to get "Black Pete" out of the curriculum of, first, the Milwaukee Public Schools and then later, the Omaha Public Schools, the fact is my children learned from the first case. And when another, somewhat different version of Black Pete was forced on them in Omaha years after the Milwaukee encounter, they let me know. In fact, the text of that short story, read aloud before hundreds of elementary school students just before Christmas break, follows:

> Sinter Claes and Black Peter
>> When people in other countries heard about Saint Nicholas and the three bags of gold, they adopted him as their gift-bringer. The Eve of Saint Nicholas (December 5, his birthday) became the time to give gifts.
>> In Holland Sinter Claes arrives late at night. Dressed in his bishop's robes, he rides through the quiet streets on a white horse, accompanied by his servant Black Peter. Black Peter, a fearsome creature, has a soot-covered face, fiery red eyes, and horns on his head. He carries a huge sack filled with presents for the good children and birch rods for the bad. It is he, at the saint's bidding, who climbs down the chimney and leaves gifts in wooden shoes that children have placed by the hearth …

The story is racist, pure and simple. The linguistic racism is more symbolic, since the saint is a white man on a white horse. All that is negative is associated with the dark "creature" whose name is "Black Pete." And although he gets to place presents in the shoes of the children, it is upon the "command" of the superior white man. It is he, Black Pete, who must climb down the filthy chimneys. What do you think this does to the mindset of the black child who must listen to this story in front of his white peers?

In actuality, Black Pete is the personification of the devil – hence, the horns on his head. Black Pete is, in effect, sub-human ('a fearsome creature') and is at the beckon call of sinter Claes. As the story puts it, Black Pete is the "servant." And finally it is Black Pete who must be the bearer of bad tidings, and mete out the punishment on the children – corporal punishment at that (using those birch rods).

While this is taking place, we juxtapose the dark and brutal chores of Black Pete with the pristine purity of Sinter Claes who is, after all, a "saint." I think you can see what time it is.

And remember: if this kind of "worldwide Christmas storytelling" took place in the Milwaukee Public Schools and the Omaha Public Schools, you can bet it exists in public schools throughout the nation. Nothing but racism in the guise of a "Christmas story." And the public school system that distributes these "Christmas packets" ought to be ashamed of themselves.

And bear in mind that there is a link between such messages and the overall reality of "mis-education" of children of color all over this nation. White people want to present that it doesn't exist. But such mis-education can be proven and has an effect on that child's behavior once he continues to get inundated with myths on how the white man created the air. Following is but one example from the Milwaukee Public Schools.

ST. NICHOLAS, SINTER KLAUS, SANTA CLAUS

Along with Little Black Sambo, Snow White and several other "fairy tales," this myth of Santa Claus has perhaps done more damage to the black psyche and to black family life than any other image-oriented white supremacist mechanism ever devised. Whether you claim that white folks don't know any better, whether you think it was just an innocent story or if like me, you know that the concept of black being negative and white being positive, makes no difference: it is the effect, the impact and the cumulative damage that has been done that should be assessed.

And that is what this analysis intends on doing. We begin with background and origins of the myth:

> The origin of Santa Claus actually begins in the 4th century, with Saint Nicholas as Bishop of Myra, now Turkey. St. Nicholas was a generous man, particularly devoted to children. Some of the current traditions surrounding "Father Christmas" or Santa Claus can be traced back to Celtic roots. His "elves" are the modernization of the "Nature folk" of the Pagan religions, and his reindeer are associated with the "Horned God", a Pagan deity.

It's all the same. During a holiday that includes songs like "Joy to the World," "White Christmas" and other bullshit-laden messages that nobody believes in or practices, we now have the myth of a white man delivering presents and of course, in at least one society, he has a black sidekick who is the embodiment of the devil. This character, "Black Pete," even gets to beat the children with a birth rod.

Dr. Carter G. Woodson wrote an incredible book back in 1933 called The Mis-Education of the Negro. And in it he outlined some of the atrocities that were being imposed on the young black mind by both white teachers and uninformed negro lackeys. This continues to exist today as black teachers can now stand in front of the classroom imparting information that they learned from their white "masters" and the few good teachers there are can be then promoted to principalships and transferred to the suburbs. Promotion for them, demotion and being "lost in emotion" for black kids.

CONCLUSION

The question you want to ask yourself is why I had to come along and were it not for my youngest son, only become aware of Black Pete after he shared his take home packet with me. Why do we continue to trust schools as if they are surrogate parents? You can see in my examples – Black Pete and the North High incident – that these schools are, to put it mildly, fucked up. I don't just mouth rhetoric I hear from some white person: I am a scholar in the field and I've done research. I've attended their best schools and out-debated their best minds. I have evidence that when all is said and done, "white people in general, do not like black people, in general." More specifically to this particular issue, "white teachers, in general, do not like black classrooms, in general.

After reading this, you can now say that you have been effectively *warned.*

FOOD (PRODUCT) DIVERSION, THE MARKETPLACE AND THE BLACK COMMUNITY

When the discussion is about product or food diversion, most articles speaking generically and/or about the various forms of fraud that may take place from time to time. Very seldom is the variable of race interjected and that is why I am interjecting it. I have lived in black communities all my life and I've seen the quality of goods that are offered to the residents. I've lived in suburban areas because, as a college student, that is where the apartments are located near these university campuses. The quality of goods offered at these supermarkets is visibly superior. There are hardly any Sentry, Krogers or other supermarkets located in "the 'hood." What we are left with in many cases are inferior meats, vegetables, fruit and goods that have an limited shelf life.

The difference between my interests and the relationship of these stores and these sales to the black community – which I deem as a form of "detrimental reliance – is the thrust of this section of my book. The differences in the way that the existence of food diversion is addressed when the variable of race is not interjected is just as important.

As an example I located an article titled, "The Shadowy Business of Diversion," which appeared in the August 4, 2009 issue of *Fortune* magazine. I will use its contents and provide analyses that will show how, in my view, the practice of detrimental reliance is alive and well.

The article begins:

> (Fortune Magazine) -- You might not have heard of product
> diversion before, but odds are you've bought diverted goods. Visit
> the nearest big supermarket, drug, or electronics chain and you
> may find diverted merchandise. Just about every product sold,
> from cars to crackers, can be diverted. (Bandler & Burke, 2009).

No, that's bullshit. The diversion that these writers are referring to doesn't really have to do with quality. I'm talking about the diversion of food that has an expired expiration date that mysteriously is loaded onto trucks and then brought into the black community and sold at these corner markets and these former "mom and pop" stores. Generally speaking, they are correct; racially speaking, they missed the boat and they probably did it on purpose so that they could get a magazine of the status of *Fortune* to publish their bullshit.

Moving on:

> Diversion is a big business, with annual sales in the U.S. in the tens
> of billions of dollars. The industry has its own lawyers, lobbyists,
> and friends on Capitol Hill. (Bandler & Burke, 2009).

Again, while the information is generically true, it is not of the type of "detrimental reliance" that low-income and minority people are victims of. By relying on stores to sell them quality goods, poor people venture forth to the market that they have access to and purchase what appears to be a head of lettuce or a loaf of bread. Many might check the expiration dates on the bread, but if it's marked down, then cost might make them purchase it. That is why there are small stores around the country that sell "day old bread" or food stuffs that are marked down because of their quality. In a society where the economy is spiraling downward, poor people catch the most hell. Therefore, detrimental reliance on the people selling the food and on the government to inspect it is the end result.

Moving on:

> There is not necessarily anything illegal about diversion. The term
> simply refers to merchandise that has somehow shifted from the
> intended distribution channel. The practice, which advocates
> describe as a form of arbitrage, takes advantage of price
> differences -- either by geographic region or between customers
> who are sold differently priced products at different times.
> (Bandler & Burke, 2009).

An act doesn't have to be illegal to be unethical, and that is the problem. America is a nation of laws made by lawless men. Judges have "discretion" and that means that the white man can interpret a law any way he wants to. He will defend his racial relatives to the last straw. So it's not about being illegal or legal. It's about the people who are being poisoned by bad food: meats, bread, and canned goods beyond the expiration date.

I recall reading an article about a decade ago about Coca-Cola. A brutha who unloaded the stuff spilled his guts and said that the carbonation in the sodas that went to the black areas of town was far less potent than the fresh stuff that went to the suburban markets. This should not be new: as black people we sit and watch these store keepers dust off bottles of soda and then place them on the shelf or in under-refrigerated freezers. Sometimes we find mold on the cheese or on the loaves of white bread that they saturate our stores with. That is, after we walk past rows and rows of various alcohol, donuts and pies so that our kids can see it and view it as all one perfectly harmless "package."

The authors want to tell the truth when they write, ". The practice, which advocates describe as a form of arbitrage, takes advantage of price differences -- either by geographic region or between customers who are sold differently priced products at different times." They might sell hillbillies in the Ozarks or rednecks in small Texas towns some inferior stuff, but the ghetto and the barrio get the really messed up foodstuffs. There are poor whites – but they ain't poor because they're white. One way to control a people's fate and future is to slowly poison them – kill them softly, as Roberta Flack might say. That is why diabetes, high blood pressure, hypertension and other preventable diseases are so high in these low-income areas. And that's why the black infant mortality rate remains sky high.

The authors introduce product diversion as a form of "arbitrage." In case you don't know it, arbitrage is the practice of taking advantage of a price difference between two or more markets. So you have the white market that can buy in bulk and therefore reduce the price of each individual unit; what's left is shipped to the black community and those stores buy less of the product and therefore mark it up so that they can enjoy a profit as well. The "sales" that take place at the end of the month (when these stores know black people get their fixed income checks and food stamps) are really mark downs from the mark ups that were made when the goods arrived earlier in the month!

The authors then provide an "example" of what they are talking about:

> One of the most benign forms of diversion works like this: A retailer orders steeply discounted promotional products, fails to sell them all, and then sells off the surplus to a third party without the manufacturer's consent. (Bandler & Burke, 2009).

The manufacturer doesn't give a damn! Once he unloads the product his job is done! It's up to the retailer to dump the leftovers! And guess where they look?

The ghetto and the barrio, more the former than the latter. But the fact is the inner city stores, usually under the cover of night. Allow the trucks to back in and unload the leftovers. And then voila! A sale! And the residents, many of them unaware of consumer rules and rights, simply shell out their money and take home a bag of groceries that are truly "gross."

In other words, the "third party" is us because that is where we join the economy – on the tertiary sector. The primary is the planting and growing of the goods, the secondary sector is the harvesting or preparation of the goods and the tertiary is where we come is – as the consumers of the goods. Gale Sayers wrote a self-deprecating piece of trash called I Am Third. According to him, God was first, his friends and family were second and he was third. I don't have time to cut this crap to shreds but have you noticed that we are always "third" on most lists. And in baseball, three strikes and "you're outta dare"!

Continuing:

> The largest diverter, Quality King Distribution of Long Island, does more than $2 billion a year in business. It made news in 1998 when it appealed to the Supreme Court and won a copyright case involving diverted hair products. The unanimous court ruled the copyright holder or manufacturer could not prohibit the reimportation of its own authorized goods. (Bandler & Burke, 2009).

Of course the ruling was in favor of product diversion. How else would you dispose of excess goods? If you throw them away, that's just a waste. So what do you do? Once the expiration date is passed, pack everything up and ship it to the ghetto or barrio. After all, "those people" have been convinced that what white people consume and buy is what is "normal," so why not give them a chance to purchase some brand goods, even though they be outdated? They won't care. That is the thinking of these retailers.

And yet according to Bandler & Burke,

> But diversion is illegal when it involves fraud, as was the case, the government charges, in the Dina Wein Reis business. Her alleged sampling ruse is just one of many forms such deception can take. Another common one, called "the U-boat," works like this: A diverter orders merchandise ostensibly for sale in a foreign country and loads it onto a cargo ship. The ship sets sail, then turns around and docks in the U.S., where the goods are resold. (Bandler & Burke, 2009).

To begin with, I had never heard of the Dina Wein Reis case, so because it is my job as an educator to learn things ("he who learns must teach"), I looked it up so you wouldn't have to. Therefore, the general aspects of the case are, as follows, courtesy of Wikipedia:

> In October 2008, prosecutors claimed that for over a decade, Wein Reis's company had tricked manufacturers into selling her merchandise at a low price … She and her associates would call company executives with an offer of a high-paying job … Then, she would ask an executive to send her a shipment of merchandise, and she promised access to lucrative markets through her "National Distribution Program," which did not actually exist … Instead of handing out samples for free as stated, she would sell the products to middlemen who then sold them to retailers, in a practice known as product diversion … Diversion is not necessarily illegal (see Quality King v. L'anza), but in Wein Reis's case, the diversion allegedly involved fraud. … In October 2008, she was arrested for conspiracy and wire fraud .. The police took much of her personal property, as the search warrant authorized them to seize the "fruits of the crime" … However, a judge later ordered some of the seized property to be returned … On May 19, 2011, Wein Reis pleaded guilty to conspiracy to commit wire fraud … (Wikipedia, (2016).

As far as I'm concerned all of it involves fraud on some level, especially when we are talking about what I'm writing about and that is the intentional and willful shipping of inferior goods to certain parts of a community based on that community's low-income or racial characteristics. After all, fraud is defined as, "In law, fraud is deliberate deception to secure unfair or unlawful gain. Fraud is both a civil wrong (i.e., a fraud victim may sue the fraud perpetrator to avoid the fraud and/or recover monetary compensation) and a criminal wrong (i.e., a fraud perpetrator may be prosecuted and imprisoned by governmental authorities).(Findlaw, 2016).

So if it's intentional and profit is the motive, the concept of detrimental reliance is an act of fraud by those who are perpetrating the sales of inferior goods. And the victims are those who are victims of "detrimental reliance." And once the variable of race is interjected, why can't this product diversion "scam" that targets low-income communities with an emphasis on the ghetto and the barrio not be listed as a "hate crime"? In sum, those who are diverting the products are "poisoning" those people who purchase those inferior quality goods.

On some levels such diversions have been deemed criminal or some form of violation:

> Manufacturers periodically have tried to stamp out diversion with civil lawsuits, but there have been few big criminal cases -- until now, with the Wein Reis matter. That's mainly because manufacturers generally prefer to settle the civil cases quickly and quietly. One reason: The manufacturers themselves are sometimes complicit, having willfully sold goods to diverters in order to hit sales targets or dump out-of-date products. (Bandler & Burke, 2009).

Again, there is fraud being committed on several levels. Just because the fraud is committed in the name of "savings" or "a good deal" doesn't make the victims any less safe or "made whole." Black people have been victimized by the sale of inferior goods in corner markets for decades. In the name of a "good deal" or a "savings," far too many families have purchased these goods and gotten sick; the diabetes, high blood pressure rates and other preventable ailments could easily be traced to these foodstuffs. And when that is added to the chemically engineered crops that these farmers are providing, then it is clear that "product diversion" is alive and well and the food stamp recipient and user is one of the most obvious targets.

The Bandler & Burke article closes down, still looking at and focusing on upper level instances of product diversion:

> Quality King and another big diversion firm, Victory Wholesale Grocers, were, at different times, Wein Reis customers, according to court records. Milt Cantor, founder of Victory, says he stopped doing business with Wein Reis soon after Unilever (UL) filed suit. "I never dreamt she was doing anything dishonest," he said. "I never knew how she got her product." A lawyer for Quality King said that that firm, too, didn't know where or how Wein Reis obtained merchandise. (Bandler & Burke, 2009).

That case is irrelevant when it comes to caste, class and race. The issue is product diverstion and what the law is that could possibly target and then prevent it. But there is nothing going on. As long as the issuing of inferior goods is clandestine and the targets are communities that are already being locked out of the system, who will defend them? Will their elected officials see it as a cause worth supporting when the stores that are involved on both sides may well be financially supporting those political campaigns?

DETRIMENTAL RELIANCE: OMAHA'S BLACK COMMUNITY, "RACE COMMISSIONS" AND "HUMAN RELATIONS"

In January of 2000 when the city issues a study which claimed that race relations were never better, I was angered by such a false conclusion. At that point I issued a "counter-document," in rebuttal to a "report" that was subsequently issued.

The method was not a new one. In fact, it represented what now, in retrospect, appears to be an historical tendency, documented in a work written in 1971 called, *Odyssey: Journal Through Black America*. In one segment, long-time Omaha dentist Earle Person had this observation:

> "When the whites put together their new downtown area, their slogan was: "Can do." We [blacks in Omaha] saw that the slogan for the Near North Side was: "Won't do." The prime movers just say, "Well, we'll try a few little things, form a committee, call in an outside research organization, make a study." And they do survey after survey after survey, and al of them get stuck away in some file..." (Selby & Selby, 1971: 290)

How prescient Person was!

North Omahans – the most oft-studied group in the history of the city and, as a result, we remain the poorest. Why? Because if we empower ourselves, there will be no one else left for them to study; no one else for them to exploit; no one else for them to document as being poor, and then taking that information and sending it to Washington, D.C. in exchange for Federal grant monies!

The city's philosophy, based upon the research of their spending patterns, appears to be clear: if they are going to do anything to help North Omaha residents, it will *only be if there are Federal grant dollars available*. Even in this "race report," as you will see, the employment section tells the reader that the key is the "economic development section" of the report. And when you turn to that section, all you see being discussed are Enterprise Zones – a federal program! The message: if blacks want jobs, then they had better pray that Enterprise Zones works! Meanwhile, local employers will continue to discriminate, refuse to hire, arbitrarily fire and otherwise neglect any blacks who apply for jobs in the conventional manner.

Generally speaking, the "Report" by the so-called Commission would receive a grade of "D-minus" if it were handed into me in a college-level course. Take note of what these white people and their "colored quislings" have done.

They begin with a report on race and divide it into sections. But alas, each subcommittee digs in only to find none of them knows anything about race relations and indeed, that they are themselves at least partially responsible for its existence. So what do they do? Each section degenerates into a "how to guide"! And that is what you can expect if you read a copy of it: a dialogue on how each of the areas – health care, housing, education, employment, economic development and media – can improve its training, its outlook, its promotional materials, its examinations, its recruiting and so on. Very little in terms of concrete ideas about how each of these areas has harmed North Omaha.

The fact of the matter is, there can be no serious social change if the players who prevent such change are in charge. This is a common sense reality that the "leadership" of Omaha appear to be too ignorant to understand. As I've written elsewhere,

> Black Omahans , with few exceptions, have very low self-esteem and apparently do not care what takes place in their community. Whites have traditionally known this, and they knew it as far back as 1977. The Urban League quotes "one city official who has boasted that 'Omaha today is host to one of the neater, more law-abiding black ghettos in the country." (Urban League of Nebraska, 1978: 7) And in a 1977 survey by WOWT, it was found that race relations, as a perceived problem, ranked tenth behind such areas of preoccupation as recreation, transportation and city sewers. (Stelly, 1998: p. 12)

The Commission was an inept, cowardly group of people who didn't attend most of the meetings. Dr. Everett Reynolds of the Omaha NAACP documented the poor attendance at many of the meetings, and the black community knows that this is just another, in a long line, of attempts to make it appear as if Omaha is changing for the better and that race relations are improving when, in reality, nothing could be further from the truth.

On the cover of the document is a quote by of all people, Robert F. Kennedy Jr. A savior to many, Kennedy's track record with blacks is questionable when you remember the role he played in the arrest of Dr. Martin Luther King Jr., and his incessant attempts to try to get civil rights advocates to "slow down."

No Kennedy had any love for black people. And, like far too many white people, he was a racist. But these white people view him as a liberal and a progressive. So the question is, why would Hal Daub, a conservative Republican who is also a racist, have a quote from Robert F. Kennedy on the cover of this report? Why would Hal Daub have a picture of the hands of black and brown and white kids joined together when, in reality, he has hurt the families of brown, black and red people ever since he took office?

With such hypocrisy evident on the cover of the report, you can imagine the depth of contradictions that lie within the covers. Following is documentation and discussion of the foolishness, shallowness and perfidious contents of the *Omaha Commission on Community and Race Relations Reports and Recommendations, December, 1999.*

The Name of The Organization

While claiming that there was no governmental influence or input into the document, the very fact that they call themselves a commission puts the lie to such claims. A "Commission" is defined as "a group of people given official authorization to perform certain functions or duties." Furthermore, in her section of the report, Director of Job Training Diane Thomas puts her report in memo form, addressed to guess who? Mayor Hal Daub.

None of the people on the Commission understand the gravity of the race problem in Omaha. But they do, however, have one thing in common: they all benefit from it. From Eddie Staton, who will do anything to remain on the government dole and Danye Etchinaw, a woman who belongs to the money-grubbing organization which calls itself La Belle Afrique, to Carrie Murphy who works at the racist KMTV-Channel 3 and Rita Melgares, queen of the conservative Latinos, they are all Daub supporters on some level, or they are the minions of people who ARE Daub supporters.

And this explains why the report amounts to nothing even resembling a relevant report. That is why they call the group who wrote it the Commission on Community and Race Relations. Had they left out the community, the lack of experience and knowledge on race issues would have been even MORE obvious; by adding the "community" dimension, those who miss the boat – meaning most of them – can claim that they were speaking "generically" or "didn't see race as a concern."

Kellie Paris-Asaka, the director of the Human Relations Department, appeared on Channel 7's "Kaleidoscope" on January 9, 2000. She was concerned about the criticisms of the report and made some statements which showed that, indeed, there is an ulterior motive to the recommendations put forth in the Commission's report.

For instance, she expressed disappointment that the City Council did not allocate her the $40,000 she needed for a "race survey." But she claims that she still wants the money and, if the Commission no longer wants a survey, she hopes "we can use the money to effectuate the recommendations of the Commission." Well, before her appearance, nowhere in the document does the city, the county or anyone else devote or commit money to any of the "recommendations" in the Report. On the contrary, one of my major criticisms is that what few good recommendations there are appear to be part of things already taking place. No money then, was committed.

One thing about her appearance was that she admitted that this was the best that she and her cohorts could do. In her words, "I put a lot of work into getting this report published … it was a powerful recommendation … this was a sincere effort to start a dialogue on race relations in Omaha."

Back in 1995 when I went on the air on Channel 22, I vowed to the community that it was my goal to take the issue of racism out of the bar and the interracial bedroom and to raise it to the level of social debate. Ernie's show came along and did the same thing. Programs like "Black Male Roundtable,""The Khalil Ben Ashanti Hour of Power,""Protecting the Village," and "Show of Truth" did the same thing. The Triple One Neighborhood Association and the Parent's Union, both created by me, did the same thing in the areas of community development and education, respectively.

How then, can Ms. Paris believe or open her distended mouth to say that this poorly written document and its pretentious authors have "started a dialogue on race relations" or anything else, for that matter? When I was addressing the race issue on my show, it was people like Paris and her cronies who were cowering at home gasping for air and acting shocked and amazed. Like her boss, Mayor Hal Daub, she is a hypocrite.

She told "Kaleidoscope" host Ben Gray that it was the findings of the Commission that "race played a significant role in" the particular problems that the Commission addressed and finally, that "race is an issue." Where has this silly woman been for the past decade? She handled the Crossroads Mall case back in 1995, after I brought the parties together and exposed the racism in the case. *And she was so inept, she had a fling with one of the plaintiffs and ended up losing the case, anyway!* This is the kind of track record that the woman who now heads the Human Relations Department brings with her. And if she couldn't handle an easy, slam dunk case like *Kemp, Kemp and Colthirst vs. Crossroads Mall and Simon Management*, then who is she to make it appear as if she knows anything about race, racism or race relations? Like her boss, she's a jack of *few* trades and a master of one: tommin'!

She claimed that the survey was "a tool to measure progress." Here's how you measure progress in race relations: look at the segregation of Omaha today and compare it with segregation of 10 years ago. Is there any change? No. Are more blacks being hired? No. Has the relative income between whites and blacks narrowed? No. If there was no racism, would there be any need for her department? No. And finally, if there was no racism, why did her own boss, Hal Daub, attempt to do away with the Department as recently as three years ago?

So it's clear what's on his mind: if he can't destroy it because of black community support, he'll put someone in charge of it who will run it into the ground. Enter: Kellie Paris Asaka! Her ignorance of racism shows when Ben Gray asked her why they didn't use the discrimination data from the files of the Human Relations Department or the Nebraska Equal Opportunity Commission. She said that while they had information in the areas of employment and housing, there wasn't enough data in the areas of health care, media, education and so on. After all, she explained, "we determined that racism could go beyond the traditional areas."

Oh, really? Paris is an attorney. The "traditional areas" of discrimination are the ones which paved the way for the others! She knows that housing and employment discrimination were both sanctioned by the system as recently as 1950! She has to know something about the racist mindset because that is what discrimination is: it is the action based on a racist attitude. Now since that is the case, if you find it in an area like employment, that paves the way for the exercise of racism in other spheres: where you can afford to live, how your children fare in school, the quality of health care you receive, where you can go socially and so on. If this woman doesn't know this, then she is an insult to the Nebraska Bar, the North Omaha community and anyone who is sincerely committed to learning about now to improve race relations in Omaha.

To paraphrase an age old adage, you judge a Commission by the reports it bears. And in this case, it is clear that the Commission created by Hal Daub and monitored by Hal Daub reflects the same naivete, racism and backwardness which Hal Daub exhibits every time he opens his mouth. This kind of ineptitude is evident in his cronies, from Mike Saklar and Brinker Harding, to Jim Cleary and now, Kellie Paris-Anaka.

As stated, this document is an exercise in futility, and starts off with what I view as "grandiose quotes" by the League of Cities.

The first such quote, from the 1991 League of Cities document, titled, "Diversity and Governance," reads as follows: "The first requirement of city leaders is that they embrace diversity and affirm equal rights for all. From that there can be no retreat." This is not true. City leaders need to ACT on that which has already been confirmed by law and by God. Their affirmation is unnecessary if they would but just act.

On the same page is another quote, this one from "Building a Nation of Communities," also by the League of Cities: "Deep-seated problems such as racism, economic exclusion, and a sense of political powerlessness often stand in the way of residents feeling they have a equal stake in their communities' success."

"Often stand in the way"? Are there times when racism, economic exclusion and a sense of political powerlessness WORK for people of color, or anyone else, for that matter? This statement, by being quoted, is a case of the blind leading the blind. This proves that what white people (and their Negro lackies) find relevant, black people feel the opposite about.

To ensure balance, no doubt, there are two more quotes from the League of cities, the 1999 Futures Report. The question at the top of the page asks, "How Can We Undo Racism?" The first answer is "By Changing Ourselves," and the explanation reads,

> On the one hand, working against racism means changing what we, as individuals and elected leaders, are doing to keep racism alive – for example, by separating ourselves, intentionally or not, from individuals of different races, or by not speaking up when those around us make racist comments.

The question is, why haven't white folks done it? The answer is, because they cannot. As Dr. Frances Welsing teaches, racism is a matter of genetic survival for those people. If they fraternize and have sex, the product is a child of color. For their own survival on this planet, they must shield themselves from the brown gene, which is both sociogenically and genetically more powerful than the "white" gene.

The second answer is, "By Changing our Policies and Institutions," and the quote says:

> Dismantling racism also means changing the policies and the social and institutional systems that allow racism to remain an oppressive force – for example, by enabling police to stop motorists because of the color of their skin or by permitting banks to treat loan applicants of different races differently.

The policies and institutions are aimed at maintaining the white supremacy structure which protects them genetically. Segregation is one way that they maintain social separation. One need only read "The Cress Theory of Color Confrontation and Racism" or *The Isis Papers: The Keys to the Colors* to better understand why white people act so foolishly when they must confront their neighbors of color.

The selection of these quotes shows that Commission members are out of tune with the racial reality of the times. Even the "Negroes" who were members of the Commission, had they cared anything about their white colleagues, would not have allowed these dunderhead quotes to be used. But it appears that neither side really cares about the other and the key was to hurriedly construct a document that the Mayor could use as evidence that he "cares about the negro people."

Well he failed and they failed. Following is evidence of these collective failures and reasons why the Report by the Commission on Community and Race Relations should be read carefully.

And then burned.

Next is the "Executive Summary."

The writers of the report were so limited in their research skills that they attempted to masquerade their shortcomings with irrelevant quotations, outmoded data and generic conclusions. An example lies in the following passage:

> Since the spring of 1998, volunteers from across this city have been actively engaged in research, analysis and assessment of race relations in Omaha, Nebraska … Racism in all its manifestations is an emotional topic for many, and is extremely difficult to talk about. Members of the committees experienced this as they strived to create actionable recommendations organizations, government and even individuals can embrace and implement. (p. 3)

More than half a year of research by all of these people, and their findings are as relevant as a term paper written by a third grader. The topic is only "emotional" to those who have practiced and benefited from it; blacks, Latinos and American Indians have been dealing with racism for so long, there is nothing to get emotional about. So the statement about emotion shows you which group constituted the majority – white folks. And that is why they "strived to create actionable recommendations" and didn't really create any. They tried to do all they could, but failed. They attempted to find solutions but didn't know how to define the problem, where to look for solutions, or how to analyze what they came across.

Furthermore, what are the academic credentials of these "volunteers"? What makes them think that they can conduct research? Not only that, but the report claims that these people were "actively engaged in research, analysis and assessment of the state of race relations in Omaha, Nebraska." If these people were so smart, they would have already found a "solution." The fact that they are, as a collective, intellectually inadequate can be seen in the difficulty that this town has in luring and keeping major businesses; when all is said and done, the State of Nebraska and Omaha lose out to such hinterland capitals as Alabama and Utah!

But this raises an important point: these people, both subconsciously and consciously, have such a low regard for race relations and improving race relations, that they feel that any layman, any clown off the corner can conduct "research." If we were studying the way to make relations better between white men and women, do you think the League of Women Voters or the Omaha chapter of the National Organization of Women would allow just "anybody" to conduct research in their behalf? No.

Only when it comes to the blacks and the Latinos do these arrogant white people think that they – the source of the problems we face – can also provide the solutions. They want to conduct research and do analysis on data when the problem stares them in the mirror every day; when they are sleeping with the problem; when they are employed by and do the bidding of the problem. This dishonesty is the basis of the report which explains why honest people must reject its contents, root and branch.

The poorly written and shabbily presented "reports" were explained, as follows:

> The reports in this package appear just as members of the subcommittees have submitted them. This is the information that these volunteers have compiled in each individual committee, on their own time over the last twenty months, without influence or input from any political factions in the City. (p. 3)

Almost two years of preparation, we now learn. And they want us to believe that during this period, the people who didn't know what they were doing didn't seek any assistance from anyone who works with the city, the university or anyone with expertise that they lacked? This is an absurd lie. The people involved had been benefiting from racism all their lives and most of them live in segregated neighborhoods. When confronted with having to challenge that which has become a way of life, it is no wonder they were left dumbfounded and why, after twenty months, the best they could come up with was 62 pages of dunce-like drivel.

To further the like, a "nonpolitical disclaimer" of sorts was provided by these intellectual midgets in the following passage:

> Subcommittees recruited members who were interested in making positive impact in the race relations arena. Political affiliation was a non-issue as subcommittees met each week or month to hammer out the essentials for improving race relations in our city. They sought out

> individuals who freely gave of their time and resources to look at
> Omaha race relations issues from a 360 degree viewpoint with the
> intent of finding facts, causes and solutions – not placing blame … (p.
> 3)

First of all, these people found no solutions. They simply regurgitated some general truisms that most people already knew. This, again, is attributable to their backwardness and dishonesty. Furthermore, they talk of not "placing blame;" it is not a matter of "blaming" anyone. It is a matter of "attributing responsibility," and we know on whose shoulders segregation, redlining, steering, consumer fraud, pilfering of Federal grant money, mis-education, and police harassment should be placed. It is not a matter of "blame," but a matter of those who practice these things to own up to them and realize that since they are so intertwined with the problem, they cannot possibly be a part of any solution.

If the subcommittee recruited members "who were interested in making positive impact in the race relations arena," why did they not share with the readers of the Report how they went about making those selections? How was the recruitment mechanism set up? Was it by word of mouth? Or was it by picking people who shared the same views and values? And since it most likely was the latter, how can one expect change when what we have on this subcommittee is really nothing more than the blind leading the blind?

How do you look at something with a "360 degree viewpoint?" What is a 360 degree viewpoint? How would you know if someone had the capacity to look at something with this kind of viewpoint? How did those doing the recruiting know who had or who did not have this viewpoint? If the subcommittee knows who has this view point and who does not, then does that mean that the committee can tell who is racist and who is not? The thoughts are flawed because the words used to describe the process are flawed. That is why nothing that comes from such divided approaches and mixed up ideas will work. As Karenga writes, "to divide the process is to deform the product."

The lies continue to mount, as the need to cover up the shabby work increases. Take note of the following attempt at an explanation:

> Cross sections of people from across the metropolitan area participated
> in the Omaha Commission on Race and Community Relations.
> Individuals from all walks of life were actively involved in all
> subcommittees. This means that leaders from community
> organizations, private and public sectors as well as front line concerned
> individuals were actively engage in the work of the commission. (p. 3)

This is a lie. Ultimately however, what they really mean is that everyone involved was selected, picked or recruited by someone else. And this means that what you ultimately had was a "clique of the unconscious," a coterie of kooks, a circle of pseudo-intellectuals. By banding together, they make it appear as if the issue of race is so complex and that they do not know what the problem is. The more people they recruited, the bigger the problem became because when it comes to race relations in Omaha, white people are the major problem, and their handpicked flunkies of color make solving the problem even more difficult.

In addition to the pervasive stupidity and racism that permeated the subcommittee, paternalism was also present. That is the only way to explain the cultural arrogance that lies behind the following statement:

> People of Color were able to openly discuss how they were affected in the seven focus areas … The impact of those leaders' participation is evident in the community partnerships that have been formed, and small, yet important change that have happened as a result of those forums. (p. 4)

How would white people know if people of color were "able to openly discuss how they were affected"? If these people of color felt some comfortable, then why even bother discussing racism, why not leave everything the way it is now? After all, they are sitting in the midst of racists and they are comfortable enough to say how they feel. This means that "equality" existed in that situation? Where then, is the equality and the "open ear" of the white man in the society at large? Nowhere to be found. And the reason it can't be found is the same reason why it didn't exist at these "playtime sessions" sponsored by the subcommittee: because both sides are being fake, with white people feigning liberalism and black people fooling those whites by "tomming." No sane solution can come out of a situation when the two parties involved are behaving in such a duplicitous and perfidious manner.

The preceding statement claims that the impact of "those leaders" participation can be seen in the community partnerships that have been formed. As a grant writer, I know that the buzzword of the 1990s was "partnership," just as the buzzword of the new century is "collaboration." At any rate, the only partnerships that are formed revolve around going after grant money and then splitting it; the white groups need the minority input for ideas and to meet Federal guidelines, and the blacks need the white resources and clout. This is not a "partnership" – it's an alienated arrangement.

Knowing that they were woefully inadequate, a day late and a dollar short, the charlatans who made up this subcommittee began applying qualifiers to their already shortsighted efforts. At one point they write,

> … **The original purpose of the commission was to assess the status of race relations in Omaha – not "fix" the problem** … The gathering of this diverse group of people to discuss the nature of race relations in Omaha, Nebraska is **a strong first step.** Many recommendations for improvement of race relations in the seven target areas have been made from the best efforts of this Commission … (p. 4—emphasis original)

The first sentence is an outright confession, confirming all that the community has been saying all along: that the subcommittee was a joke and that they were studying what had already been studied to death. By "assessing the status of race relations in Omaha," these lazy cowards relied on information and insights already studied – secondary information. If you want to know the status of race relations in Omaha, you have to interview the people who are the victims of racism, because they know where it comes from, how intense it is and what form it comes in. You don't bring together a cadre of people from the oppressor class and then claim that you want to "assess the status of race relations in Omaha." You know how those relations are because, as a racist, you enjoy the benefits and the segregation that the "status" has brought to you and your family.

Notice that the quote says that the recommendations for improvement of race relations were made "from the best efforts of this Commission." Not from concrete results; not from quantitative analysis; not from objective longitudinal assessment and comparison. No. From "the best efforts" of the Commission. So if the Commission is filled with people who are ignorant of race relations, then their "best efforts" are going to culminate in a a collectively foolish conclusion. And that is exactly what happened.

After this confession, the overall weakness and inadequacy of the committee is addressed, in a backhanded way, but addressed nonetheless. Note the following "well-at-least-we-tried" foolishness:

> … Challenges that Omaha and the nation have faced concerning race relations did not happen overnight. Subsequently, the on-going recommendations and solutions will not "fix" the problem of racism – intentional or not – overnight … The Omaha Community must be constantly vigilant of inequities or opportunity, and be change-hardy and solution-driven about processes or behaviors that perpetuate those inequities … (p. 4)

These people are local and they are part of a subcommittee that is supposed to be looking into racism here in the River City. Why then, do they write begin by writing about, "challenges that Omaha and the nation have faced concerning race relations?" The answer is because they know that they failed but they want the reader to know that the entire nation has failed to deal with racism, so Omaha is not by itself. In a word, misery loves company. After indicting the entire nation in an attempt to ameliorate their own racism and segregation-oriented tendencies, the subcommittee then stoops to clichés: it didn't start overnight so it won't be fixed overnight.

These people realize that Omaha is a wealthy city and that racism played a major role in building that wealth. The master of the subcommittee, Hal Daub, knows that it is racism and his hatred of North Omaha that is going to generate Federal dollars for the city—money that he can steer away from North Omaha and use to improve his downtown skyline, build more places where white people can engage in freakishness and frolic, and use to entice more companies into the city, companies that won't hire people of color.

That is why all this subcommittee could come up with, after all those months, is sweet-sounding, liberal rhetoric like that which follows:

> What IS needed if Omaha, Nebraska is to continue to strike to be an
> inclusive community that values differences of all types, is for MORE
> people to continue to come together in a spirit of unity … (p. 4—
> emphasis original)

And finally, after realizing that their efforts were abysmally inadequate, they conclude, nonetheless, by trying to make themselves look like civil rights pioneers:

> The Omaha Commission on Community and Race Relations has laid
> the groundwork for open dialog … several of the subcommittees have
> decided to continue their work by sharing and partnering with
> community organizations. Let the good work begun by these dedicated
> volunteers continue. … (p. 4)

This is the product, not of white trash or some high school dropouts. This is the work of the best that Omaha's white community can produce. This is their ultimate effort. And you see what it looks like and what it entails. And as you read it, things don't get better. They get measurably worse.

The next section of this "race commission" study carries the heading, "Overview From the General Chairs." Following is that interview and my analysis of it

***   ***   ***

Racism makes you do stupid things. In order to feign a concern for race relations, Mayor Hal Daub knew that he had to pick a chairman that would make him (Daub) appear "wise." He couldn't pick a white one because that would look like paternalistic racism; he couldn't pick a black one because he (Daub) distrusts and despises African-Americans. He couldn't pick a Latino because it might make the Blacks and other racial minorities feel left out. So what do they do? Three people are picked to serve as "general chairs." The three are Eddie Staton, a system-oriented "Negro" whose words and actions prove he is beholden to the mayor; Rita Melgares, a conservative Latina lawyer; and Roy Smith, owner of a white car franchise and a very rich man. This "menagerie," then, served as the leadership for a "Commission" that was supposed to address race relations with some semblance of seriousness.

The paper is supposed to be apolitical, but what do they write in the document? Take note:

> We want to also express appreciation to Mayor Hal Daub for his support and vision in the creation of this commission. We hope that this will be the first in many efforts to publicly denounce racism and discrimination of all types in Omaha … (p. 5)

If he supported it, then that means he was around when they were writing it. And if the commission was the creation of Daub's vision, then that explains why it was filled with racists and incredibly unqualified people of color. It also explains why the committee's statements, like the actions of the mayor who created it, are also contradictory.

For instance, the commission writes that, "we hope that this will be the first in many efforts to publicly denounce racism and discrimination of all types in Omaha." That statement translates to mean that racism and discrimination are always going to be around, hence the need for "many efforts" in the future. This is the kind of foolishness that exposes racists for the imbeciles that they are. This Commission is surely no exception.

And because they know that they are visibly making themselves look like fools, they immediately launch a reaction formation and attempt to place the blame on those who can see through the cheap scam that they are trying to pull of. They write that,

> … Let the critics say what they will – if they did not actively participate in this process they personify the adage: "If you're not part of the solution, you're part of the problem. …"

The only way to "actively participate" was to be "recruited" by one of the members of the Commission. Therefore, if you weren't recruited, what they are saying is that you are part of the problem – as if they and only they are part of the solution. Anything created by Hal Daub is going to be racist because that is what he is. And those Commission members know what they are doing – they just don't give a damn. And it is this very lack of values and morals which prompts them to attempt to transfer the blame onto others.

The whimpering idiots know their shortcoming, and that is why they cover them up by claiming that they have just started:

> Racism in America has existed for over 300 years. While the efforts and recommendations of this Commission are not a quick fix, it is a beginning …

A beginning to do what? Moving on, they write,

> If change is to happen, it must begin at the top! We challenge all arms of City and County government, as well as leaders of Corporate, community Educational and Religious organizations to take an adamant moral stand of denouncing racism, bigotry and hate. We urge these leaders to weave a culture of understanding, respect and valuing of differences among people .. TODAY! (P. 5 –all emphasis original)

This suggestion about change beginning at the top is how racism is maintained. The change has to start at the bottom, collectively amass influence and power, and then influence those at the top with the numbers of people who want to influence and determine new policy. Why would a racist who has things going the way he wants – practicing racism in full view and still not have any opposition from most whites – stop in the middle of the stream and reverse his position? It doesn't make sense, but the suggestion once again shows how silly the people on this Commission are.

How can they "challenge" anyone in the corporate, community, educational or religious community? They are beholden to these interests! That is why the meetings were so poorly attended; that is why of the three General Chairs, only the "Negro" member came forward and tried to justify the contents of the report. This was because that "Negro" was the only one with the tombstone courage to condemn the head of the local NAACP. Had Smith done it, he would be exposed for his racism; had Melgares done it, she would have been attacked by the Latino and Black leadership. But when a "Negro" does it, the attack is legitimized by those white people who believe that he is really a leader. But the black community knows better.

With that said and done, the following section of the "study" is titled, "Recommendations of the General Chairs." The recommendations (pages 6 and 7) are shallow, generic and written as if the chairpersons were in a hurry. Following are excerpts from some of those recommendations:

> … Organizations should create a statement of personal commitment of zero tolerance for racism and discrimination and make that statement public no later than January 31, 2000 …

A statement of personal commitment? This implies that these organizations should go to each of their employees and get a statement that they will no longer hate black people. No, what we need is an "organizational" and an "institutional" commitment and, from there, an ideological and philosophical commitment that these people will no longer practice the stupid doctrine of racism. We need financial, legislative, judicial commitments – not personal ones. If a white person never says "hello" to me in life, that is fine by me. But that doesn't preclude him or her from supporting and turning their head while their institutional representatives destroy North Omaha and then lie and claim that "the negroes did it to themselves."

Furthermore, *how can a city, steeped in a history of racism and segregation, have the temerity to issue a zero tolerance edict?* That would be self-incriminating! They would have to issue a statement against all of their white leadership, from Daub, McKiel and the County Board, to all of the banking and business interests who are behind the evil that is done to North Omaha on a daily basis. They would have to expose Creighton University and how it controls the board of the Charles Drew Center and how it is gradually encroaching northward. They would have to expose the sexually perverted and racist hijinks taking place at Boys Town, the elitist racism at UNO, and the discrimination at its malls, restaurants and movie theaters.

After the preceding ridiculous recommendation, the General Chairs continued the pattern by suggesting that,

> … People of Color must be vigilant in reporting acts of discrimination and bigotry promptly to appropriate authorities (i.e., -- human resources departments, City Human Relations, Nebraska Equal Opportunity Commission, Urban League, NAACP, ADL , NCCJ, Chicano Awareness, etc.) …

This statement was put in the report to imply that people of color were not reporting incidents of racism and discrimination. This is a dupe. People of color have "reported,""blown whistles" and "exposed" so much, and have paid such a high price for doing so, most of them are just burned out. When they do report such acts, who do they go – the nitwit who now heads the Human Relations Department and claims that a "race survey" would do some good? The same Mayor who, upon learning that a Native American child had gotten shot in the back by a white clerk, basically said "if you shoplift, that's what you can expect?" A police department that is responsible for saturating North Omaha with drugs and arbitrarily arresting black males? An Equal Opportunities Commission that is, at best, a joke?

Then, when you do report these incidents what are you really doing? You are, as Malcolm X would say, "running from the wolf to the fox." The employers who own the big companies are the same ones who backed the racist Mayor we now have. The Mayor controls the Human Relations Department and all of its verdicts. How then, can black people find justice with such an existing state of affairs? Not to mention a judicial system which includes judges who draw swastikas on reports, say "fuck you" to female attorneys, and who allow even worse "pranks" to take place and say nothing.

Black people must fend for themselves and if the Report was honest, that is what it would have said.

But if the preceding suggestion showed an abysmal ignorance of what black people are up against, the following one most certainly over-estimates the moral fortitude of this community's white population when it suggests that,

> … It is the responsibility of People (sic) who are NOT of color to also be vigilant in taking action when they see occurrences of racism, whether it be confronting the perpetrator of the racist behavior or refusing to patronize an establishment who (sic) is guilty of such behavior …

Now the board is asking the racists to spot and respond to other acts of racism! If white people had the collective capacity to do this, there would be no residential segregation in Omaha; there would be no District 66, for surely their racism and the subsequent "white flight" led to the creation of far west Omaha! Those members of the Commission who allowed this report to go public did themselves a grave disservice. Not only did they expose their collective ignorance, but they also insulted the intelligence of those of us who are out here fighting racism on a daily basis. According to them, we are misguided: all we have to do is sit back and wait for white people to put an end to it themselves!

> Have the Human Relations Department; (sic) with community groups
> (i.e., Nebraska Equal Opportunity Commission, Urban League,
> NAACP, ADL, NCCJ, Chicano Awareness, etc.) create a community
> database of verifiable incident reports by December 31, 2000 …

First of all, the Human Relations Department is supposed to be already doing this. But who are these Commission members to talk of "having" the other organizations create a database of future incidents. These groups need to get on about the business of making sure that no more incidents occur! And as for those Jewish groups – the Anti-Defamation League and the National Council of Christians and Jews – they are of no use to the black community whatsoever. They sit on our boards and dominate our lives through so-called "philanthropy," but they are just as responsible for the condition of North Omaha as their gentile buddies are. To even include them in this list is a slap in the face of both the black and Latino communities.

Since Daub is behind this madness, and since the director of the Human Relations Department is his water carrier, what they are trying to do is "control" complaints of racism so that these complaints can be more easily discarded. That is why many of the recommendations have the "solutions" funneled through a department run by a woman who knows nothing about race relations and who was handpicked and appointed by the Mayor.

Still as yet they suggest that some unnamed entity,

> … Create a process where Douglas County employees can register
> discrimination complaints with City Human Relations Department by
> February 28, 2000 …

What has the Human Relations done for the black community in recent years? One of the General Chairmen is a former director and even he, as mealy-mouthed as he has been lately, knows that the work of the Department has been watered down since the times when he held the reins. The Department is intentionally being made worthless so that it can be eliminated altogether – that is why Daub appointed an incompetent to run it. Who else, but an incompetent, for example, would make the following suggestion.

> … Create a citywide public relations campaign to promote valuing of
> differences and reporting of incidents by December 31, 2000 …

Money can now be spent. But on what? A stupid public relations campaign! Daub and Paris-Anaka want that money so badly that now they're grasping at straws. A citywide public relations campaign against racism? Where are you going to put the billboards – in west Omaha? Because you're preaching to the choir if you put them in the north or southside.

The foolishness continues and concludes with perhaps the most absurd suggestion of all:

> … Have City Human Relations host awards event for groups,
> corporations and individuals who contribute to bringing the city of
> Omaha together in valuing differences by December 31, 2000. …

The key to the preceding statement is that the suggestion calls for the Human Relations Department HOSTING an awards banquet. How timely. This is one way to give the department credibility that it lacks. To give this department the power to bestow awards for people who promote racial harmony. This relieves the Department of the responsibility of having to do it! Daub would be present and would give a speech; the Omaha World Herald would be there with cameras flashing. And before you know it, you've got a press release, a campaign brochure and billboards showing how Daub "unified" the city. And every entity that gets an award would represent a real or potential vote.

Secondly, why "award" these groups? If they are so "anti-racist" or progressive, then why should they be awarded for it? This suggestion shows the true commitment of the Commission: surface level only. *Pretend* that you are not racist. *Pretend* that you will work to combat racism. *Pretend* that your Department is committed to people of color when, in reality, you're in the mayor's pocket. *Pretend* that the Report you just produced has real merit. *Pretend* that the Commission you are on is actually working. And then, when you are rewarded for your deceitful behavior, *pretend* that you deserved it.

Detrimental reliance is perpetuated through perpetuation of the perversely parasitic ploys, programs and paragraphs just outlined by politicians and policymakers.

<u>Cultural Tenderizing": Inclusion, Diversity, Engagement, etc.</u>

Before you baste or bask a race of people in continued racism and segregation, it helps to "tenderize" them so that you can dupe them into thinking that despite your disdain for them, you nevertheless have their own best interests at heart. The "tenderizing" process of the 21st century rests in the on-going saturation of the community with buzz words like "inclusion," "diversity," multiculturalism," "cultural competence," "community engagement" and so on. Following are examples of each.

Christopher Columbus is alleged to have once said, "By prevailing over all obstacles and distractions, one may unfailingly arrive at his chosen goal or destination." Those in power are aware of this general truism and over the centuries have, on varying levels, used it to their advantage. If there is one thing that the American media is able to do it is to "district" the oppressed masses from what the system and the government has been doing to them. The media, which is part of the system ("the fourth estate") has a job to disguise, camouflage, dupe, trick, circumvent and confuse the already confused American masses.

In recent times one of the leading distractions has revolved around the system's attempts to convince Blacks and Latinos that it truly gives a damn about them. Without providing resources, funding or any tangible proof, what comes out of this myth is the proliferation of programs, projects, special events, forums, workshops, cultural centers, museums and the like – anything to take attention off the dirt that is being done and is taking place in Washington, D.C. and the controllers of the system.

Following then, are a few buzz words that serve as perfect distractions that are aimed at "softening up" the American public, "tenderizing them" into believing that "race relations are really getting better."

<u>Multiculturalism –</u>

Multiculturalism is a watered down version of reality and in the hands of white people, almost any group can be channeled into this catch-all category: white ethnics, especially the Jews; foreign nationals; and while Asians are an important group, they are still as yet immigrants, meaning they CHOSE to come to this nation. Their success in terms of structural, marital and cultural forms of assimilation too often pit them against us and, indeed, in at least two Asian countries I know of, the black man is mocked and caricatured (Japan and China).

A different interpretation brought to light by someone who had experienced what was taking place, someone who lived the life. And this is what multicultural education brings to the perennially lily-white world of academia: a perspective rooted in "feeling" and knowing what is right. Can a member of the oppressor class feel what it was like and remains like, to be a member of the oppressed class? No. Can they read it and study it and gain inspiration to go out into the world and battle oppression? Yes. But can they impart to young kids of color and future generations of whites what need to be understood to combat oppression? No.

Without alternatives, stripped of viable options by system-oriented and reactionary black leadership, all we are led to believe that we have is "one-way integration," of which multiculturalism is but one prong. But there are other components of the "cultural tenderization" process, the next one being the concept of "cultural competence."

Cultural Competence

On its face it appears to be a step in the right direction: if white people can become culturally competent, they are less likely to be less racist and xenophobic than they have traditionally been. The only problem is that it's a scam, an illusion. It is a myth along the same lines as that old "contact hypothesis," remember that? The thesis was that the more "contact" you have with people who are different from yourself, the less likely either side is to be prejudiced against the other. That turned out to be bullshit: white folks kept thinking they were superior and forced us to have to knock some sense into them, which in turn reinforced their beliefs that we hated them and wanted to do them wrong.

The concept of "cultural competence" operates in quite a similar fashion. You see, white people can flash that buzz phrase all over the place, claiming that they are culturally competent or their writings are or their organization is. But it's just white nationalism with a bullshit window dressing, Their version of cultural competency, like their version of diversity, is saying "the n--- word" instead of calling you a nigga outright. To them, that's progress. It's all part of the cultural tenderizing process: dupe the niggers, make them think we are and that we have changed, and then when they let down their guards – take 'em to the cleaners.

Diversity

The logical question to ask is can a system that has made tens of octillions of dollars discriminating and excluding and legally segregating a people overturn itself in the name of becoming more "diverse"? Or is it more likely that the gradual "browning" of the country – demographic transition – is going to cause a new program, plot or "tactic" to be implemented where there is the façade and appearance of diversity when, in reality, campuses and other societal institutions remain as white-dominated and therefore discriminatory, as ever.

There is no doubt that there is much media attention and lip service being paid to making claims that such programs are aimed at increasing the numbers of minorities on predominantly white campuses; however, this paper seeks to ask the 'right' questions in finding out what the intentions of administrators really are in implementation of such programs and in fact, if such intentions are sincere for the long-term or just another band-aid short-term grant-oriented "scam" that these institutions tend to run on a regular basis.

To begin with, nonwhite people cannot and should not lead or run programs that are truly committed to "diversity." How could they? Their version of diversity is akin to their commitment to being "color blind," and we know that such a term is an insult to people of color. If you're "blind" to a person's color, then the only way you can treat that person is as if he or she is another white person – tanned and ethnically different perhaps, but another white person nonetheless.

The white version of "diversity" is what they call "inclusion." What arrogance! Who is going to determine who is "included"? Furthermore, "included to be among whom"? Included to do what? Their version of "inclusion" is akin to the military's version of it: "include" people of color to fight in the war and once they're in, send them to take "the point" or "bring up the rear." Control them through the use of "total institutions" where their clothes, the time they go to bed or take a piss, and eat are all controlled by the people doing the "including." In other words what I call forced one-way integration. To be "included" is viewed as an "honor" while those who are not included are deemed somehow "unfit."

More profoundly, diversity, to date, has not allowed people of color to "close ranks" and formulate strategies which would, indeed, allow for true diversity. The concept of "designing diversity" was first made public and prominent by Dr. Kenneth Shaw when he was the president of the University of Wisconsin system. With the assistance of then Chancellor Donna Shalala and "Special Assistant" James Sulton," the "Design for Diversity" was given headlines and headway in major publications all over the nation.

But it accomplished very little. Why? Because of the lack of commitment, follow-through and continuity by those in positions to make a difference.

Within one year of instituting the "Design for Diversity" and still falling short of its publicly stated goals, the three key players mentioned all left the UW system for other venues; Sulton to another institution with the same position, Shaw to another educational institution with a major position, and Shalala to become Secretary of the Department of Health and Human Services under president Bill Clinton. What happened to all that diversity? One campus newspaper at UW-Madison pasted in a picture of blacks and whites together in the stands and tried to pawn it off as their own school. And that's another tenet of diversity: a "cut and paste" approach to complying with some federal mandate or grant, or to push a recruitment effort so black athletes will come to your school and run touchdowns, dunk basketballs and chase white coeds.

In this paper, I offer four approaches to "designs for diversity" that will be proposed and analyzed. From this information will come analyses, answers and inspiration pointing to similarities between these programs and highlighting the potential positives that each program might possess. There is no doubt that such programs are aimed at increasing the numbers of minorities on predominantly white campuses; however, this paper seeks to ask the "right" questions in finding out what the intentions of administrators really are, why all this sudden concern about "colorization," what awaits these kids once they arrive, and what types of behind-closed-doors "benefits are in for once these schools engage in implementation of such programs.

For the sake of future debate and discussion, I offer four (4) reasons, all of them less than "moral": (1) The Ideological Response Approach, (2) The Federal Compliance Reaction, (3) The Oasis Syndrome and (4) The Qualified Intentions Approach.

The Ideological Response Approach.

This approach is nothing more than a knee-jerk reaction to what other institutions are doing and to the buzzwords of the time period. There is no real commitment, but the over-use of such terms as "multiculturalism," "diversity programs," "prejudice reduction workshops," "racial harmony" or as the University of Nebraska Omaha once had the gall to sponsor, "Pathways to Harmony." These terms and buzz words are used time and time again when the reality reflects that the campus remains lily-white and racist. This approach is one that is aided and abetted by campus and community media, which make pronouncements of what "will be" and what "is on the way" when nothing to bring about true substantive change is even being considered.

An integral aspect of Ideological Response Approach is the promotion of existing blacks to highly visible areas: director of Multicultural Affairs, Dean of Minority Recruitment, Special Assistant to the Vice-Chancellor and the like. The fact is, the people have no experience, there is no job description and there are no objectives or goals. These are people of color who could serve in any administration in a role that is more "mainstream" and less token. But they are used and highly paid to do what the real estate "manager" does for the actual homeowner: serve as a buffer between the decision makers and the minority students.

In truth, the individual, as Senator Ernie Chambers taught, receives a set of keys that fit nothing. Another equally humiliating characteristic of this approach is the competition between campuses that both practice the Ideological Response approach. It is almost as if they are competing to see "whose Negro" or "whose Latino" can be displayed more prominently in the newspaper, whose has the most degrees or credentials and whose has received the most air time. It is paternalistic racism at its most insidious.

Remember that the Ideological Response Approach may have an end result of the creation of diversity programs, minority affairs departments and the like, but the foundation is still white supremacy. The end result is still offering black students few social alternatives because heaven forbid they should hang around and remain on campus. These commuter campuses get black students into the statistics that the campus needs for grants and then it's back to the ghetto. Separate but equal has been inversed to equal but separate, plain and simple. That's the ideology, and it keeps the state and federal dollars pouring in.

<u>The Federal Compliance Reaction</u>

Remember: the federal research grant is the white man's government cheese. They go after Federal money the way a bee goes after honey. They will apply for any grant and then lie on the application that things will get better. These "outcomes" may never materialize, but who cares: the government is made up of the same idiots who run these schools. Just like HUD turns away from the abuse of Community Development Block Grant funds by cities like Omaha, Milwaukee and Dallas, so it is with the education money: the Pell grants and student loans. These "incentives" bring kids of color onto campus, duped them into accepting that diversity exists, but then when they don't see any taking place, they become frustrated and drop out.

Furthermore, realizing that the campus numbers are fading, many campuses rush out to find "qualified minorities" who can quickly be used to place on a chart which, in turn, is immediately faxed to the Federal government to protect or retain contracts. This kind of "diversity" is always publicly described as being "an idea whose time has come" without ever really stating what the real reason is. Examples will be provided of several institutions, some of them from the Associated Colleges of the Midwest, which continue to operate in this fashion.

Moreover, the existence and rise of students from other countries – Nigeria, Pakistan, China and so on – are convenient because they are "factored in" as minorities even though they are not. The only thing that makes them a minority is that their skin color places them in a category of "few numbers" on campus overrun with spoiled white kids who are there because if they don't "do something with their lives," mommy and daddy will take away the Porsche.

If the Federal government walked onto any of the campuses of the University of Nebraska or University of Wisconsin systems, a lot of those schools would flunk. I don't mean calling ahead and "arranging a meeting in two weeks" so that they can line up a bunch of brainwashed kids to talk about how "wonderful the diversity experience is." No – surprise visits. There's not enough money to keep giving these schools Federal aid so that they can turn around and hire their cousins, kids and mothers who are unqualified to boil water, let alone work in a higher education setting.

These individuals don't know anything about diversity because the neighborhoods they hail from don't have any and further, they were hired by people who were themselves, ignorant. And the Federal government knows this, but has to be careful lest they come under scrutiny from the rest of the world. You can't point your finger at human rights violators and be guilty of it yourself. So you play games with "programs," "projects" and "activities" that make it look like you give a shit. People of color are quickly learning the truth.

<u>The Oasis Syndrome</u>

Third, the Oasis Syndrome. We call it a "syndrome" because it represents a set of signs and symptoms that occur together. On the one hand is the belief that "integration" can best be captured through imagery: on the covers of course schedules, in yearbooks or in publicity shots. When this is done, it simply points out the disingenuity of the campus and its politics. The approach used to capture such "integration" is evidence of the "oasis syndrome," an attempt to make it appear as if people of all colors sit, talk, study, sleep, eat and interact together on these campuses when, in reality, nothing could be further from the truth.

On the other hand is the hypocrisy of the Oasis Syndrome, since it does not exist in the communities where most of these universities are located. In fact, in the information provided in this paper, we will show that the opposite is the case: in college towns where there are attempts at "designs for diversity," the black community for the most part is extremely segregated from the rest of the community. It is then, an "oasis" for another reason: the campus promotes an ethic which is not reinforced by the community that the campus serves.

While campus presidents are being forced to write speeches, responses and platitudes about race – an issue they know nothing about – the reality was perhaps captured in recent comments by Supreme Justice Antonin Scalia. According to a December 9, 2015 issue of Mother Jones, and as was reported on major networks including PBS, Scalia made the following statement:

There are those who contend that it does not benefit African
Americans to get them into the University of Texas, where they do
not do well, as opposed to having them go to a less-advanced
school, a slower-track school where they do well. One of the briefs
pointed out that most of the black scientists in this country don't
come from schools like the University of Texas. They come from
lesser schools where they do not feel that they're being pushed
ahead in classes that are too fast for them … I'm just not impressed
by the fact the University of Texas may have fewer [blacks].
Maybe it ought to have fewer. I don't think it stands to reason that
it's a good thing for the University of Texas to admit as many
blacks as possible."

Much of what he said was at least *partially* correct. I am going to share some truths with you that are based on first-hand research and analysis and that show that the "Oasis Syndrome" that I have defined is a conflict between utopian reality and the real world.

To begin with, Scalia is right: entry into the University of Texas is not going to benefit Black students. Graduate will. That's what's wrong with the diversity movement: as part of the Oasis Syndrome, it is more committed to skin color walking the campus than it is to people of color walking across the stage with degrees. This is the same treatment these schools give to black athletes: show them some white cheerleaders, get them on campus, have other people do their papers for them, get them on the field and if they graduate – leave it up to the gods.

Secondly, the concept of the "slower track school." Just take a look at Omaha and the public schools: they can't get the job done so a matriculation agreement is signed promising kids that couldn't cut it that if they opt to attend Metropolitan Community College and graduate, then they can come to the University of Nebraska Omaha (as if that's a big step up) and attend the four year school. During slavery there was a "seasoning process:" blacks were first taken to the Caribbean and beaten up and "taught" to submit once they got to the American plantation. How is that different from the yeoman's work that Metro teachers and staff have to do in order to get OPS graduates "in shape" to go to UNO, a campus that has a history of ignoring students of color by giving them short shrift?

Third, black social scientists may come from black schools (that's what Scalia was hinting at) but they are directed to make a contribution to the community – which is something that these lily-white institutions aren't doing. Furthermore, a college education is just that, no matter where you go to school. The only differences are in the research skills you can acquire. I was on scholarship at the University of Nebraska-Lincoln, the University of Iowa and the University of Wisconsin-Milwaukee and trust me, in those classrooms the students are all idiots and the teachers, for the most part, could care less. (Except in the technical fields like Urban Planning and Research Methods).

Fourth, the Oasis Syndrome's "gap in reality" can be seen in another Scalia contention; that, "I don't think it stands to reason that it's a good thing for the University of Texas to admit as many blacks as possible." This is exactly what the University of Nebraska Omaha seems to think as it "assigns" OPS graduates to Metropolitan Community College; this is what the University of Wisconsin thinks when they assign under achievers to Milwaukee Area Technical College. This is what the University of Iowa thinks when they direct high school graduates to Kirkwood Community College or another nearby two-year school.

Why is "diversity" being viewed as an oasis when the very actions of administrators and this nation show that skin color is not valued? Why strain to have a diversity program and a myth of "diversity" on your campus when you sho' ain't got none in the Omaha suburbs, the Milwaukee suburbs, or nearby Coralville, Iowa right near the University of Iowa?

The Qualified Intentions Approach

How can you "design" diversity? The formula is quite simple: a certain percentage of minorities are going to be "allowed" on campus, and that's that. So is this diversity just because you've made your ten percent? There's no quota on black athletes when they're recruiting; hell, most of the teams are predominantly black, and the majority of those gladiators will never see a sheep skin. The ones who don't make the pro ranks will find a token job as some local corporation or head back home to find a job at a 7-11 or a Wal-mart.

This paper provides example upon example of where the "design" for diversity is just that - a "formula" that while, on the one hand, allows for increasing numbers of minority students, faculty and staff on predominantly white campuses, nonetheless contains a CEILING as to "how many" will be "allowed" onto the campus. Therefore predominantly white campuses merely "adjust" so that the control of white males at the top is simply increased to include control of a larger minority student population, control over a more diverse staff and control over a more widely represented faculty corps.

With whites in power, the people of color who are "put in charge" are those individuals whom they (whites) feel most comfortable with and, for the most part, these are individuals who do not represent the best interests of African-Americans, Latinos, Asians or Native Americans on campus. In fact, the opposite may be the result: the "special assistant to the Chancellor for Diversity" or the "Dean for Multiculturalism and Diversity" may not have the trust of staff or students, may not understand what is needed in the nearest low-income (minority) community and may, indeed, have a mindset that more approximates that of the whites in charge than of the persons of color whom all purport to want to "include." Karenga (1967) said it best when he wrote, "White doesn't represent a color; it represents a mentality that is anti - black."

It is for these reasons that I call this particular mind set and strategy the "qualified intentions" approach. The intentions are not sincere or bereft of considerations for quotas, control systems and monitoring. Were it not for the Federal government's fear of black reprisals, few of these campuses would have any black students on them at all. The intentions are "qualified" because they have pre-determined parameters and boundaries. There were no boundaries on the slave system that got our ancestors over here. There are no parameters on the percentages of Blacks and Latinos locked up in penitentiaries around the country. And there sure ain't no boundaries on who gets shot in the back, killed while handcuffed or pulled over because they "looked suspicious."

Qualified intentions.

In sum, true *diversity* cannot be "designed," but most flow. True diversity cannot be implemented by those who do not understand diversity or those who have never seen it in operation. True diversity is not just a matter of numbers, but a matter of quality. As the late, great Albert Camus once wrote, "The evil that is in the world always consists of ignorance, and good intentions may do as much harm as malevolence if they lack understanding."

<u>Inclusion</u>

Another of the buzz words that lend to the "cultural tenderizing" that seems to be a goal of the controlling decision makers is that of "inclusion."

This book addresses two of the "cultural tenderizing" buzz words mentioned in this book – diversity and inclusion. Both will be briefly addressed before moving on. The name of the book is The Inclusion Breakthrough: Unleashing the Real Power of Diversity (San Francisco: Berrett-Koehler Publishers, 240 pages). The book was written by Frederick A. Miller and Judith H. Katz and published in 2002.

This book was selected because after reading the information presented in the text regarding diversity and affirmative action, it was clear that much of what was presented was an ideal-- statements on how things should be as it related to rule, rights, recruitment, promotions and so on. And that is what these buzz words are about: ideals, hopes, dreams and those things which have not yet come into fruition. This book, claiming that there can actually be a breakthrough in creating an inclusive work environment, seems to also believe in a brighter future, but relies on several assumptions that are at best superfluous.

One of those assumptions that I regard as superfluous can be found in the following claim by the authors, where they posit, "Equal employment opportunity, or the employment of individuals in a fair and nonbiased manner, commands the attention of the media, courts, legislators, HR managers, and their firms alike." (p. 96). The assumption is that there is such a thing as "equal employment opportunity" in the first place. Where is the evidence other than posters, written documents and truth claims by those who have jobs promoting this myth.

Since it never existed in the real world other than as a dupe to "culturally tenderize" the words of Snell and Bohlander (2013) appear more valid as they write, "In 2010, a record 99,922 private-sector workplace discrimination charges were filed with the U.S. Equal Employment Opportunity Commission (EEOC), the federal agency that enforces the nation's fair employment laws." p. 96). If charges are being filed then that means that the concept of "equal" is sheer and shallow. Once you get to the workplace, the REAL deal comes down when no one is looking. Compliance was only a reality to get the Federal government to look the other way, or so it appears.

Furthermore Miller and Katz claim,

> A more diverse and multicultural workforce has also made it increasingly important for managers to know and comply with a myriad of EEO laws. When managers ignore or are unaware of fair employment laws, they and their firms run the risk of costly and time-consuming litigation, negative public attention, and potentially lower sales, lower employee morale, and even damage to their own individual careers. Because even unintentional discrimination can be illegal, supervisors need to be aware of their personal biases ... (p 96).

Again, note where "inclusion" ushers in more bullshit mythology. How can there be such a thing as "unintentional discrimination"? In many ways this term is an oxymoron. Books like the one selected, *The Inclusion Breakthrough: Unleashing the Real Power of Diversity*, are easy reads because they imply harsh realities such as the ones just cited, and claim that these harsh realities can be altered or somehow neutralized. The authors (and all of those who accept these mythological concepts) offer a utopian explanation of what "can or might be" in the area of inclusion -*not necessarily a realistic one.*

Using an economic model it seems that discrimination should be stopped because it costs the company money and hurts profits. Although this is true, he real reason it should be topped is because it is wrong and immoral and in many cases, illegal. But despite claims of "diversity," "inclusion," "multicultural workplace," "cultural competency" and "affirmative action," what takes place in the real world?

That which comes most naturally: exclude those who are different and favor fellow members of the white race – qualified or not.

Another point in the book states that, " … capitalizing on diversity requires more than simply hiring a diverse workforce. Radical changes are needed also in both the structure and culture of most organizations—in their policies and practices, the skills and styles of their leaders, and the day-to-day interactions among all their people. Many organizations will fail to make these changes because the changes seem too radical. Those organizations will not survive (p. 13).

Again, more superfluous assumptions. The first one is that diversity actually exists. The only "diversity" these white folks are talking about are diverse groups of their own people: Irish, Italians, Slavs, Jews and so on. The blanket term "diversity" means nothing unless you qualify it with a descriptor; for instance, *racial* diversity or *gender* diversity. And those in power full well know that even as they use the blanket term to feed into their "cultural tenderizing" process.

Writing about diversity now that the nation is becoming increasingly black, brown and female seems to be a good way to get a book published, to get programs approved, to get structures build that talk of "community engagement" and to create jobs that dupe the Federal government into thinking that there is compliance. Printing general truisms that have been covered decades ago doesn't seem to matter. In this book, Miller & Katz (2002) believe in "leveling the playing field (uttered decades ago by Martin Luther King, Jr. Gloria Steinem and others), which they refer to as "Leveling."

They describe thusly: " Leveling involves removing the negatives of barriers, 'isms', and biases in appointment, assignment and promotion, while raising the playing field involves proactive practices to build cross-difference partnership, ensure continuous individual and team development and create systems to enable all people to do their best work (i.e. to allow for individual and cultural differences in approaches)."

Some people, such as myself, believe that the status quo is not equipped to offer a "playing field" that is anywhere near "level' when it comes to inclusion, and that women and minorities are best served developing a playing field of their own rather than seeking a level playing field when the person who owns and controls the field (and the rules of the "game" being played) is the same person who made the field uneven in the first place.

A second idea by these authors calls for an "Inclusion breakthrough cycle," and a third, "creating an inclusion breakthrough," which are four phases: Building the Platform for Change, Creating Momentum, Making Diversity and Inclusion a Way of Life, Leveraging learning and Challenging the New Status Quo. They add that, "Each phase contains specified actions, which are detailed in the four chapters of the part."

This is an oversimplification of a complex social problem.

Before you can humanize the workplace it seems that you would first have to change the attitudes of those who control the workplace. How can you have inclusion where you work when you don't have it in the way you think? Sidney Wilhelm wrote an article called "Equality: America's Racist Ideology" and he made it clear that separate but equal has been changed to "equal but separate." In other words, we may live in similar areas and attend movies and schools together, but when we leave those movies and churches and schools, we drive back to our own separate communities. How then can there be workforce inclusion when there is a segregated reality when it comes to quality of life issues?

Using the concerns that the text offers about the financial costs and burdens of discrimination, it seems that the authors of *The Inclusion Breakthrough* are not concerned about the time and money that goes into various workshops, seminars, and programs aimed at "educating" their supervisors about inclusion, diversity and so on. In fact in the book's final chapter the authors claim that by following their guidelines, the "inclusion breakthrough" can, " make diversity a central and profitable part of an organization's strategy for long-term success rather than merely a peripheral program" pp. 221-222).

This is utter bullshit and a key to the "cultural tenderizing" and "blue skies promises" that I outlined elsewhere in this book.

The ideas put forth in the book, *The Inclusion Breakthrough: Unleashing the Real Power of Diversity* are generalist and based on the history of race and gender relations in American workplace, almost superfluous. People make money and pad their professional resumes writing and publishing books such as these (and creating programs and "special projects" and "events"). *But incorrect perceptions of the problem can only lead to incorrect solutions to it.*

The merit of an idea has to include how major an impact it is going to have, not only on its contemporaries, but on subsequent generations. This cannot be done with piecemeal approaches and these idealistic sounding "phases" and phrases such as those laid out in the Miller & Katz book. If there is a breakthrough, then it deserves to be duly noted; but in my professional opinion there is nothing positive to be gained from telling people that progress in acceptance and tolerance have been made when the statistics prove the very opposite!

Any idea that is going to bring about serious change has to be rooted in reality. Miller & Katz seem to think the opposite. For instance, the following claim made on page 129 where they opine: "Given the choice between other equal products, many people choose the ones made by organizations they perceive to be more aligned with their values, more responsive to their needs as customers, and more willing to treat them with respect as individuals and identity-group members."

Anyone can claim that "many people" do this or opt for that. Where are the numbers? Were these people in majority numbers, there would be serious change and perhaps no need for the "inclusion" concept. People are like buffalo when it comes to the marketplace. Scott H. Young once wrote in regard to "the herd effect" that, "When buffalo were still common in North America, Native American hunters learned a trick to hunt the herd animals. Buffalo don't look up when moving as a group. In fact, if a few buffalo in a herd were startled into running, the entire herd would charge, even if most of the buffalo had no idea what they were running from. The Native American hunters learned that if they encouraged a few buffalo to start running towards a cliff, the entire herd would run off the edge. The buffalo followed the group thinking, and couldn't stop themselves–even when it meant their own deaths" (Young, 2009: p. 1)

This seems to be the mentality of far too many Americans. Even if a product is equal to another, too many people buy based on family history. For instance, just because Uncle Ben's Rice and Aunt Jemima Pancake Mix have black people on the box doesn't mean that all black people will support it. The fact is, black people seem to buy based on what they see majority group members buying. And white folks well know it.

Finally, I don't think that any undertaking that is still in development or still as yet only marginally proven should be considered a "breakthrough" on any level. In this particular instance, to write or talk of an "inclusion breakthrough" is ludicrous. *Inclusion means acceptance; there are increasing numbers of Hispanics and Blacks, and women ate the nation's majority.* And yet because those in power belong to neither of these groups, both groups earn pennies on the dollar when compared with the white male. This is the way it has historically been and any "chances" are determined by the group in power. How is there a breakthrough when the source of the problem remains in a key decision making position in the workplace and in the society that determines what transpires in that workplace?

How can you apply that which is rooted in inaccurate information and homespun assumptions? Even with credentials far too many minorities and women continue to be viewed as "not the type" to hire, promote or recruit. Both the Inclusion book and our text seem to miss the mark when it comes to distinguishing between which is legal and that which decision makers deem "comfortable."

Snell & Bohrlander (2013) posit that, "The Supreme Court's emphasis on the prevention and correction of discrimination means that the employers that do not have an EEO policy are legally vulnerable. Antidiscrimination policy statements must be inclusive; they must cover all applicable laws and EEOC guide- lines and contain practical illustrations of specific inappropriate behavior. For the policy to have value, it must be widely disseminated to managers, supervisors, and all non-managerial employees. A complete policy will include specific sanctions for those found guilty of discriminatory behavior. (p. 125)

And as for the "inclusion" model, look at the data – exclusion seems to be continuing.

An article from the *Huffington Post* is a reminder. Titled, "Workplace discrimination costs businesses $64 billion every year," it is noted that, "Discriminating against your employees can cost you. Workplace discrimination against employees based on race, gender or sexual orientation costs businesses an estimated $64 billion annually, a recent report from the Center for American Progress finds. The businesses incur costs in a variety of ways, including through the turnover of about 2 million employees who leave their jobs due to discrimination. Litigation related to workplace discrimination also costs employers a significant sum. Just this week, FedEx paid $3 million to settle claims that it discriminated against job applicants based on race and gender in 15 states" (Bradley, 2012).

Employers can afford to pay. That's why they have insurance – they anticipate and expect lawsuits. Therefore the ideas offered in the book by Miller & Katz (2002) sound good just like the laws offered by policymakers and even the Supreme Court. But when all is said and done, the "equal opportunity" insights offered in the text are still falling way short when it comes to the inclusion of minorities and women.

Empowerment

This is truly one way that "cultural tenderizing" can be most successful: dupe the powerless into thinking that if they join a group called "the Empowerment Network" that they will, by extension, gain power. So even when they don't, they are led to believe that if they are patient, it will eventually come, In the meantime, the white man gets his "power" by encroaching upon and taking control of the black community that you live in RIGHT NOW.

Empowerment means "to make stronger" in some capacity, it has a hypnotic quality. But black people should have learned over the past 300 years that the white man is not about giving power to a group of people that he both hates and fears.

But that is understandable: mine was a grass-roots movement, a bottoms-up kind of approach. Stripped of the word "self" and employing more of what we urban planners call an "elitist model," today's empowerment movement has been true to form: it is truly "empowering" a number of people. But the question is whom—and for what??

Can there be any doubt that with all this construction going on—new sewers, 75 North, North Star, expansion of Girls, Inc., riverfront development, a so-called Fair Deal Plan and a North Omaha Village — that there is someone making money and planning to make even more? Here's my point: what does any of this have to do with the residents of Omaha's 68111, 68110 or for that matter, 68104?

Councilman Ben Gray – who surely knows something about playing both sides of the fence as it relates to race issues -- told the Omaha World Herald back on or about October 9th his views of North Omaha, the area he represents. He said that the area was "a neighborhood inhabited by people of various income levels, with businesses and offices mixed with the residences … That's the way North Omaha used to be," he said.

Then he cogently and correctly added that, "This is a prime opportunity to re-create that in North Omaha" and that he is confident that the rest of the development will happen because of "the caliber and commitment of people willing to invest and of the people doing the groundwork."

What does this have to do with "empowerment" of black people? Nothing. It has to do with empowerment of the people that Councilman Gray described, and that sho' don't mean the residents of the area that Triple One represents. You had your chance, and sat back and waited for lions and lambs to fall in love and pose for pictures. The "Empowerment Movement" is not about empowering those who don't already have power; it's about providing more power and opportunities to partake in it for those who can appreciate it.

I'm telling you after almost 40 years of organizing in black communities around this country: *our halcyon days are over.*

Most of you came here from the South acting as if you were free when you landed jobs at the packing houses. Jobs were so plentiful that you can get fired from one packing house and walk across the street and find work at another one. You moved your families up here and then, for someone reason, you forgot where you came from. You started thinking that you had it made because you didn't see any lynch ropes or "for whites only" signs. And it went to your head.

From there, you used the resources you scrounged up and started spoiling your kids. Now look at 'em: pants and draws sagging, talking back atcha, skirts as short as blouses and no idea of their history: too weak to do anything but wander. The key to their lack of power is one of the fundamental sources of city, county, state and federal revenue! That would be counter-productive, would it not?

The low-income folks from North Omaha—black, white, Latino and Asian— they are the ones supporting this city. They do it with the social service jobs that other people get, they do it by riding the Metrobus line, they do it with their on-going ordering of premium cable channels while suburbanites stick with basic cable because they're never home, they do it with higher interest rates on that rent-to-own crap and so on.

You can't "empower" people who wouldn't know what to do with power if they had it. The only people of color you see directing and leading the neighborhoods are not people who have power — they are influence peddlers! And that's how and why the neighborhoods have deteriorated and outsiders have bought up the housing and the vacant lots—empowerment means investing and then building so that your kids can have something to live on.

Community Engagement

An article by Leah Betancourt that appeared on a website called Mashable.com (December 16, 2009) titled, "10 Rules for Increasing Community Engagement," provides the basis for elements that I will now re-direct and tailor for the needs and proposed future "vision" and "strategy" of higher education in general and the University of Nebraska at Omaha, in particular.

Before she begins with her "ten points," Betancourt offers this preface:

> Getting people to interact with others and upload content to a community-driven site enough may sound easy, but engagement doesn't happen automatically. It takes time and work, and much of the right formula is deduced through trial and error. Here are 10 tips for increasing user engagement that work for news community web sites, but can apply to all types of online user-engagement communities.

Here is why the University of Nebraska at Omaha is a conglomeration of its own contradictions: as you can see in the information above, in order to have engagement you have to interact with others and be community-driven. These two acts are contrary to the segregation that permeates Omaha. If the community is segregated and the majority still have the mentality of farmers from the 1800s, what other kind of "engagement" can you have other than hailing back to the times when "the nigras knew their place"?

This mentality still persists. The black people that are visible have no semblance of power and are either elected or appointed by whites or ill-informed negroes. Bringing it home to the UNO campus you have black people who have to suppress the knowledge that they have so that they won't insult the racial ignorance of their supervisors. No group of black people could be so backwards as to actually believe that their university – a hick institution in the middle of Omaha, Nebraska – is going to usher in relationships that don't even exist at UC-Berkeley, Harvard, Florida State or other schools with credibility.

Engagement is so shallow in and around Omaha that even white kids want to leave as soon as they graduate. The inducements being offered by employers are not enough; they'd rather brave the wild than to spend another minute in a town that offers nothing more than restaurants, a small spot called the Old Market, and one football team that is fifty miles away. Add that to the fact that Nebraska ranks No. 7 in the nation in the highest property taxes, and you can see why many of these kids are going to be joined by their parents and other relatives who don't see why they should be paying high taxes to live around a bunch of ranchers and septagenarian snake oil salesmen.

Now for the "10 Rules for Community Engagement" as postulated by Leah Betancourt.

1. Make It Easy to Participate

> This sounds like a no-brainer. If it is not clear that people can do things on a site, they won't. Create multiple entry points and ways to access the online community and use actionable language to turn observers into contributors.

Before you can develop a "site" to open up communications you have to first of all (1) have something to communicate and (2) know what to do if someone attempts to communicate with you or poses a question you're not equipped to answer.

In the case of UNO any of these possibilities could well be the case, and it is a situation that students can "sense" more than they can actually "prove." It's like discrimination in a court of law: you have to now prove "intent" which is almost impossible in this day and age of liars, sabotaging of personnel files, and "benign neglect."

> "I've gotten feedback from people who didn't quite know how to participate and if it seems to be a problem for many, we reevaluate how we're displaying the message. Sometimes you need to put out

a call for action: 'Post your own blog,' 'Upload photos,' and the like. Sometimes the registration process is just too cumbersome," said Angela Connor, WRAL's managing editor/user-generated content and author of *18 Rules of Community Engagement: A Guide for Building Relationships and Connecting With Customers Online*, in an e-mail interview.

When these people who are writing about "community engagement" produce these manuals, articles, and other publications, they are not talking about cross-cultural, inter-racial or inter-racial communication. Oh, there may be a blurb or snippet about it, but they don't know. They've been well-trained by people who see the world in a "whites only" framework, despite their admonitions of the opposite. As the old saying goes, "you can't teach what you don't know and you can't lead where you won't go." When white people say "community engagement," their first and oftentimes only focus is their fellow white folks.

Each week CNN's iReport.com posts at least one new topic to its Assignment Desk page for people to respond to by submitting photos, video or audio. iReport.com has more than 412,000 registered users who have signed up and contributed content, according to CNN.

All she's doing is showing that the blind can indeed, lead the blind. Making referrals to people whose "racial vision" is just as myopic as hers only delays real solutions, and solves nothing. The white folks' network is a large one but that doesn't mean it's culturally competent.

"Our hope is that once they're comfortable with the system and they happen to be in breaking news, they'll think of iReport.com as a way to have their footage seen," said Lila King, a senior producer for CNN.com, who leads the site's user-participation efforts.

"Hope." When you see that word you know that the writer doesn't know his or her ass from a hole in the ground. Hope? When you are talking about a topic as important as "community engagement," you need raw facts and tangible, outcome-based action. Anything short of that is pure bombast.

That strategy has paid off. For example, there was an Assignment Desk topic on beating the heat and a man in North Carolina submitted content for the topic and then a few months later a

tropical storm came through his town and he filed an iReport.com
about it that was used on the air at CNN.

This is irrelevant to the topic at hand, mere filler akin to that which permeated the UNO Strategic Plan to make it look more comprehensive in terms of page numbers than it was in terms of content.

> Andy Carvin, senior strategist at **National Public Radio**'s social media desk, said in an e-mail interview he's a firm believer in getting people to rally around an editorial project that has a specific goal with a beginning, middle and end. Those who want to get involved have a clear understanding of what's expected.

And what was just described means that Carvin did more than what UNOs administrators do: he came in with a vision, a process and outcomes already stated. UNOs administration wants to come in with utopian ideals that they can never live up to, grandiose claims about what they claim to have already done, and then they bring people on board who are as culturally incompetent as they are. Now can you see what I've been getting at in all of these "counter-documents" that I issue? Is it now clear – now that a white woman has said it – that I know what the hell I'm writing and talking about?

Another example drives home a similar point as she writes,

> For example, during last year's hurricane season NPR signed up hundreds of volunteers to create tools like Google Maps of evacuation routes, a wiki of state and local emergency resources, and galleries of user-generated content.

Again, this was proactive and reactive at the same time. This is what UNO is going to have to learn how to do. These people act just like farmers: waitin' around fer time ta harvest de crops." No! You have to deal with community engagement on an on-going, proactive basis. You have to stay on top of the issues and know what the community is thinking, planning and what it needs. In the absence of the caliber of "student leadership" that was there when I was leading that campus, grownup administrators are going to have to take the lead. And there's no time like the present.

2. Be a Leader

This is an area that UNO surely needs to work on. They have the titles and may be a little top-heavy with all those "assistants" and "vice-chancellors." But that's their business. My concern is to make sure that each and every one of them knows that North Omaha and South Omaha exist and that the students who hail from these areas no longer receive short shrift from that institution.

> Connor said she feels strongly that every community is different and a manager must adapt accordingly. She described the skill set needed to be a good community leader.

The key word is "adapt," and this is not the one-way street that UNO has traditionally assumed it to be. The institution is so busy working to make students "adapt" to campus, that they don't understand that they need to "adapt" to the needs of the community from whence these students come.

Now comes the skill-set that Betancourt claims that these leaders need to have:

> "I'm talking about razor-sharp interpersonal communication skills, the ability to exhibit an enormous amount of tact, an extremely thick skin and a boatload of compassion for people you would rather not give an ounce. Did I mention grace under pressure, courage under fire, openness to criticism and tolerance beyond belief?" she said.

UNOs administrators appear to be lacking in the qualities that have to deal with the "communication skills" component. Elsewhere in this analysis I dissect an email by one of UNOs administrators and in past documents I've done the same to others. They can't write and they apparently don't engage in much long-range thinking. As for the "tolerance," the "thick skin" and the "openness to criticism," I am going to *personally* see to it that those particular skills are honed. After all, practice makes perfect!

Now read the next section carefully because it indirectly speaks to me and my skill set and what I have to offer to the culturally moribund members of the UNO administration:

> Matt Thompson, interim online community manager for the John S. and James L. Knight Foundation, said in an e-mail interview, the best communities tend to coalesce around leaders. "The best leaders inspire leadership in others. In news site comment threads, people tend to respond to the story, not to each other, leaving behind a long stream of essentially unrelated comments," he said, which is why strong leaders are important for building community engagement. A good leader can step in and encourage users to interact with each other.

The previous paragraph speaks to me because I have proven leadership no matter where I've gone – even my enemies will attest to that. But there are some issues that should be addressed before moving on to the next point.

To begin with, it is easier to become a leader than to be one. This is especially true in Omaha and one need only look at the UNO administration to see this is the case. But in all fairness, one can arrive at the same conclusion when one takes a look at African-American leadership in Omaha as well. Many of those people couldn't make it anywhere else. Most of them lack the intelligence, the credentials and definitely the commitment necessary to do what they do in some other city. Most of them are anointed or appointed and essentially carry water and rubber stamp whatever the white man tells them to.

The best leaders, as it states in the Betancourt passage, "inspire leadership in others." This can be done in one of two ways: either mentor them and show them the way to lead, or tell them to get the hell out of the way because what they are doing in the name of leadership is so screwed up that they are actually impeding the leadership process. I prefer a combination of the two.

Finally, the statement that, "strong leaders are important for building community engagement." So if there is no community engagement, that says something about the caliber and quality of leadership, does it not? And when you have to build a "community engagement center" that is not "engaged" when it comes to North Omaha's grass roots masses (not handpicked negroes who make white people feel safe), then that is also a reflection of the lack, not only of leadership, but also in direction, scope and its very nature.

3. Interact With the Community

My track record at UNO dwarfs that of most of the people who have been here since 1977 (when I arrived as an undergraduate). I have done more to link the state's largest black community with the UNO campus than anyone on this campus, including all the Black Studies professors, Goodrich personnel and Multicultural Affairs officials *combined*. My efforts range from spearheading the "give back the krugerrand donation" movement, the South African divestment movement and charging the Regents with racism, to a petition for a police-civilian review board, creating the multicultural programming slot on the Student Programming Organization, creating awards named after local and campus leadership and sponsoring the first and only "Student Unity Day" on the UNO campus. If you do a search of names in the UNO Gateway since 1977, mine is in there over 260 times – no other minority or non-minority faculty member even comes close.

With that having been made clear, let's now deal with the foundation of most of my efforts: the need for enhanced community interaction and my focus is on North Omaha because that is the context to which I owe my existence ("If you are black, your purpose is to build black"). What you are about to read undoubtedly echoes issues I've raised in writing on campus and in the community for the past four decades.

> Don't ignore participants in the community — they're the ones behind the content. Thompson suggested talking to site commenters, being colloquial, and laying out guidelines for participating.

This is what I've been warning these white people about. They want to use North Omahans as guinea pigs for their research papers, surveys and participant-observer studies, and they don't mind gathering northside demographics to include in their grant proposals that they submit to local and national foundations. But other than that, UNO has always given short shrift to the state's largest black community. When I was a student on campus (1977-1982), I generated more publicity among black people in north Omaha regarding UNO than was done before or since. Just ask the folks who were there. They remember well.

UNO's current crop of "leaders" doesn't seem to remember that the original institution, Omaha University, started off with its campus in North Omaha. From that time on the school would allow black people on campus through open admissions, not because they gave a damn, but because those bodies represented financial aid revenue. The school tried to deny the coming of Black Studies but Senator Ernie Chambers, Dr. Milton White, Dr. Edgar Tidwell and Dr. Melvin Wade countered that racist move. Now the Department is one of the oldest in the nation. Thanks to the fact that they know that the community is watching them. Again, "participants in the community are the ones behind the content."

Moving on:

> "Don't hesitate to delete contributions that shut down rather than encourage discussion; don't listen to anyone who tells you doing so will leave you open to liability. At the same time, contact people one-on-one before you delete their comments or ban them," he said.

You can see that this essay is referring to UNOs actions, actions that have to be shut down. I will go further: those actions should be condemned and then corrected through the introduction and establishment of their opposites. In fact, "being open to liability" would give UNO a positive shot in the arm because at least such a situation would show some semblance of life and energy! Right now the campus just sits there with its ritualistic professors, new buildings going up, a growing influx of foreign students rife for assimilating while north Omaha, less than five miles way, withers away like the last leaves of a painfully prolonged autumn. And UNO, with all its resources, it partially to blame for the latter situation.

> Interacting with the community lets them know someone is listening. Connor blogs and comments on content posted by others in her community. "You can never go wrong when you respond to your users. Answering e-mails in a timely manner is engagement when those e-mails are from community members," she said.

See? UNO needs to do more listening and a little less writing, talking and obsessing on getting grants. They need to listen and slow down on construction, expansion and development plans. That goal that Christensen expressed in his earlier statements of having 20,000 students at UNO by the year 2020 is a pipe dream unless he plans on targeting foreign students. Why do I say that? Because with the matriculation agreement that they've got with the high schools and Metro Community College, Omaha kids are going to get sick and tired of the same old bullshit and are going to vacate this hick town with the quickness. Unless UNO does what is suggested above – let them know someone is listening – they are going to have slim pickings as they compete with the likes of UN-L, the University of Iowa, Grinnell, Coe, Cornell, Union College, and so many others within a three hour commute.

Another echo from one of my early essays or articles can be seen where Betancourt posits, "You can never go wrong when you respond to your users." And in this case by "user" I mean community people, the grass roots masses":

> iReport.com's contact with contributors starts with its vetting process, which means the content has been approved by a CNN producer for use on any of CNN's platforms and is labeled as such. King said the staff also reaches out to regular iReporters who do interesting work.

I don't know what this has to do with "community engagement" other than the fact that it mentions the importance of "vetting." "Vetting" as defined by an on-line encyclopedia hits the nail on the proverbial head. It means, "Vetting is the process of performing a background check on someone before offering them employment, conferring an award, etc. A prospective person or project may be vetted before making a hiring decision. In addition, in intelligence gathering, assets are vetted to determine their usefulness." So what does this have to do with UNO, its "focus group" and its claims of being committed to equity, inclusion and in this particular instance, "community engagement."

The truth of the matter is, the existing background checks that are being run are evidently falling short, because "new blood" is not ushering in any new results. The fact is, as I've outlined in other reports, UNO tends to hire from within. Oh sure, they bring in candidates from other parts of the country, but all that is window dressing to comply with whatever requirements they have to meet. When the dust clears it's the same old people – that's how current UNO Chancellor John Christensen got the job.

The idea of what I call "cultural vetting" might be good. But on the other hand I've met some of the "minority hires" in several of these departments and they are just as loony and weird as the white ones. They may have credentials, but there is nothing in the vetting process that gauges or evaluates "commitment:" commitment to black students, commitment to the black community, commitment to defense and development of the black intelligentsia. Just white boys and girls in blackface for the most part.

Point number 3 concludes with the statement, "The whole thing works because of the relationships we've been able to form," she said. "I don't think it would work if we stopped communicating." And this is a key: but communication among the ignorant and out-of-touch is stagnating and leads to repetition of the played out. Once someone is brought on board that person has to be willing and allowed to implement new approaches and ideas. The people who brought him on board have to learn from what they see so that they, in turn, can implement something new if they are given or are forced into such an opportunity.

4. Welcome Newbies

While the topic seems to be about "online" concerns, what is written can be developed for "community engagement" across the board. For example, where it says,

> As an online community grows and becomes more established, newbies might feel like intruders. That's where a community manager comes in. Thompson said a good community manager will constantly be seeking opportunities to diversify the community in a productive, organic fashion.

Let us make the UNO campus the "community" for the sake of the focal point of this paper.

So as it grows and becomes more established (stable), people who are new are made to feel like intruders. This is the perfect description. For decades black students were made to feel this way. My predecessors on this campus had to fight for what little they got in the way of programs and clubs because white people felt that what they had was good enough for everyone. Luckily for white people that I didn't arrive here until 1977 because the black students who were here did not study; they were not scholars on my level. They were just kids on a campus looking for a good time. Even the over-rated "Omaha 54" sit in on former Chancellor Kirk Naylor's office was mostly about the inability to have black ticket takers at a party. There were other issues, but this is mentioned to show you the low level of consciousness that these kids had at the time.

They were nevertheless intruders, hence their concerns about the lack of black ticket takers, not being allowed to have parties on campus, the lack of black cheerleaders and so on. They fought for what exists now. Were it not for Sen. Ernie Chambers and some out of state black men, there would probably not even be a Black Studies Department. These "intruders" had to force those Chancellors and their minions to do the right thing. And since what they demanded was taking place all over the nation, UNO submitted and did the right thing. But it was not because of white beneficence; it was because of the pressure applied by these "intruders."

Now let us consider the "community manager" as the Chancellor or the Vice-Chancellor for Student Affairs. Now we look at the statement that was made earlier by Betancourt where she cogently contends that, "a good community manager will constantly be seeking opportunities to diversify the community in a productive, organic fashion." There is a Dr. Shipp who is on campus who came from elsewhere and is responsible for bringing qualified people of color on board. Were it not for him, would this have been done? Who would have done it? Why hadn't it been done before he made his moves?

There must be more Shipps of this ilk in the educational ocean that is UNO. Without that, UNO will be drifting afloat in a sea of racism, discrimination and misogyny.

> "The danger is creating a community that feels insular, groupthinky, and hostile to outsiders. I've heard horror stories about online mom communities that slowly warped into being totalitarian enforcement regimes for particular ideas about maternity," he said.

The "online mom communities" that Betancourt babbles about are trumped in the real world by these "real world paternalistic communities" that permeate higher education. And since the inception of this institution, UNO has acted in a totalitarian manner toward minority students. There is not a single member of the administration that could win a debate with me if the subject was race relations or inclusion. That is because they simply don't know or care about what needs to be done. They will make "mad grabs" at pseudo-solutions to the point of publicity or promotions and make the claim that they did their best, but that's the best that they can do.

The article makes the point that, "Connor said it can be hard to get newcomers to engage the way the older members do, so she specifically reaches out to newbies." Reaching out to these newbies (in this case I'm speaking about incoming minority students) is a good idea. But you got to have something to reach out them with! What are you going to do: give them a Hostess Twinkie or a pat on the head? The latter action will lead you to getting your ass kicked, let me tell you that right now! At any rate, they are "newbies" because they are different, because they have been long denied, and because the white man is fearful of them. Out of that fear (veiled envy) comes the late arrival of these "newbies." The administration should keep this in mind.

> "Once that culture develops it isn't easy for others to go against it, even in a good way. I am working hard to be supportive of newcomers. I even have a group called the Welcome Wagon that reaches out to newbies. They've even created tutorial for newcomers that I had nothing to do with, and they are awesome," said Connor.

This is an idea that I will now elaborate on. The concept of "Pathways to Harmony" is defunct because it was a crappy idea from the get-go. But how about sifting through your old files and dusting off my proposal (1980) for a Third World Cultural Center? I had more than 15 letters of support, including letters from Dr. Thomas Gouttierre, Dr. Peter Suzuki, then Goodrich teacher Helen Hiatt, Senator Ernie Chambers, then NAACP president Buddy Hogan and many others. And it was still rejected. Do you know why?

Because my commitment to these "newbies" is on-going and perpetual, that's why. The "welcome wagon" concept is just that: something on wheels that stops, doles out some crumbs and then hastily beats a path to the next welfare recipient. Even lily-white Cornell College in Mount Vernon, Iowa, where I served as its first Minority Student Advisor, has the foresight to have a house for the "Black American Cultural Organization" (BACO).

Instead of tearing down all those homes to the west and expanding and building to the South, how about taking a couple of those rooms in Arts and

Sciences Hall, knocking out a few walls, and creating something more than that "human aquarium" that these racists refer to as "American Minority Students" and "Multicultural Affairs"?

5. Identify and Nurture Power Users

How else do you fine-tune "community engagement" and of what benefit is it to a school like UNO that has an entire building that claims to be committed to such engagement, but does little for the state's largest ghetto, which lies less than five miles from the campus? Let's look at this component and allow me to continue "schooling" you so that you will no longer be able to feign ignorance in the future.

This section begins:

> Don't forget about frequent content contributors in the community.
> They can offer great insight and feedback from a point of view
> potentially better than the site's own manager.

Every community has those "frequent content contributors." In this case, many of them are on the rolodex of UNOs administration. The only problem is that they work for some white man who UNO can pick up the phone and contact. And that's how they keep control of their "negroes." They find out their weaknesses and use it against them. They can't do that to me. If anything, I'll flip the script and do it to them. And they know it. Ask BJ Reed if you don't believe it. Ask Del Weber. Ask Richard Hoover, who went to Hastings College and got busted for plagiarism. And the list goes on and on.

My version of "frequent content contributors" means the sources that UNO can rely on to tell them the facts. People who aren't tied to the political system or some bullshit religious group. It means grass roots people, preferably retired elders, who know what's going on and aren't afraid to let them know about it. I can provide a full list upon your request.

> "One of my constant findings is that you have to identify, befriend
> and nurture your super users. Especially when you're small and
> starting out, interact with your users to a degree one step shy of
> creepy," Thompson said. "The culture you create amongst your
> most hardcore users early on will be the biggest influence on your
> site's culture when it's, God willing, flooded with loving users."

In the context in which I am operating and focusing this critique, the "super users" are those administrators who deal directly and most regularly with students of color. This includes the director of the student center, the director and staff of Multicultural Affairs, the Vice Chancellor for Academic and Student Services, some representatives and advisors of student clubs and someone from International Studies. This committee – let's call it the "Optimum Interaction Committee," would address important student issues from a number of perspectives, from problems to prospects, to teaching them how to study, write grants, and prepare for conferences around the nation. It would include writing them letters of support and assisting with locating part-time jobs.

So when Betancourt writes that, "The culture you create amongst your most hardcore users early on will be the biggest influence on your site's culture when it's, God willing, flooded with loving users." The campus "culture" that I am most focused on is that for students of color. UNOs ranks are abysmally low and that is by design. The combination of the OPS failure to educate graduating black seniors and the greed-based matriculation agreement that was made between Metropolitan Community College and UNO combined to reduce the ranks of black students on the UNO campus.

Add to that the mind numbing lack of social outlets of kids of color, and it only stands to reason that black ranks would be low. But as one cultural nationalist taught long ago, "culture is the basis of all ideas, actions and images. To move is to move culturally, i.e., by a set of values given to you by your culture." Since this is the case at the macrolevel (societal), then it can also be applied to the campus milieu. A Third World Cultural Center on campus would be more productive than the half-assed programs and outlets being offered at the present time.

> Getting to know the community doesn't have to be exclusively online. The Public Broadcasting Service held a national unconference called PublicMediaCamp that bought together more than 250 people who represent the general public, developer community and public broadcasting, according to Carvin.

Bringing together people like this has always been a part of the problem in Omaha. For one thing, Omaha's leadership is controlled; there are few independent thinkers among them. Most of them are more committed to making the ride home to suburbia or wherever they live than they are to improving and upgrading life for everyone. The segregationist mentality has two components: the mindset of oppressors (the city and county government, higher education, state government) and that of the victims (kowtowing blacks and Latinos, corporate minorities afraid to "say the wrong thing" and the outright ignorant who are just window dressing on the set, e.g., male and female concubines of some power broker). And when it comes to the latter example, don't you think for one minute that I don't have evidence, names and dates.

Getting to know the community would be easy if UNO had the inclination to do so. They've got the space, the resources and the justification. They don't mind until you start considering the fact that inviting the community in would be out of their control and too many niggas might show up. So they have what I call "controlled recruitment," "selective solicitation" and "anglicized invitations." That is why that which is lily-white remains that way, and even if a few people of color get in, they are basically Uncle Toms, tio tacos (uncle toms for Latinos), bamboo (yellow on the outside, hollow on the inside), or apples (red on the outside, white on the inside).

If serious communication is accomplished, the following can take place, even at a lily-white bastion like UNO:

> "By getting together with them as equals and co-conspirators, it helps bring more volunteers into the fold, because we give them a vested interest in our success. Remember, 'Public' is National Public Radio's middle name. The community is perhaps our biggest asset, so we're creating new platforms and strategies to strengthen that relationship, and hopefully strengthen our journalism in the process," he said.

This is the kind of approach that UNO would use if it was serious about all this "equity" and "inclusion" that it is incessantly talking about but rarely acting upon. Check out the following statement from the previous excerpt: "The community is perhaps our biggest asset, so we're creating new platforms and strategies to strengthen that relationship, and hopefully strengthen our journalism in the process …" There is no "perhaps" to it when it comes to UNO and the community, and I speak of the black community.

How soon these white people forget in terms of how black students and other students of color have bailed them out over the years with their unquestioned payment of tuition for the lily-white and limited education they get. Paying for courses and then facing teachers who are racist and who I have personally had to correct and deal with from time to time. Teachers who will deflate their grades knowing that these students, so "whipped" by the maltreatment of the Omaha Public Schools, will not protest or contest a "C" when they know they should have gotten a "B" or a "D" when they should have gotten a "C". UNO is notorious for such actions and I can prove it.

The creation of "new platforms and strategies to strengthen" UNOs relationship with people of color in the immediate community (north and south

Omaha) should be a priority. And if it was such a priority, the need for these "equity" programs and committees or the projects revolving around "inclusion" would be already in progress.

6. Showcase and Cross Promote UGC

"User generated content" in this context (my report) will refer to student-generated content because they are the "users" of the resources provided by UNO. And they are – or should be – the focus and fulcrum of both campus- and community content on all levels. I will explain later in this analysis of this section of this report.

Betancourt asserts the following:

> Curating and then showcasing community content energizes and motivates users and can help get new content contributors. User-generated content can also add depth to stories reported by news organizations.

For this Report, the preceding can be interpreted as showing that students on campus who are treated fairly and feel as if they are a part of the process will pass this information on and in turn, "can help get new content contributors." As for the news organizations, I have written extensively on the racism and selective reporting that permeates the Omaha media. I am the former editor of a major black newspaper (The Milwaukee Courier) and I excelled in journalism classes at the university, as old school instructors like Warren Francke, Robert Reilly, Todd Simon, Hugh Cowdin and others can and will attest to. In other words, I write what I know. Can UNOs administrators make the same claim? Or do they just idealize, plagiarize and then pawn off conjecture as racial facts?

Continuing:

> Connor said she's been successful with featuring a member each month with GOLO (short for Go Local) Profiles. "I ask probing, introspective questions that allow members to see another side of the person and people love it." She also compiles and posts lots of lists such as top 10 blog posts, top 20 commenters and most visited profile pages.

This is what real "inclusion" is about. When you "engage" the community you automatically include that community. The problem with Omaha in general and UNO in particular is that they have a particular definition of what constitutes "the community." When they say "community," when they talk about "our community" on those grandiose television commercials that promote the city, they are talking about white people. UNO has not found away to combat the national belief that Omaha "has no blacks in it." And yet this is a common belief that most black people in Omaha hear wherever they go.

Here's some evidence. I am fortunate enough to have stayed in some of the most expensive hotels in this city. From Embassy Suites, the Hilton, AmericInn, and the Sheraton, to a host of others. When I stay there I look at the reading materials and what do I find? Publications like Omaha magazine and several tourism related "guides." Black people are invisible in these publications. Under "places to go" or "things to see" there is nothing about North Omaha. KMTV-Channel 3 regularly thanks various parts of the city for its viewing – "thanks South Omaha," "thanks West Omaha" and so on. Never do they mention North Omaha. And their division of the city for weather information skips over North Omaha locations but mentions Hanscom Park and Eppley.

These are visible messages and that is why I dog the media every chance I get. After I distributed my analysis of UNOs so-called "strategic plan" (of 18 pages), some 60-plus pages of insights, ten days later the Omaha World Herald – which got a copy – published a fluff piece on all the good work UNO was doing in recruiting minorities. The statistics were faked and so were the comments. I called the World-Herald to confront the writer, Henry Cordes and, as is the tendency, he didn't have the guts to return my phone call. I wonder why?

My point is this: UNOs people of color cannot expect the Omaha media to assist in bridging the gap between the campus and the black community. Such a link simply does not jibe with the traditions and history of a conservative and backward city such as this.

The final clause of this section of the "10 ideas" is irrelevant to UNO and Omaha but I include it for the sake of the readers:

> iReport's King said their site gives CNN a new way to tell anniversary stories. For example, an iReporter submitted a photo of her grandmother walking down the street with Calvin Coolidge for an Assignment Desk topic on Presidents Day.

'Nuff said.

7. Reward Contributors

It is the tendency and tradition of UNO to present awards to those who are the top-ranked water-carriers or flunkies for the administration. Those receiving these awards know well that they are not deserving. They take turns presenting plaques, certificates, trophies and the like to one another, padding each other's resumes based on barely recognizable contributions or ideas.

For the sake of this report, "contributors" would be those who donated the most to assisting UNO in actualizing or realizing its claimed vision of "inclusion" or "equity." Those who promoted on a basis that was devoid of selectivity and discrimination when it came to 'community engagement' would be 'contributors' to UNOs journey toward practicing equity and inclusion. With that having been said, we refer now back to the words of Betancourt:

> iReport labels its top members "superstars." The designation is
> determined by an algorithm that tallies members' contributions,
> ratings, popularity and site activity, and scores in the top 20
> percent every week make Superstar status, according to
> iReport.com.

I don't like rating systems because in almost every instance, it is the white man's standards and norms that serve as the basis of any "point system." Frantz Fanon once wrote that, "A racist in a culture of racism is therefore normal." What goes in is what comes out. Even when these white people talk about wanting to recruit more minority students, they go through the motions knowing full well that there is a ceiling that they will stop at; there is a formula based on percentages. They want the numbers of black men and women to be nearly equal, and they don't want the percentages of black students on the campus to exceed ten percent. They feel most comfortable when that percentage hovers around five percent as it does now.

I cite this to support my belief that people who have a tradition and history of this type of perfidious behavior are in no position to have a ranking system that involves students of color on any level. Their long titles protect them from being seen for what they really are, but I have defeated and embarrassed enough of them to know what they really are. I have out-debated their best minds at the doctoral level, the master's level and surely all over the community. I have gone on radio shows and humiliated the host if they got out of line (e.g., Steve Brown, Tom Becka, Milwaukee's Mark Belling, and many more). If there is to be a "superstar status" accorded to someone, it should be to me. It's been done in cities far larger than Omaha, but these racists have been so embarrassed by me they simply refuse to accept the fact that I am their intellectual superior.

Even when I produce documents like this one.

At any rate, Betancourt's essay continues:

> Thompson described a reputation management system called karma that is used at Vita.mn, a site he managed, which rewards people with points for contributing particularly engaging content."We gave a prize monthly to the users who accumulated the most karma over the previous month, and that worked like a charm. Eventually, the super users stopped aiming for prizes, but settled into a regular, engaging rhythm," he said.

A system like "karma" should be immediately implemented at UNO. But in order to acknowledge those who believe in and fight for true "inclusion" and "equity," those who have traditionally been on the other side, those who want to talk the talk but never dare to walk the walk would be exposing themselves and admitting that indeed, they have been and continue to be a part of the problem.

8. Be Timely About Posting UGC

Again we have the reference to UGC – "User generated content." But the point here will deal with the issue of "postings" and the like. More specifically, what is being posted around the campus that would make students of color feel as if UNO was an advocate of or believer in "equity," "inclusion" or "community engagement.

Postings can make a difference, which is why those hanging around UNO promote those things that UNO does not really believe in. The fraternities and sororities hang up their bullshit and no one says anything, although knowing full well that these groups are racist, exclusive and filled with freakishness and frolic.

> Time lags on user-submitted content getting posted to the site interrupts the conversation. Connor warned that moderated comments that do not post in real-time are a killer. Why would a user, who is interested in starting a conversation, submit a comment knowing it may or may not post within 24 hours, she asks.

Metaphorically, UNO is also "late" and "behind in the times." What UNO is concerned about now has been addressed on campuses all over the nation. Even their recruitment of minority staff lags behind its own professed goals. This has been the tendency for decades, with black people coming in, leaving for greener pastures, and then being replaced by whites or some black person who is even more reactionary than the sellout that they replaced.

The final statement of Betancourt's section truly represents UNOs fate and future when it comes to recruiting and retaining American students of color:

"If I continue to come to your house, and you're not there or if I'm dying of thirst and you know it but refuse to offer me a glass of water, I'm not coming back," she said.

And that's what UNO is up against and well they know it. That's where the influx of foreign students come in, cash in hand and dorms waiting. And the crooked admissions people count them as "minorities" when, in reality, they are not. But for Federal purposes and to keep that tuition money coming, UNO has turned in lies for decades.

9. Allow Profile Creation

As it relates to what she calls "community building," Betancourt writes,

> Fleshing out a community site with user profiles, preferences and even UGC stats for each member helps contributors to get to know each other and fosters community building.

The administration doesn't even "know" one another. The black ones might get smiled at or talked to, but they are not a part of the "clique" that those white boys belong to. These men are the hillbilly version of "The Skulls," and their decisions show that this is the case. The fact is there is already a "profile" that exists: it is the profile of "the perfect black administrator." And each one of them fits this "type." They are quiet, they smile a lot and they have a bunch of keys that don't fit anything. They have these grandiose titles and oftentimes have to do double-duty in addition to their "administrative roles." They are not the first because UNO has a long tradition of such exploitation and abuse.

Much of what remains is irrelevant but I share the final part of this 9th point because it does hit home:

> iReport **profile pages** list details such as bio information, stats for comments posted, iReports posted, page views, iReports on CNN, how many iReporters the user is following and how many are following that person. "Good online communities tend to allow users to have profiles, where records of their contributions are stored. A profile is the foundation of reputation management," Thompson said.

Remember what I said earlier about the "(negro) profile"? Betancourt is correct when she adds, "A profile is the foundation of reputation management." Let's take it to the macrolevel for a moment.

What is UNOs reputation? Does it have one? If it does, it cannot be positive because they play second fiddle to another mediocre institution, its sister campus in Lincoln. So if UNO would only upgrade its profile, it would be able to better management its reputation. And how can it improve or enhance its profile?

The question has to be asked, "Does UNO relish its position as a mediocre institution"? How else to explain the on-going placement of sports over academics, the on-going leeching for grants and subsequent bricks-and-mortar projects over basic essential issues? And then, in spite of all this, have the unmitigated gall to whisper about "inclusion," "equity" and "community engagement." What will these hillbillies come up with next?

10. Engage With Popular Existing Communities

As stated, before present-day University of Nebraska Omaha was where it is now, it started off in north Omaha as Omaha University. Like the Nebraska Furniture Mart (now the largest in the world) and Canfield's Sporting Goods, these white people start off in the low-income area, gain stature mainly due to black customers and revenue, and then they get big and move out west. The fact is, UNO has always relied on black input but did so under the veil of "doing the negroes a favor" so that unsuspecting blacks wouldn't realize that indeed, UNO needed them as badly as they needed a college education.

Forgetting about the social media crap outlined by Betancourt, the key in this section deals with both "community engagement" and strategies to achieve it. For instance, she writes,

> Starting a new online community might seem like reinventing the wheel compared to behemoths such as Facebook. Hooking a community site up to these social media sites gives users the best of both worlds.

In this case we are not talking about starting a new online community. We are talking about a major modification of a campus culture, the creation of what I would call "a community of concern and consciousness." If this were to be done, then all that talk about "community engagement" would be a logical extension and a key part of the UNO vision for the future. With m y approaches and ideas instituted, Chancellor John Christensen's "dream" of having 20,000 students by the year 2020 would be achievable and more importantly, that increase would also be parallel to an increase in support from the minority communities (north and south Omaha) in the surrounding area.

In terms of engaging people in their own comfort zones (communities), this is another area where UNOs racism and fear of black people has historically come to the fore. First, the following statement by Betancourt:

> Carvin said NPR believes strongly that it's important to engage people in their own online communities rather than assume they will engage with theirs. He said that means having a strong presence on communities such as Twitter and Facebook. He pointed out that NPR was one of the first news organizations to partner with YouTube as part of its YouTube Direct service, which allows them to embed YouTube upload widget onto the NPR site and create curated content galleries. They recently launched their first experiment with it called the WonderScope.

The talk of "online communities" is not a major issue for my report; it is location, location, location! These white scholars, academicians and administrators are going to have to venture forth and go into North Omaha and open up their minds to the community. For instance, if you are going to major in urban studies, social work, criminal justice, black studies, sociology or education, then there should be classes taught in an area that is predominantly minority. The Chicano Awareness Center (or whatever they're calling it now) would be an excellent location. As for North Omaha, there are a number of sites, including the Charles Washington Library and several community centers where classes could be offered.

White students who want to major in "the caring professions" and other areas where they will be interacting with people of color are going to have to move beyond the sterile atmosphere of UNO and their suburban locations. They are going to have to, as the old saying taught, "get your ass in the water and swim like me"!

The "10 ideas" offered by Betancourt and analyzed by me are only a beginning. But it's far more than the administration, as a collective, have dared to put in writing in terms of self-analysis. The article by Betancourt concludes as follows:

> "It never surprises me that an NPR story that got 25 comments on our site gets 250 comments on Facebook, or gets retweeted 100 times on Twitter. It's the nature of those communities to contribute and share," according to Carvin. "That's why tools like Facebook Connect, Open Social, etc., are so interesting — they lower the

<blockquote>
barrier of participation for people in more active communities, making it easier for them to participate in sites that may not have as much of a history with social media."
</blockquote>

And even in an article where there is no apparent connection some truth can nevertheless be found. Note where the preceding excerpt offers that by lowering the barrier of participation, it is easier for them to participate …" And that has been one of the problems that impedes a more positive and productive link between UNO and the north Omaha community. First someone came up with the bright idea to "land lock" the campus. Secondly, those in power believe that "making the campus more student friendly" is a matter of bricks-and-mortar, video games and brightly painted walls. That is not the case.

You need to take your asses out to the communities that those prospective and actual students live in and interact with their neighborhoods and their parents. You need to be seen in those communities even before they graduate from high school. In the words of the ghetto, you need to act like you give a shit! I believe that all of that expansion and construction is aimed at two groups of students: suburban white kids and incoming foreign students. There is very little that is cultural that would make a Latino or black student feel as if his or her background really matters.

DETRIMENTAL RELIANCE: THE FARMLAND CRISIS

Everybody's gotta eat. We're human beings. Some people eat better than others because they have more money, and still others have access to better shopping outlets and as a result, a higher class of foodstuffs. Much of this latter statement has to do with race and geographic location of certain stores, and chain stores are no exception. As black people our reliance on aliens of our race to provide safe food stuffs for us and our family is perhaps one of the most extreme examples of "detrimental reliance."

But the farm is dying as is the state. And black people, reliant upon both for food and protection, will once again be let down.

According to an episode of "Elementary," diabetes kills four million people every year. When I heard that number I researched it – and guess what? A 2012 article from United Nations radio said that in 2012, the United Nations health agency estimated that 3.4 million people died every year from diabetes, and that almost 80 percent of the deaths occur in developing countries (United Nations radio, 2012). And according to the American Diabetes Association, 1.4 million Americans are diagnosed with diabetes every year.

You may ask, what does diabetes have to do with the farmland crisis. I blame farmers DIRECTLY for the rise and proliferation of diabetes because of what they have been placing in their crops and their livestock, that's what it has to do with it! In order to make more profit, these hicks are injecting their animals and their crops with all kinds of steroid-type ingredients and are genetically engineering bigger and larger crops and animals. What goes in is what comes out. And once we digest it, the human body cannot adjust – the result is diabetes and related diseases.

Nebraska is a rural state, which means that the concept of "agribusiness" and the commitment to farming are vital to the state's survival. In February of 2016 it was learned that the farm economy's values were plummeting. According to the article,

> FOURTH QUARTER 2015
> Farmland values in the Tenth District softened in the fourth quarter of 2015 as farm income continued to weaken. Looking ahead, bankers generally indicated they expect further moderation of both farmland values and cash rents alongside relatively low prices for agricultural commodities and low farm income. Reductions in farm income continued to affect credit conditions, and bankers expected loan repayment rates to deteriorate further in the coming months. (Kauffman & Clark, 2016).

When bankers talk about anticipating "further moderation" of anything, that's going to affect the way they loan money in the future. With no loans, the farmers are screwed. In the past they've been able to borrow money and repay it using the interest that was generated after they deposited the loan in an interest generating account. With that scam over, what are they going to do? They can't "rely on their wits" because the track record makes it clear that Nebraska farmers are also lacking in *that* area. What to do, what to do?

When credit conditions are affected, the state's overall economy is also impacted. Once again, the state is falling short, continuing to make the same kinds of projection-related, hiring and management errors, and they pay the price each and every time. I believe that Nebraska's best days are behind it. But the only way to break the news to a low-intelligence public is to piecemeal out the bad news, to break it up so that the situation won't sound as catastrophic as it really is. For instance, note the following:

> Farmland values in the Tenth District dipped again in the fourth quarter. According to respondents of the Tenth District Survey of Agricultural Credit Conditions, values of nonirrigated and irrigated

> cropland decreased 4 percent and 2 percent, respectively, from a
> year ago … With the fourth quarter declines, irrigated cropland
> values have fallen modestly in four consecutive quarters, and the
> value of nonirrigated cropland generally followed the same trend
> through 2015. (Kauffman & Clark, 2016).

What is being posed as an issue in the "Tenth District" or "the fourth quarter" is a piecemeal way of hiding the fact that Nebraska, as a state, is in trouble. The key word above is "trend" and you know what the old maxim teaches us: once is a fluke, twice is a coincidence and three times is a trend (or a pattern)." Nebraska's on-going woes signal a trend, and the source of that trend is easy to pinpoint once you take note of certain decision making policies, hiring policies and the on-going greed and malfeasance of political officials. The "invasion of the booty snatchers" is a survival tactic that brings in money for the state. And they will pimp whomever or whatever they have to in order to keep the farmland state solvent.

Continuing:

> Growth in the value of ranchland also stalled in the fourth quarter
> alongside sharp declines in cattle prices that persisted to the end of
> the year. From January 2015 through December, feeder cattle
> prices plunged more than 25 percent, causing profit margins in the
> cattle sector to deteriorate significantly. Alongside these price
> declines, year-over-year growth in the value of ranchland dropped
> from an average of 8 percent in the first three quarters of 2015 to
> zero in the fourth quarter. (Kauffman & Clark, 2016).

When the "growth in the value of ranchland stalls," then this only proves the point I made earlier. Texas is now the beef capital – not Nebraska. So the farmers are in trouble which leads us to the issue of genetically engineered food. The bigger the cattle and the larger the stalks of corn and the more soybeans, the more you can make up for any perceived or actual losses. But when you spray that food, feed those cattle and genetically alter those foodstuffs, you are poisoning the people who consume it. When you ask why America is getting so fat, just look at what the farmers are providing in the form of food, meat, vegetables and so on.

They are killing not only Americans because their genetically engineered food leads to diabetes, high blood pressure, cancer and other diseases, but they're shipping these foods out to the rest of the world – just like they did with cigarettes. Once banned in America, these white men immediately found markets in the Phillipines, China and other Asian nations. The international version of "the invasion of the booty snatchers."

Look at how other states are doing:

> In contrast to most other District states, farmland values in
> Oklahoma continued to rise modestly. Oklahoma was also the only
> state where bankers reported increases in average cropland values
> when compared with the previous year. Ranchland values also
> continued to rise modestly in Oklahoma, in addition to the
> Mountain States (Table). Changes in farmland values in most other
> states, however, generally were consistent with average changes
> for the Tenth District as a whole. (Kauffman & Clark, 2016).

Oklahoma's farmland values continue to rise, albeit modestly. Why? Proper fiscal management at the state level. Even when it comes to "most other states," according to the article, the farmland values were consistent. But not Nebraska. So then what can you say? What can they do to get the values back on par and at the same time, bolster a dying economy? It's time for "invasion of the booty snatchers" and they have been doing it for decades but their management and leadership teams are so inept, so morally bankrupt, that they can't seem to get their acts together. So instead they cover up failure with glossy pictures of rewewed tourism, the construction of new soccer and football fields, and other fluff pieces that the media just loves to air and place in print.

Is it going to get any better? You be the judge:

> Survey respondents expected farmland values to fall further in the
> coming months. In fact, bankers expected the value of each land
> type – non-irrigated cropland, irrigated cropland and ranchland – to
> decline again in the first quarter of 2016 (Chart 2). However,
> between the three land types, more bankers expected further losses
> in the value of non-irrigated cropland. Moreover, bankers expected
> slightly larger adjustments in non-irrigated cropland values in the
> coming year than what was expected at the same time a year ago
> (Chart 3). (Kauffman & Clark, 2016).

When bankers start worrying that is when the farmland economy is really in trouble. Those farmers are constantly leeching for loans, using their land as collateral, and then depositing the loan in interest-generating accounts and using the interest off the borrowed money to repay the banks. It's a game that's been going on for a long, long time. Also known as "dryland farming," there are certain crops that use the winter water stored in the soil and don't depend on rainfall during the growing season. These include grapes, tomatoes, pumpkins, beans and other summer crops. Corn is not one of them.

And then there is the issue of land leasing and rents, another revenue steam for the farmers. Farm rents, quite simply, take place when a farm is rented for a fixed amount per acre for all acres in the farm (e.g. 160 acres in a quarter section) regardless of the number or acres of cropland, pasture, buildings, or waste. This is referred to as a whole-farm rental rate. Or, the farm may be rented for a fixed amount per cropland acre (i.e., 145 acres cropland in a 160-acre farm) with a different rental rate for any pasture or buildings (Edwards, 2016). Once again, the same white people that pointed fingers at black people getting welfare subsidies knew all the time that the "food stamps" were basically welfare for farmers. After all, who grew the food that was in the supermarkets that black people and others were purchasing?

But even deeper than that, look at how these farmers leech for loans and then "rent out" their farmland – land stolen by their ancestors from various Native American tribes. And it's easy money. Edwards (2016) explains,

> Cash rent lease agreements are popular because the lease is simple, the rent is fixed, and the owner is relieved of making operating and marketing decisions. Likewise, the tenant has maximum freedom to plan and develop the cropping and livestock programs. The risk and returns from changing prices, yields, and costs are all borne by the tenants.

What "risk"? They either make the money or lose it but they still retain the land. And land, no matter where it is located or how white boys manipulate the market, never loses value. The farmers who rent the land do so banking on there being a profitable crop. Just like they did the black sharecroppers just after slavery when everything rested on "trusting" and having faith in the white landowner. Now they know how it feels. Put into a more contemporary context,

> This squeeze is starting to attract more attention, even outside of agriculture. Recent reports hint at farmers "walking away" from land leases due to the inability to pay high cash rent rates with corn, and soybean profitability falling into the red. If that happens, it could dramatically change the land market in areas where highly productive land fetches up to $400 an acre cash rent. (Caldwell, 2015)

This is just what the black sharecroppers had to do back in the day – pack up with their families and "walk away." They would then head up north hoping for a better way: no land, highly visible because of their black skin, and without a clue about what to do about "finding work." The white farmer is white in a nation that is predominantly white and therefore benefits from some semblance of "white privilege." He can still "muster" up enough capital to survive, sell his land or use his "contacts" to lobby the legislature. He can continue to plant his poisonous crops, spray them with toxic insecticides and if those crops don't pass government muster or inspection, peddle the food overseas to some developing nation – even as he is know doing is tobacco crops.

Caldwell (2015 adds that, "Supply and demand will decide rental rates as they have before. It may reduce rental rates, or it may change the players. But it will be a competitive market as before," adds Farm Business Talk senior contributor ... "What made rental rates high was people willing to pay it, and that will be as always." (Caldwell, 2015).

The key words are "people willing to pay." In a capitalist system, that is the way it will always be. Greed begats more greed, which is why Ponzi schemes are so successful. These farmers get by on their image of being "people of the soil" and "down to earth folk," but they've been bilking various state governments – Nebraska being no exception – for centuries.

While consoling "Black Bart," fast draw Jim (Gene Wilder) has a line in the movie "Blazing Saddles" that not ony points to the racist reaction of the farmer-type townspeople to the new black sheriff but also their overall mentality on social issues. It goes like this:

> **Jim**: [*consoling Bart*] What did you expect? "Welcome, sonny"?
> "Make yourself at home"? "Marry my daughter"? You've got to
> remember that these are just simple farmers. These are people of
> the land. The common clay of the new West. You know... morons.

And because the leadership of Nebraska is equally bereft of management skills, creativity and innovative leadership, they continue to capitulate to these farmers, cater to their every need and then when the economy begins to sink, they bail them out. Even with farmland going down, what reputation would a state like Nebraska have without its hayseeds? Speaking of farmland, Kauffman & Clark (2016) posit,

> The volume of farmland sales also dropped in 2015. Historically,
> changes in the volume of farmland sold and farmland values have
> moved together (Chart 4). Landowners may be less inclined to sell
> when prices have recently fallen, in hopes that prices might
> rebound in the future. A more limited supply of farmland available
> for purchase, then, may partly explain why farmland values have
> retracted only modestly, as demand has remained relatively strong
> in the meantime. (Kauffman & Clark, 2016).

So what can be done? The Nebraska economy's main industry, the farmer and the land, is being threatened. They know this because they have agricultural committees, agricultural leaders, they air TV shows on "agribusiness" and they have a multitude of farmer types being voted into the Nebraska Legislature every election. They have no choice but to engage in what I call "the invasion of the booty snatchers." They'll make up for any losses at the expense of the poor and ignorant. They only have one real black community, so they exploit it to the hilt (as I show in this book), the Indian reservations are paying hundreds of thousands in management fees and taxes to the system and the alcohol that these white boys keep plying the reservations with, and the various Latino enclaves around the state are rife for exploitation.

Free federal grant money and on-going poverty pimp programs help to offset some of the shortfalls, but the Cornhusker State still has a long way to go. It's tourism is failing and the only real source of statewide entertainment is its lackluster college football team, the Nebraska Cornhuskers. In my view, the future does not look good. Read it for yourself:

> Farm credit conditions in the Tenth District also deteriorated somewhat alongside lower farm income. Farm loan repayment rates slipped further in the fourth quarter while farm loan demand remained high (Chart 10). Moreover, both loan demand and repayment rates moved in similar directions in all District states … (Kauffman & Clark, 2016).

Loans slipping. Farm credit conditions deteriorating. Farm income waning. Such conditions require extreme measures, and again, it's time for the state to rely on its largest city and the mis-managers at the state level to find new ways to pimp, exploit and bleed dry the social service money and the poor people whose poverty generate that free Federal funding. Just as the Democratic party relies on" the black vote" and just like the enslavers of old relied on "negro labor," the state of Nebraska is relying on social service block grants and related monies being allocated so that they can turn around and "divert" those funds to pay bills or to help out white farmers and others.

The banks are no friends to these people because they have no honor or commitment to the community. They only care about the bottom line. For example,

> Through the fourth quarter, softening repayments rates and strong loan demand appeared to be a reflection of persistently weaker farm income and reduced cash flow. Yet, commercial banks generally continued to report low delinquency rates on agricultural

loans, as shown in the Federal Reserve Bank of Kansas City's first quarter (Kauffman & Clark, 2016).

This same Federal Reserve Bank of Kansas City, which has a branch right here in Omaha, nevertheless has a "community" division where token negroes are sent out to talk these hicks and small business "negroes" into believing in what they (the Federal Reserve Bank) has dubbed, "entrepreneurial momentum." This is putting a band-aid on a cancerous sore. It is a pacification measure aimed at keeping Nebraskans constantly believing that "this is only a temporary condition." But it's not. Nebraska is on its way out because its main exports are inferior to other areas of the country (corn and beef from Kansas and Texas, respectively). Their home grown products are anxious to leave and see "the real world" and the old guard has been exposed so many times for their outright buffoonery and ineptitude that banking interests and others don't want to give them the time of day.

Skipping past a lengthy and repetitive paragraph in the Kauffman and Clark article, we (mercifully) arrive at the conclusion:

> The effects of weakening farm income continued to ripple through the farm economy in the fourth quarter. Reduced income pushed cropland values lower and developments in cattle markets halted growth in ranchland values. In addition, lower farm income trimmed cash rents somewhat and was expected to continue to pressure agricultural credit conditions in the coming months. (Kauffman & Clark, 2016).

And there you have it. The "invasion of the booty snatchers" will continue on, unabated, with the targets being low income areas, from the Native American reservations and the small Latino areas in the panhandle to the state's only real "black community" in Omaha, Nebraska. As long as poverty can generate free money from the federal and state governments, then poverty will be maintained by the powers that be. The money will be used to pay bills and to promote antiquated tourist attractions. Abuse of Tax Incremental Financing and other enticements and inducements may lure businesses to the state, but it won 't last long.

The state's leadership should come clean – or go away dirty.

DETRIMENTAL RELIANCE: RE-DRAWING OF POLITICAL DISTRICTS

I would like to be able to say "it was a good run" or how "those times will be missed." But looking back on the people who the black community of Omaha elected to represent them from City Council District 2, such comments would be totally ridiculous. Four straight representatives since the early 1980s and the community looks worse today in 2016 than it did in 1977 when I first arrived here from the California Bay Area.

Nebraska State Senator Ernie Chambers, a lifelong resident of what came to be known as District 2, should be commended for fighting for years to get district elections for the school board, city council and county board. The fact that the representation that was selected for the positions was barely mediocre is not his fault: the black community voted for the people that they felt best represented this community, which in my view is a symbol of the caliber of African-American that exists in Omaha, Nebraska.

It will soon no longer exist – not as a black district at least. The white people, in their quest to upgrade their long-term hillbilly status, have sought annexation as a solution. They think that by increasing the population this will bring in more money and make them appear more "urban" and "cosmopolitan." But being urban is an attitude and is one that these Nebraskans will never have. As the saying goes, "you can put lipstick on a pig but it's still a pig," as President Obama said recently. In like manner, Nebraska is hemorrhaging money, Omaha continues to commit political mistake after political mistake, and the farmer mentality is alive and well in everything they do and say.

They need money and they will continue exploiting black poverty in order to get it: money for cops, money for social workers, money for drug rehabilitation, money to fight crime, money to combat teen pregnancy, money for this and that. It's all free and coming from the "look the other way" Federal government which has busted Nebraska time and time again for various forms of mismanagement but nevertheless continues doling out the dollars. Were it not for the black "pocket of poverty" of North Omaha, the state wouldn't even qualify: it has more millionaires per capita than any other state in the union.

This brief essay will document the issue of "district elections" and District 2, the black community of Omaha, Nebraska.

<u>DISTRICT 2: POLITICAL EVOLUTION AND NORTH OMAHA</u>

In March of 1974, the Omaha Star reported that the names of nine blacks would appear on the ballot for various offices, but the officers were all at-large and there was no chance of a black being voted in. For example, hose who sought a full four year term for the 1974 election for school board were John Guy, who had previously run for the school board two years previously; Ruth Thomas, who had been appointed to the school board in an attempt to pacify the black community; and Michael Adams who had just retired as the president of the Nebraska Urban League.

Four black women were named to the Mayor's Commission in the Status of Women, appointed by Edward Zorinsky to two-year terms in September of 1974. The four women were: Barbara Hewins, Elaine Levison, Velma McFadden and Clody Wright (Omaha Star, 1974: 10).

Getting a black on city council had long been a concern among blacks in Omaha's north side, many of whom had grown weary of expecting all-white city councils to address the needs of the black community. By February of 1977, a move was again afoot to get someone black elected to the Omaha City Council. As the World Herald reported it,

> The Interdenominational Ministerial Alliance plans to act as a catalyst in forming a coalition to elect a black to the City Council in May, the Rev. James S. Allen … He said a meeting to form the coalition will be held at 7:30pm Friday at the Zion Baptist Church, 2215 Grant Street. The Rev. Mr. Allen, who is president of the alliance, and other officers expressed disappointment that the City Council did not fill its recent vacancy with a member from a minority … He said political clout is needed to deal with the panorama of problems facing blacks in Omaha in the areas of education, housing and community development. The Rev. Mr. Allen said the City Council's reasons for not choosing a black to fill the vacancy were "escape clauses, not good reasons."

The Omaha chapter of the NAACP was not standing still. In March of 1977, the organization elected attorney James C. Hart to serve as its president, with Jesse Sharpe being elected as first vice-president. Others elected to the executive committee were: Giza Coleman, second vice president; Dorothy Eure, secretary; A. Buddy Hogan, treasurer. Others included: Jesse Allen, Joe Allen, Mildred Althouse, Bobby Bas, J. Fred Bishop, Phyllis Brown, J.E. Butler, Virgil Chandler, William Cooper, Herb Davis, Homer Early, John Guy, Willie L. Harper, H.C. Harris. Paul Jefferson, Lawrence McVoy, Nebraska Morrow, Pearline Mosely, Hurbie Rhodes, Jeff Ross, Charlotte Shropshire, Evelyn Smith, J. Andrew Thompson and Fredrick D. Williams (Omaha World Herald, 1977).

In November of 1977, Faye Mullen of Hastings, Nebraska became the first Black woman to serve on a City Council in the state's history. Lincoln had elected two blacks to city council, Harry Peterson and John Robinson, but they were males. Ms. Mullen visited Omaha in December of 1977 and said that she was "shocked and surprised" that Omaha had never had a black on the Council (Omaha Star, 1977: 1).

In late 1972-early 1973, State Senator Ernest Chambers began to vigorously work toward instituting elections-by-district in the City of Omaha, a process that would enable the poorest section of town to finally be guaranteed a representative on the City Council.

In February of 1973, then president of the Urban League Michael Adams endorsed the idea, stating, "The old City Hall machine must now yield to fair and democratic processes. People from North, South, East, Central and Millard areas have concurred with us in our review and evaluation of all the available alternatives and we heartily recommend that it receive over-whelming support from the good people of Omaha" (Omaha Star, 1973:8).

Prior to the move to bring district elections to Omaha, most of what was done was rooted in relying on the "morality" of the majority population. A front page article in the July 31, 1974 issue of the *Omaha Star* is an example of the kind of "hoping" that blacks would hope for in order to acquire a political voice. The article reads, in part,

> Within the month after the new City Council and Mayor took
> office last year, they were guests of the Urban League at a public
> meeting held at the Logan-Fontenelle Multi-Purpose Center. One
> of the speakers that Sunday afternoon was Michael B. Adams, then
> president of the League, who sought to evoke promises from the
> Council and Mayor that in the event a vacancy occurred on the
> Council, it would be filled by a Black. No hard fast assent was
> given. Only the statement that a Black would not be precluded
> from being considered.

In other words, Adams got bullshitted. White people speak in this "political doublespeak" when it comes to making any kind of commitment in general, but if the issue has to deal with race, you can bet their words sound like something that is totally unintelligible. In addition, how can you "evoke" a promise out of a city council that is perfectly happy with the lily-white way things are going and the on-going bottom-of-the-barrel status of "the negroes"? After all, according to most of their logic, that's the way God planned it!

The July 1974 article continues:

> Now with Jerry Hassett running for County Assessor, a vacancy
> might happen and this has lead to speculation who will fill the
> vacancy if he wins and if it is a Black, who that Black will be.
> Some of the names making the rumor circuit are Human Relations

> Director A.B. "Buddy" Hogan, Parks and Recreation Member
> Kenneth Shearer and R.L. "Bob" Boozer, the ex-NBA star and
> now an executive with Northwestern Bell Telephone Co. Other
> names being spread are Robert "Bob" Rodgers, sportscaster and
> Bryant Center coordinator; Paul B. Allen, a Zorinsky
> administrative aide; and Adams.

Not a single one of the people who were mentioned above made the cut. The Council would remain lily-white for six more years. But in 1974 both sides – white and black – were insulting the black community by singling out particular "qualified negroes" to sit on the council. It was if both sides were admitting that there was an abysmal shortage! Moving on:

> Zorinsky said this week he hoped he would have something to say
> about a replacement for Hassett if the situation arose. While
> stressing that he was not committed to seeing that a Black was
> selected, he said he had no objection to the naming of one. He was
> asked to comment on the possibilities of Hogan, Boozer and
> Shearer. He said he thought Hogan 'would make a great council
> member.' Of Shearer, he said that he was "a Parks and Recreation
> Board member" and cited the fact that Shearer has toured the
> various Parks and Recreation facilities and noted where some
> improvements are needed. Zorinsky said he had sought to name
> Boozer to a Board but found that he lived outside of the city limits
> (Omaha Star, 1974: 1).

See? The fact is that A.B. "Buddy" Hogan was head and shoulders above the other people mentioned, and the white man knew it. But he was also the kind of Black man who didn't take any shit and spoke out against racism whenever he got the chance. He was director of the Human Relations Department and the host of the KETV-Channel 7 show, "Kaleidoscope." The white man knew that Buddy could organize the community at a moment's notice and this was something that those in power in Omaha could and would never allow

History tells the tale. Dan Goodwin would have been a great member of the city council, but he was too closely aligned with Ernie Chambers. There was no way the white man would ever go for that because they feared Chambers' militancy. Others were considered:

> Rodgers and Allen have both ran for the Council before. Adams is
> now seeking a seat on the Omaha School Board in the November
> election. It is certain that some effort would be made in behalf of
> Dan Goodwin, who was the top vote getter in the Black
> community in the last Council election. Some support would

probably also be garnered for Fred Conley, who scored well in the
last election in his maiden try for office. Conley is to enter
Creighton Law School this fall (Omaha Star, 1974: 1).

But the absence of district elections (which would come in the years ahead) did not stop one black woman for testing the mayoral waters. Rowena Moore, a long-time community activist, the chairman of the Douglas County Democratic Party, and the owner of the property where Malcolm X was born, made a bid for the mayor's job in 1973, stating that she would represent all the people and would be "unbiased and unbought" (Omaha Star, 1973: 1).

When she filed as a candidate a few months earlier in December of 1972, Moore chose the 27th Anniversary reception of the Friendly Hearts Club to make her announcement. The Friendly Hearts Club was an organization that Moore of which Moore had served as a past president. Moore, who had lived in Omaha since 1924, said during the Anniversary that, "I live within the community where a lot of unresolved problems reside," and she got more than 500 signatures on her petitions for her mayoral candidacy, although only 150 signatures were required (Omaha Star, 1972: 1).

A year earlier Moore had filed as a candidate for delegate to the 1972 National Democratic Convention. But this was not a city council seat, the one thing that black Omahans had longed for – someone nearby (not in the Legislature in Lincoln) who could address immediate, day-to-day needs of the people.

At the end of February 1977, the Interdenominational Ministerial Alliance was working diligently to act as a catalyst to elect a black to the City Council. One of the key organizers, Rev. James S. Allen, along with others, "expressed disappointment that the City Council did not fill its recent vacancy with a member from a minority." Allen said, "We believe with unity we can succeed in securing enough support from the larger Omaha community to elect a black in the City Council … We want to form a unified coalition out of community agencies that will move forward to deal with problems facing the community." According to one article, this was the first time that ministers had taken the initiative to create such an alliance. Allen said that political clout is needed to deal with the panorama of problems facing blacks in Omaha in the areas of education, housing and community development (Omaha World Herald, 1977).

One reason why Senator Chambers' quest for district elections continued to stall year after year was because most whites opposed the measure. For instance, in an editorial titled, "Elections By District Could Have Impact," the Omaha Star quotes Creighton law professor Dick Shugrue whose comments are typical of the comments of white people who do not want to confront their own racism:

> Dr. Richard Shugrue, a law professor at Creighton University who
> formerly taught political science, was quoted in a recent article as
> saying that whether the City Council is elected at large or by
> districts, minority citizens would be treated the same … He
> maintained that regardless of the system used, the basic demands
> citizens make on the city don't change. They generally want, he
> said, police and fire protection, garbage pickup, street cleaning in
> bad weather and repair of chuckholes (Omaha Star, 1978: 1).

Even after district elections became law for the school board and city council, there were those who continued to attack the black resident of Omaha, usually launching charges of apathy. But what was really taking place was in order to offset black representation, whites were using various means to "relocate" the black community – population transfer, as it is called in urban planning terminology.

In both 1973 and 1977, Fred Conley ran for city council in the at-large format and each time he finished 18th – just like Overall some seventy-plus years before him. Four of the 51 candidates in the 1973 election were black, and five of the 62 candidates in 1977 were black (Flanery & Brown, 1986: 12).

When Senator Chambers was able to get the law passed for district elections for city councilmen in 1979, there was no shortage of North Omahans circulating petitions to get their names on the ballot. The front page of the Christmas Eve issue of 1980 of the *Omaha Star* captures the confusion and hype surrounding the bid to become the city's first-ever black councilperson. Following is that article with my analyses filtering in and out:

> Check off the names of City employees Michael B. Adams and
> Ruth F. Jackson; Omaha Board of Education member-elect
> Lawrence W.M. Mcvoy III; Community Volunteer Rowena
> Moore; Creighton Law senior Gregory Rhoades and NOCD
> President Carl Tyler from the list of possible candidates next
> spring from the heavy populated City Council District 2. All had
> been previously mentioned as giving some thought to seeking the
> office. A recent check by the Omaha STAR reveals that all now
> have made up their mind not to seek the post. (Omaha Star, 1980)

With the exception of Michael Adams, the names above would have all failed miserably on the city council, surrounded by some of the most conservative white people in the history of the city. Ruth Jackson, a great woman who would end up serving as director of the Human Relations Department, would have been far too nice and passive to get the job done. Rowena Moore, the founder of the Malcolm X Memorial Foundation, had always craved political power, but had dubious ideas, at best; Greg Rhoades ended up being a city attorney and carried water for the system and didn't put in any work in the black community, although he owned one of the most visible homes in the area (corner of 33rd and Hamilton), and Carl Tyler, as president of North Omaha Community Development, played a role in the beginning of the takeover of the black community under the guise of "community development."

But wait -- there's more:

> Other names in the rumor mill as possible candidates a month ago were Jackson Graham, defeated by McVoy in November for the School Board; Ronald McGruder, re-elected last month to a four-year term on the School Board; Mortician Ruth Thomas, recently retired School Board member; Fred Conley and Robert "Bob" Rodgers, both who have sought Council seats-at-large. New names to surface in the past three weeks are NOCD Executive Director George Garnett and Businessman Dan Goodwin, who operates the Spencer Street Barber Shop where State Senator Ernest W. Chambers works. (Omaha Star, 1980).

None of the people mentioned above, except for Dan Goodwin and Ron McGruder, would have been viable councilmembers. Ron did an adequate job as a member of the school board, but Ruth Thomas, who was also mentioned above, couldn't even stay awake as a member of the same board that McGruder was a member of. She would sit there and knit and then nod out in full view of TV cameras. McVoy made grandiose statements but did very little during his short stint on the school board, and Conley showed what he would have done once he finally made it to the Council in 1980. Bob Rodgers was known around the neighborhood for his yeoman work with young people, but he would never have been able to cut in on the city council.

But one old school bootlicker is never afraid to back a "new wave sellout" when he finds one. Check it out:

> In announcing that he would not be a candidate, McVoy said he was trying to entice Garnett into running. Garnett said he had been approached by several persons but that he would not be running. Goodwin said he would seek the office. Tyler has given Goodwin his support. Conley is running and has the backing of Rhoades and Mrs. Moore. McGruder said his name will appear on the ballot next spring. (Omaha Star, 1980).

The "Garnett" that is being alluded to is George Garnett, the city-sponsored "boy wonder" who graduated from Yale with a bachelor's degree in political science and who returned to Omaha to become the president of North Omaha Community Development – the same group that Carl Tyler had been president of. Although Garnett would eventually become the director, the direction f NOCD remained the same: to keep on doing the bidding of the city as it worked feverishly to take control of the black community, its land and its buildings

It is now 1980 and the first city councilman would be voted in. The two finalists for the City Council seat were Ron McGruder and Fred Conley. Conley edged out McGruder for the position, and in 1981 became the first black on the City Council. At the time he told a reporter for the *Omaha World Herald* that he had always wanted to become a councilman so he could make a difference in the community. He added:

> "The most important thing about being the first is the fact that you serve as a role model for the people you represent .. Whites as well as blacks saw me as a role model for African-American people. You are watched as to how you conduct yourself, whether you understand the issues and so forth … And I think I overcame that test" (James-Johnson, 1995: 2).

You don't "overcome" tests – you either pass them or fail them. In my book, Conley – and those who came after him – failed the black community. Four consecutive black representatives of District 2, and four people who left the community worse off than when they inherited: Fred Conley, Brenda Council, Frank Brown and now, Ben Gray.

Merely take a tour of the community today in 2016 and as I've written elsewhere, it looks worse today than it did in 1977 despite the fact that black poverty has brought in more than $215 million in Community Development Block Grant dollars to the city coffers. When they get it, they hire fellow whites and spend money on expansion, freakishness and frolic, Not a few of their mayors and city planners have had alcohol and drug-related issues. They practice nepotism whenever they can and they get away with it.

Now, we come to 2016.

REDISTRICTING AND THE DECLINE: A RESPONSE TO A WORLD-HERALD ARTICLE

As stated at the outset of this book, the definition of the word "fatalistic" is, "relating to or characteristic of the belief that all events are predetermined and therefore inevitable:" Since the passage of election by district by State Senator Ernie Chambers in 1979, the area of the city known as District 2 – the largest black community in the entire state – has had four representatives as of 2016. All of them share in a common history and I believe fate: though marginally successful prior to being elected, once in office, they became visibly flawed individuals, lending to the stereotype of the area they represented as being somehow "deviant."

This brief essay is an excerpt from a much longer piece that I titled, "The Rise and Fall of the Fatalistic Four," which makes reference to the four people who were elected to serve as council representatives for District 2 after Senator Chambers forced through district elections: Fred Conley, Brenda Council, Frank Brown and Ben Gray. A copy of that document addressing each politico in detail can be provided upon request.

As a result of the buffoonery, ineptitude and misfeasance of the "fatalistic four," the white power structure has bought enough time for continued political abuse of the North Omaha community to become a reality. In August of 2016, yet another strategy was invoked to make sure that black voting power would be diminished at very least and nullified at worst.

As it was reported in the August 8, 2016 edition of the *Omaha World Herald* under the headline, "City Council Redistricting: New Map Lines Might Shift Political Makeup. Annexation In West Mean Eastern Districts Could Gain GOP Constituents." Following is the thrust of that article as it relates to the North Omaha community, with my analyses filtering in and out.

> When Omahans go to vote next spring, some of them will likely find an unfamiliar City Council member on their ballot. The City Council has begun the process of redistricting because the city's three western districts have gained so many new residents in recent annexations (Moring, 2016).

And so began what this writer believe as an attack on district elections. The white people of Nebraska and Omaha are cowardly, but they have long memories. Senator Chambers humiliated them, first by getting district elections by school board and in doing so, negated the power of the once awesome Orange Ticket. City Council was another issue, one that was not relegated to books, binders and education-oriented issues. So with the complicity of a backward community and the blind loyalty of various "negro" cliques, four consecutive people were elected to serve as city council representatives, four people who in their own way and in their own style, contributed to the gradual demise of Omaha's black community.

With that as a setting, the previous excerpt that states that "When Omahans go to vote next spring, some of them will likely find an unfamiliar City Council member on their ballot," is not quite fitting for North Omaha. It won't apply because it would not matter if the person was different in appearance or not; the die had been cast, and the tragic trend of mediocre city council representation had become the norm. The damage that had been done by the foursome that have been discussed, in collusion with those outside of the community who have always wanted to do it harm, set a standard that could not be reversed or slowed down.

The demise of North Omaha is eminent.

The article on re-districting continues:

> If the City Council approves the mayor's 2016 annexation package
> Tuesday, the difference between the largest and smallest Omaha
> council districts, population-wise, is set to reach 35 percent – far
> higher than the 10 percent maximum the council aims for (Moring,
> 2016).

What difference would it make? The black community's city council district was already the smallest and, as you will see later, white people attempt to translate that to mean that it has the most juice or biggest voice downtown. Nothing could be further from the truth, as this short black paper should have made clear. Continuing,

> The boundary changes will most likely be minor, Council
> President Ben Gray said, he said most likely the eastern districts,
> which have fewer people, will grow and shift westward. That could
> mean a gradual shift in the council's political makeup (Moring,
> 2016).

As you can see in the previous sections of this paper, Ben Gray speaks without studying, talks without thinking and offers little more than conjecture and bullshit theories. He dropped out of college and has no real political education other than the behind-closed-doors deals he cuts and the grandiose public claims that he makes. Put another way, he couldn't find a hooker in a whore house. So his views on what might happen or will happen are useless, and if you notice, he speaks in vague generalities: "most likely be minor," "could mean" and so on.

White people, as usual, attempt to put a positive spin on what is clearly a part of yet another black political dissipation plan:

> The City Council is officially nonpartisan but is now made up of
> four Democrats in the eastern districts and three Republicans in the
> western districts. A westward expansion of council district could
> mean the four eastern districts end up with more Republican
> constituents. "The City Council could become a more conservative

one," said Gregory Petrow, University of Nebraska at Omaha
political science professor. (Morning, 2016).

I phoned Dr. Petrow on August 8, 2016 at around 1pm. I spoke with him and what I told him about Omaha's relocation strategy and its long-time attempts to control the black vote obviously surprised him. I have a master's degree in political science from the same department he works in. When I told him what I knew he was shocked, but brushed it off, claiming he would contact me if he were ever again contacted for an interview. In other words, why he was contacted in the first place is not clear; but one thing is for sure: he is more likely to be a part of future problems than future solution.

Petrow's opinions and claims continue:

> Redistricting can be an adjustment for political leaders, Petrow
> said. Elected officials get used to serving constituents with a
> certain set of beliefs and expectations. They've also often done
> casework for their residents and neighborhoods. So when elected
> officials lose some residents and gain others, the politicians might
> have to abide by a new set of expectations (Moring, 2016).

Again, what Petrow suggests would and could not be "felt" by the residents of Omaha's district two, the black community.

To begin with the elected officials rarely "served" the constituents. Phone calls went un-returned by Conley, Council, Brown and Gray, with Brown probably having lost an election because of that very fact. They offered no town hall meetings and when they did, the meetings were short, contrived and staged. If someone were to do an analysis of how much letterhead (paper and envelopes) was used to provide information to District 2 residents, I am willing to bet that it would be markedly lower than that of any other council person. All four of these people let power go to their head and it was clear: Conley cut a deal that got him lifetime employment, Council purchased property and buildings after deserting the school board to run for a seat she was sure she could win, Brown won the seat after directing the Jimmy Wilson Jr Foundation, a racist organization that raised money for bullet proof vests and radios for cops, and Ben Gray had nothing going other than failures as the leader of an African American Achievement Council that achieved nothing, and like Council, Brown and Conley, filled his own pockets and coffers from deals made with white people behind closed doors.

Secondly, as for "a certain set of beliefs and expectations" that those constituents may have had, it is clear that the Council people were in an ideal situation. They represented a community that had a childlike understanding of politics, no real vision, and was almost totally dependent on the system for all that was life giving and life supporting. They were what Malcolm X would have referred to as "house niggers." Therefore with no real expectations, these council representatives took full advantage of their naiveté and got elected and then just kicked back and collected their city-sponsored paychecks and benefited from other perks

Third, the assumption that council representatives do case work for their residents and neighborhoods. There has been no neighborhood related commitment by any of District 2's council representatives that was serious. The creation of what was called D2NC was co-opted and taken over by sunshine soldiers who argued among themselves and finally abolished it. As the founding director of the largest black neighborhood association in the state, one that includes nearly all of District 2, I have never been contacted by any of the fatalistic four for anything other than the favors that Frank Brown would beg for (paperwork, proposals, etc.) They feared me because they knew and continue to know that I see them for what they are. That makes me a threat to their livelihoods and therefore they cower and avoid me at all costs.

A wise decision.

Fourth and finally according to Petrow and the Moring article, " … when elected officials lose some residents and gain others, the politicians might have to abide by a new set of expectations." If you never had expectations from the get-go, and your leadership is happy for that fact and in doing nothing rewards your apathy and complacency, what would be the benefit of having "new expectations"? All four of the District 2 representatives ended up in the pockets of the mayor at that time and because of that, they were reduced to keeping their mouths shut. As I've written elsewhere, the black community looks worse today than it did in June of 1977 when I first arrived in Omaha from Oakland, California.

The article further provides information that,

> Northeast Omaha's District 2, which Gray represents, is the city's smallest, with 57,091 people. Southwest Omaha's District 5 is the largest, with 77,514 people, assuming the annexation is approved. Political districts are generally supposed to contain about the same number of people, known as the "one person, one vote" principle. But because of the po0pulation difference, you might say that a District 5 resident's voice counts one-third less at City Hall than a District 2 resident (Moring, 2016).

You might also say that a piece of shit is a Hostess pie, too – but it ain't one! The fact is District 2 had no real voice or power, not even when it came to issues that impacted black people specifically. White people intervened and the four black representatives usually chose the path of least resistance. When the black community raised an issue, the councilpersons would occasionally jump on the bandwagon, but that was about it. No real leadership, no real vision, and never a strategic plan for the area. All four sat back and watch racists in the City of Omaha Planning Department apply for, receive, and then pilfer over $215 million in Community Development Block grant funding and didn't do shit about it. Even when I filed legal grievances, none of them bothered to back me. Why? Because the white man might get mad at them.

EVACUATION OF THE YALE APARTMENTS IN 2018

The Tommie Rose Gardens were the bomb when they were first built. When I arrived here in 1977 they were clean and a lot of single black women lived in them. Now they look like they were hit by a bomb. In an interview with former Omaha Housing Authority director Robert Armstrong, it was clear that the apartment complex had been "condemned" or "tagged" for at least two decades. The fact is, two reviews from 2004 – some 14 years ago were of the "one star" variety and included the following comments.

One resident claimed that the place was "not recommended" and added, "This place just needs to be torn down and made up with the Miami Heights housing project going on in that area complete dump." Another one from the same year, April 30, 2004, stated that, "Tommie Rose Apartments is still bad. To (sic) many things go there that should be the area is not comfortable (sic) and the people are still the same. Maintance (sic) is slow and not compelting (sic) their jobs." The illiterate slob who wrote this was evidently dissatisfied with the apartments and the residents.

About a decade or so ago I sent a letter to the editor of the Omaha World Herald for publication, outlining what I saw as a "relocation strategy" taking place in North Omaha. They refused to print it but Frank Partsch, then one of the editors, took the time to scrawl a personal note referring to my assertions as "clap trap," asserting that such a relocation strategy could and would never take place in Omaha. After I dogged him and sent copies to everyone in his news room, I realized that the World Herald – and the Omaha media in general - was a part of the neglect and cover-up, a part of covering up and when caught, embellishing what was taking place to look like some kind of model urban project.

I say this because reporters like Henry Cordes and Erin Grace have frequently written stories dealing with the problems in the North Omaha area. If not, stories (fluff pieces) about self-proclaimed negro leaders who are basically influence peddlers, not power brokers. There is hardly nary a mention of the low median housing value or the dilapidated structures. Slumlords like Dave Paladino of Landmark Management were given national television shows where he proceeded to slander North Omaha, claiming at one point to a Channel 3 reporter that he would often be knee deep in feces. We know this to be an absurd lie, but it played well as the 2011show, "The Super" painted Paladino as some kind of hero who was "helping" the low-income population of the Northside.

Just before the Channel 3 (KMTV) interview by Adam Racusin, the national media promoted the show as follows:

> "You see a part of American life that you haven't seen before, and just really how kind of messed up it really is," said Dave Paladino. The Omaha native turned reality star is the owner of the Landmark Group. The company manages 1,800 properties throughout the metro. Paladino is in charge of his tenants and their off the wall problems.

The show was cancelled but not before Paladino circulated lies about North Omaha akin to those most recently uttered by Yale Apartment owner Kay Anderson who acted in a paternalistically racist fashion, implying that he was somehow "helping" the refugees who lived in the 33rd and Lake apartment complex.

People like Paladino and Anderson can read the demographic reality, which is why they work hard to exploit it. And if either of them would like to publicly debate the issue, then it would be my pleasure.

At any rate, more evidence of bias on the part of the Omaha media when it comes to North Omaha - notice the following state figures that show what the area is faced with, *by design:*

- Median household income below state average
- Median house value below state average
- Unemployment percentage significantly above state average
- Black race population percentage significantly above state average
- Median age below state average
- Renting percentage above state average
- Length of stay since moving in above state average
- House age above state average
- Percentage of population with a bachelor's degree or higher significantly below state average

Paladino and Channel 3 call them "off the wall problems." The rest of the nation calls it "system wide poverty." Moving on, the report on Paladino offered the following:

> "If your mother saw what I saw she would need long term therapy,"
> said Paladino. "I mean that it's just hard to see the things we see."
> Camera crews spent months following Paladino. From his office in
> downtown Omaha, which by the way resembles the set of the hit
> TV show 24, to inside broken homes, Paladino is up to his face in
> feces, hoarding, filth, grime, and dust.

Fast forward.

According to a World-Herald report, the mayor the city of Omaha – with no background in community development or urban planning whatsoever (the same can be said for many of the members of her "F-Troop"-like Planning Department – claimed that the owner of the complex, Kay Anderson was a "do-gooder" and "a man giving back to God and his community by sheltering hundreds of refugees from Myanmar in apartments they can afford." Mayor Jean Stothert added that she considered the evacuation of the refugees as a "humanitarian mission" rather than a code enforcement. If it was a humanitarian mission, what took so long?

So we have two slumlords – Paladino and Anderson – acting as if they are doing the state's largest black community a favor by paternalistically "overseeing" the housing stock and collecting rents that the house owners don't want to collect because of their fear of the area.

When people who live in and benefit from a segregationist reality attempt to sound humane or understanding, they often make fools of themselves when they attempt to make a comment or voice an opinion on said reality. This is what took place recently when a central city apartment complex, Yale Park Apartments, had to be shut down because of unlivable conditions. Following is an analysis of what happened with emphasis on the racist complicity of the city's services and the mayor, along with the collective ignorance of those who refer to themselves as helping professionals.

To begin with, the complex was made up of mostly refugees who were placed there by white people knowingly. Tommie Rose had been formerly a mostly black complex and when it was, few of these kinds of problems occurred. After slow-but-sure relocation over the years, refugees were moved in with full knowledge, even as far back as 2000, that the complex was in need of repair. No one did a thing and the refugees didn't complain because they didn't want to raise the ire of the landlord who lived nowhere near the community.

A news report from Channel 6 (NBC) television, on the day of the evacuation of the complex, appeared on line under the title, "All Residents of Troubled Yale Park Apartments Have Been Displaced." The article appeared the same day as the evacuation and may not be quite accurate, but even if everyone wasn't move out, most of the residents indeed, were.

Equally embarrassing and slanderous were the comments of Human Relations director Dr. Franklin Thompson. According to WOWT-Channel 6, he said, "When you come from a third world country you come from an experience that's pretty, um, traumatic and so when you come to America, sub-standard here, still looks good. And the residents had to decide what was the tipping point." Third World country? Do you remember back in January of this year when Donald Trump, President of the United States, referred to Haiti and some African nations as "shit hole countries"? That is what the term Third World has come to mean which is why it has been debunked and discarded. The proper term, Dr. Thompson (who is an educator instructor at the University of Nebraska Omaha) is "developing nations."

All the inspectors, cops and firemen in the world can't alter an antiquated and racist mentality, which is what all of the main actors in this issue clearly possess. Racusin has long since left Channel 3 for California and Paladino still expands Landmark Management group. The mayor, in serious need of cultural competency training and the newly appointed Human Relations director, an intelligent man who should know better, are clearly not the sharpest knives in the drawer.

Anderson, doing his best Lone Ranger impersonation, told a World Herald reporter that he's carrying a loss of $2 million on the property and that he charges residents upwards of $500 per unit, per month, which he called a "sub-market" rate, especially considering that he has 100 percent occupancy and a waiting list. First the city downgrades the area by manipulating property values. Then they bring in these "developers" who buy up the vacant lots and available buildings. Then they recoup their investment by renting out property that would otherwise have been torn down. Anderson made money off of the backs of the poor and ignorant, just as the City of Omaha has been doing with the on-going abuse of Community Development Block Grant money since 1975. The city has received more than $200 million from the Federal government claiming they will "help" North Omaha.

And this brings us to another subject. Those landlords calling for more inspections could be a smokescreen. My proposed Affordable Housing Manager would hire a crew of inspectors who would be trained. When inspections are scheduled, those landlords should get no more than 24 hours notice (if that). No warnings to give them time to prepare the way public housing does when an "inspection" is coming down the pike.

It is clear by the condition of the Yale Apartments and the negative demographics that saturate the 68111, 68110 and 68104 zip codes that help is still a long way off.

Most of the TONA NEWS readership came northward from the South acting as if you were free when you landed jobs at the packing houses. This was known as "The Great Migration." That is what these refugees are now going through with white host families and Christian groups like Omaha Together One Community bringing them in and then posting them up in the one area of the city deemed most undesirable: the north side.

TOWARD AN AFFORDABLE HOUSING MANAGER

The Triple One Neighborhood Association has more urban planners among its members than any other neighborhood group in the city. It has produced more reports, documents and memos about North Omaha than any other group in the state, including UNO. Instead, novices are contacted and you see what kind of statements they make, statements that are a reflection and reinforcement of the same attitude that makes Omaha the "urban village" that it claims and seeks to be.

What is needed is an Affordable Housing Manager position that will make the bleeding reciprocal. When these slumlords have to "pay in" to the system for their paternalistic purchasing of housing in North Omaha, maybe they will take said purchases more seriously. Here is how it would work.

For one thing, such a position would ensure that Omaha residents have access to the city's growing number of affordable apartments and homes. That number is going to be growing because Omaha is trying to create these "high density areas" that enable it to segregate by class just as it has always done by race. Look at midtown: sprinkled with multi unit dwellings. Secondly, the position would make that that developers comply with the laws that were violated by people like Anderson and Paladino. Monitoring these people would afford the housing rights to North Omahans that have long been denied by the courts, the cops and the code enforcers.

Based on my research and the eclectic combining of positions from cities all over the country, this position of Affordable Housing Manager would be a senior-level executive role that would report directly to the mayor; none of that mid-level high visibility cubicle crap that Omaha is notorious for – giving minorities and women long titles and keys that don't fit anything.

I would recommend that Mayor Stothert, as racially naïve as she is begin the implementation of a Mayor's Inclusionary Zoning Program. No more creation of "villages" and Potemkin houses. This program and along with the Manager being proposed, would propose innovative ways to engage Omaha residents and interest groups to explore housing needs and opportunities.

All landlords pay a registration fee for every house managed or owned. Maybe then they will appreciate the manipulation of North Omaha's land valuation a little more. As the First Nation people taught long ago,

> *Maka le wakan -- the land is sacred. These words are at the*
> *core of our being. The land is our mother, the rivers our*
> *blood. Take away our land and we die. That is, the Indian in*
> *us dies. We'd become just suntanned white men, the jetsam*
> *and floatsam of your great melting pot.*
> ■ *Mary Brave Bird*

RELOCATION REALIZED: AN AFTERWORD

And the plan for relocation and political neutralization continues. There are black lackeys who go around and latch on to a candidate here or a candidate there, claiming to be able to deliver the black vote. But they are just opportunists with limited options. The stuff these negroes do in Omaha would not be acceptable in any city of similar size. The politicos do it because they know they can and the residents accept it because most of them can't spell "politico.;"

The icing on the cake can be found in the following excerpt from the Moring piece:

> During Mayor Jean Stothert's time in office the city has passed
> two annexation packages, and the council is scheduled to vote
> Tuesday on a third. Assuming the full package passes, the city will
> have added more than 235,000 residents to the city during the
> Stothert administration. Most of those new Omahans live in the
> three western council districts. *District 2 hasn't grown at all*
> (Moring, 2016 – emphasis added).

The fact is District 2 may not have grown, but part of the growth in those other districts is due to the relocation of people who at one time lived in District 2. The triumvirate of evil and division has been completed. First, the destruction of the housing projects and the dispersal of black people to other parts of District 2 thereby a partial dilution of the black vote. The second prong was the coming of the North Freeway, which literally divided the community in half, wiped out black businesses and relocated black people to the west into other areas of the city, most of them going into multi-unit dwellings (apartments) where density is high.

The housing left behind is now being forced into a "land bank" controlled by the white man or being torn down. If not that, it is being purchased by Warren Buffett's daughter, Susie. All this means that District 2, as we once knew it, is going to disappear. But this is where the buffoonery and ineptitude of the fatalistic four has a positive taint.

The third prong – re-drawn districts, further diluting the black vote and ensuring that somewhere down the road a white person will be the District 2 representative. The question is, could they do any worse?

Nothin' from nothin' leaves nothin'! Black people won't feel any "loss" because under these four representatives that they have elected to represent District 2 since 1980 – Fred Conley, Brenda Council, Frank Brown and Ben Gray -- they (the community) never experienced any gains! Senator Chambers and his well-intended district elections proposal was countered with a cowardly long-term strategy by those in power. They made sure they did all in their power to nullify black District 2 representation by appealing to the greed, low moral compass, political ignorance and desperation of the people who were elected into that office. While that was going on and while all four faded unceremoniously into the sunset, a relocation strategy was also taking place.

Relying on this cast of characters and the city to do its job, served as the basis of the "detrimental reliance" that I allege.

CONCLUSION

Native Omaha Days will have a new complexion, both literally and figuratively speaking, in the years ahead. Over thirty years of black representation with nothing to show for it but felonies, failures and on-going miscues. Another product of habitual and perennial detrimental reliance.

The masses of North Omaha residents "relied" on the city to do its job. But there was no rhyme or reason for the community to believe that the white power administration or the "negroes" who came into office (based on the black vote, I might add) would do anything but make sure that the status quo was maintained. And today in 2016, North Omaha looks far worse than it did in 1977 when I first arrived in the city.

The reliance upon these individuals, entities and institutions was therefore "detrimental" to the social, cultural, educational and political health of the black residents of Omaha. But there are lyrics that describe what you meant and what the residents enabled me to learn. The song is the Englebert Humperdink's 1976 cut, "After the Lovin'." The words to the song says it all in metaphor:

> So I sing you to sleep
> After the lovin'
> With a song I just wrote yesterday
> And I hope you can hear
> What the words and the music have to say.
> It's so hard to explain
> Everything that I'm feelin'
> Face to face I just seem to go dry.
> 'Cause I love you so much
> That the sound of your voice can get me high.
> Thanks for takin' me (Thanks for takin' me)
> On a one way trip to the sun (On a one way trip to the sun)
> And thanks for turnin' me (Turnin' me)
> Into a someone. (Someone)
> So I sing you to sleep
> After the lovin'
> I brush back the hair from your eyes.
> And the love on your face
> Is so real that it makes me want to cry.
> And I know that my song
> Isn't sayin' anything new.
> Oh, but after the lovin'
> I'm still in love with you.

Our reliance on those who are not like us proved to be our undoing. It was truly "detrimental." In simpler terms, good-bye North Omaha; we hardly knew ye.

REFERENCES

Algeo, John. (1981, Summer-Fall). As harmful as sticks and stones." *Perspectives.* Summer-Fall 1981.

Armah, Dr. Afroamerican Studies 228: Introduction to Black Political Economy. "The Theory of Cultural Racism." J. M. Blaut. University of Wisconsin-Milwaukee. Spring 1992.

Asante, M.K. (1989). *The Afrocentric Idea*. Philadelphia: Temple University Press.

Askew, N. (1993, November). The dark side." (letter to the editor). *Essence*

Atlanta Blackstar (2014, February 21). Eight disturbingly racist children's books designed to devalue black people. Retrieved from http://atlantablackstar.com/2014/02/21/8-disturbingly-racist-childrens-books-designed-to-devalue-black-people/

Bandler, J. & Burke, D. (2009, August 4). The shadowy business of diversion. Fortune.com. Retrieved from http://archive.fortune.com/2009/07/31/news/companies/product_diversion.fortune/index.htm

Bednarek, J.R.D. (__).Creating an "Image Center": Reimagining Omaha's Downtown and Riverfront, 1986-2003. ***Nebraska History Quarterly***.

Biga, L. (____). Power players, Ben Gray and other Omaha African-American leaders try improvement through self-empowered networking. ***The Reader.***

Bradley, H. (2012, March 23). Workplace discrimination costs businesses $64 billion every year. Huffington Post. Retrieved from http://www.huffingtonpost.com/2012/03/23/workplace-discrimination-costs-businesses-cap_n_1373835.html

Burbach, C. (2012, September 30). Council's taxes went unpaid for four years. ***Omaha World Herald.***

D'Antonion, D. (1987, May 12). "How to use white lies to make your marriage better." *The National Enquirer*.

DeBakey, L. (1983). "Time to call a halt to 'the mutilation of English'." *U.S. News and World Report*.

Edney, H.T. (2004, March 2). Presidential candidates understate extent of poverty. ***The Final Call.***

Evans, D.L. & Evans, O.W. (2007). ***The complete real estate encyclopedia***. New York, New York: McGraw-Hill.

Fraser, J. & Kick, E. (2005). Understanding community building in urban America. *Journal of Poverty*, 9, (1). 23-43.

Fredericks, S. (2005, June 5). The uninsured in Omaha have "hope." Retrieved from http://www.hopemed.us/news/press_releases/uninsured.asp

Gibbons, Frederick X. "Stigma and Interpersonal Relationships" in Stephen C. Ainlay, Gaylene Becker and Lerita M. Coleman (Eds.) *The Dilemma of Difference: A Multidisciplinary View of Stigma.* New York: Plenum Press. 1986.

Hammel, P. & Tysver, R. (2012, September 14). Brenda Council receives steadfast support. *Omaha World Herald.*

Huffington Post (2012, September 18). Brenda Council, Nebraska State Senator, Pleads Guilty To Filing False Campaign Finance Reports.

Kearney Hub. (2012, September 13). Charges against Sen. Brenda Council tied to gambling.

Ladson-Billings, G.J. (2000, May/June). Fighting for our lives: Preparing teachers to teach African students. *Journal of Teacher Education*, 51.

Levy, John M. (2000). *Contemporary Urban Planning*. Upper Saddle River, New Jersey: Prentice-Hall.

Los Angeles Times (1988, April 21). Councilman to fill late Omaha mayor's role.

Mitchell, S. (2000, April 18). The impact of chain stores on community. Retrieved from https://ilsr.org/impact-chain-stores-community/

New York Times (1988, April 14). Mayor Bernie Simon of Omaha dies at 60 after a cancer battle.

Nohr, E. & Burbach, C. (2016, July 14). Conley's presence on Metro College board could cost school millions in federal funding. *Omaha World Herald.* Retrieved from http://www.omaha.com/news/metro/fred-conley-s-presence-on-metro-college-board-could-cost/article_1f0fd992-f444-5f1b-9f11-b7fc299882af.html

Omaha Monitor. (1928, December 14). A city of homes.

Omaha World Herald (2004, December 13). Interracial barometer: A horrendous assault brings reminder of decline in one type of racial bigotry.

Omaha World Herald. (2002, July 22). Despite gains, blacks far from parity with whites, report says.

Silberman, Charles E. (1964). ***Crisis in Black and White***. New York: Vintage Books.

Snell, S. & Bohlander, G. (2013). ***Managing human resources***. Mason, OH: Cengage Learning.

Thomas, Emma. (2013, October 23). "Outrage in Netherlands over calls to abolish 'Black Pete' clowns which march in Christmas parade dressed in blackface". *American Renaissance.* Retrieved from http://www.amren.com/news/2013/10/outrage-in-netherlands-over-calls-to-abolish-black-pete-clowns-which-march-in-christmas-parade-dressed-in-blackface/

US Legal.com (2016). Detrimental reliance law and legal definition. Retrieved from http://definitions.uslegal.com/d/detrimental-reliance/

Welsing, Frances C. (1974, May). "The Cress theory of color confrontation." *Black Scholar.*

Welsing, F.C. (1991). *The Isis papers: The keys to the colors*. Chicago, Illinois: Third World Press.

Wilford, John Noble. (1992, October 10). Hubble scope may yield clues to universe's 'dark matter'. *Korea Herald.* October 10, 1992.

Williams, John E. & John R. Stabler. (Title not discernible). *Psychology Today.* July 1973.

Wilson, J. (2013, March 29). India Arie accused of lightening skin, singer looks very different on 'Cocoa Butter' cover. Huffington Post.

Young, J. (2012, September 12). AG: Sen. Council withdrew campaign funds at casinos. *Lincoln Journal Star*.

Young, S. (2009). Think for yourself. Retrieved from http://www.scottyoung.com/blog/about-and-contact-info/